IN HOSTILE SKIES

North Texas Military Biography and Memoir Series
Ronald E. Marcello, series editor

In Hostile Skies

An American B-24 Pilot in World War II

James M. Davis

Edited by David L. Snead

Number 3 in the
North Texas Military Biography
and Memoir Series

University of North Texas Press
Denton, Texas

10 9 8 7 6 5 4 3 2

Permissions:
University of North Texas Press
P.O. Box 311336
Denton, TX 76203-1336

The paper used in this book meets the minimum requirements of the American National Standard for Permanence of Paper for Printed Library Materials, z39.48.1984. Binding materials have been chosen for durability.

Library of Congress Cataloging-in-Publication Data

Davis, James M., 1921–
  In hostile skies : an American B-24 pilot in World War II / James M. Davis ; Edited by David L. Snead.
      p. cm. -- (North Texas military biography and memoir series ; no. 3)
        Includes bibliographical references and index.
    ISBN-13: 978-1-57441-209-3 (cloth : alk. paper)
    ISBN-13: 978-1-57441-239-0 (paper : alk. paper)
  1. Davis, James M., 1921- 2. World War, 1939-1945--Aerial operations, American. 3. World War, 1939-1945--Personal narratives, American. 4. United States. Army Air Forces--Biography. 5. B-24 bomber. 6. Bomber pilots--United States--Biography. I. Snead, David L. (David Lindsey) II. Title. III. Series.
  D790.2.D38 2006
  940.54'4973092--dc22

2005033926

In Hostile Skies: An American B-24 Pilot in World War II is Number 3 in the North Texas Military Biography and Memoir Series.

For Jean

Contents

Preface   ix

Acknowledgments   xiii

Introduction   xv

Chapter 1 – The Dream   1

Chapter 2 – Training   20

Chapter 3 – Flying the Beast   47

Chapter 4 – Topeka to Belfast   68

Chapter 5 – The First Mission   84

Chapter 6 – Our Early Missions   107

Chapter 7 – Close Calls   134

Chapter 8 – Finishing Our Tour   169

Chapter 9 – Homecoming   189

Epilogue   207

Appendix   210

Glossary   212

Bibliography   218

Index   223

Preface

In the spring of 2002 I was an assistant professor of history at Texas Tech University, where I taught a variety of courses in modern U.S. military and diplomatic history. One day a visitor, Jay Wischkaemper, stopped by my door and asked if he could talk to me. It seemed a little strange since Jay had never been in any of my classes and was older than most of my students. It turns out that Jay is a financial adviser and had been working with one of my close colleagues, Jorge Iber. Jay mentioned to Jorge that he had stumbled across a World War II memoir of a U.S. B-24 bomber pilot and wondered if he knew of anyone who could evaluate it for possible publication. Jorge sent him to my office, and a new adventure was added to my life.

Jay quickly explained that James "Jim" Davis, who lives in Midland, Texas, had written the memoir to describe his experiences flying with the Eighth Air Force in World War II. By coincidence, Jay and Jim both had season tickets for the Texas Tech Lady Raiders' basketball games and had seats next to each other. After striking up some general conversations, Jim mentioned that he had flown a B-24 in the war. Jay, being an airplane buff, was enthralled. Eventually, Jim mentioned his memoir, and Jay asked if he could read it.

When Jay told me about the memoir, I was immediately intrigued. I was most interested in reading a veteran's story that with few exceptions was unknown. As a historian, there are few greater loves than reading a newly discovered primary source. I did not hold out much hope that it was publishable since there have been numerous memoirs of the war written, but I very much looked forward to reading it. To my surprise, I found the memoir not only valuable as a primary source but also worthy of publication.

Jim's memoir reflects more than sixty years of contemplation and reflection. He had considered writing one on several occasions after the war but found little time to do so. It was only after he retired in the mid-1980s that he finally sat down and pondered his experiences. He proved to have a sharp mind for detail and was able—with his personal records from the war—to recall and record his vivid memories. While it needed some editing, I really believed that anybody interested in the American military history of World War II would find it fascinating.

Due to other projects, I could not devote much time to editing the memoir for about a year, but I remained very excited about its possibilities. I contacted Jim and made arrangements to meet him in October 2002. We had a wonderful time getting to know each other, and I came away from the meeting even more excited and determined to get the memoir published. I found Jim to be one of the kindest and gentlest men that I have ever met. We agreed that as soon as I could, I would start editing the memoir and then seek a publisher.

I wanted to do a couple of things with the memoir. While it needed some editing of punctuation and grammar, it mainly required cutting and streamlining the prose. At times Jim provided too much detail, while at others not enough. I made it my goal to keep as much of Jim's writing as possible and to let him tell the story. Whenever I needed more information, he was quite forthcoming and made the process move smoothly. Beyond the editing and streamlining, I also added notes that would provide other sources verifying his memories, as well as extra explanations when needed. I had found in other memoirs a lack of explanatory material or sources verifying the accuracy of the writer's memories. As a historian, I always found this quite disturbing and especially problematic when trying to teach undergraduate students the importance of providing evidence to support their arguments. As compelling as I found Jim's narrative, I knew the addition of explanatory information and sources would make his memoir more powerful and useful.

I relied on several different sources to obtain the explanatory material. Several published primary and secondary sources proved invaluable. The most important of these are William Carigan's *Ad Lib: Flying the B-24 Liberator in World War II,* Wesley Frank Craven and James Lea Cate's multivolume *The Army Air Forces in World War II,* Roger A. Freeman's *B-24 Liberator at War,* and Charles H. Freudenthal's *A History of the 489th Bomber Group* (see bibliography). Additionally, I examined the records of the Army Air Forces at the National Archives of the United States that are related to Jim's bomber group and the Eighth Air Force. I was able to confirm all but one of the missions that Jim flew using these sources.

Jim's memoir raises the age-old question of why do some men survive war, while others die? This question is truly unanswerable, yet clearly there are definable factors that provide some explanation. Natural skill, training, determination, and bravery are obviously important. Teamwork and the quality of equipment are often equally significant, especially when flying a bomber over hostile territory. Without question, Jim possessed a great deal of skill, determination, and bravery. Furthermore, while the Army Air Forces' training regimen was not perfect, it was quite good. Jim received almost a year and a half of training before he was sent into combat. Finally, Jim never fails in his conversations with me to commend his crew and mention the B-24's strengths. The young men who served on Jim's plane carried out their duties with aplomb. Beyond a rather humorous incident where several of his men snuck a few young ladies onboard during a training mission, Jim does not remember any problems. The B-24 was not the prettiest or most comfortable airplane in the war, but it proved to be very dependable, capable of delivering a large bombing load, and able to take a lot of punishment.

Unfortunately, however, many servicemen did not survive, even though they shared the same traits as Jim, worked effectively with the men around them, and used good equipment. Neither Jim nor I have an adequate answer for why this is the case. Some assign the choice of life or death to simple fortune. If this is the answer, then Jim was truly lucky on many occasions. Others believe some divine force determines who will live or die. Jim falls more into this category. While he does not discount fortune, he considers himself to have been blessed with a great crew, a strong plane, and dedicated support personnel ranging from his flight instructors to the ground crews to the fighter escorts. Whether it was blessing, fortune, or, as is more likely, a combination of factors that led to Jim's survival, his story should resonate with all of those fortunate enough to hear it.

Jim's memoir addresses some of the most important topics related to the air campaign against Germany in World War II. He carefully describes the extensive training that all American pilots received, the strain that training and service placed on relationships, and the toil of combat in Europe's skies. While several books have captured elements of these issues, especially Philip Ardery's *Bomber Pilot: A Memoir of World War II* and Bert Stiles's *Serenade to the Big Bird* (see bibliography), none does so like Jim's memoir. Anyone interested in understanding the difficult training process, the impact military service had on the home front, and the horror of combat from the cockpit of a B-24 should find this book useful and captivating.

Acknowledgments

This memoir could not have been written without the assistance of many people at various stages in the project. Jim's crew offered him unfailing commitment, and without question, helped him survive the war. Jay Wischkaemper started editing the memoir before passing it on to David. Dr. Gretchen Adams and Dr. Jorge Iber provided invaluable support and advice.

Texas Tech University provided David with a research grant that allowed him to examine records at the National Archives concerning Jim's missions.

Lynn Gamma, at the Air Force History Research Agency at Maxwell Air Force Base in Montgomery, Alabama, facilitated many requests for photos that are included in the memoir.

Ron Chrisman, the director at the University of North Texas Press, guided this memoir throughout the publication process with a careful hand. The anonymous reviewers for the press also made valuable suggestions that have strengthened the memoir.

It goes without saying that this memoir would never have come to print without the love, support, and commitment of our wives, Jean Davis and Lori Snead.

Davis' Missions in Europe, 1944

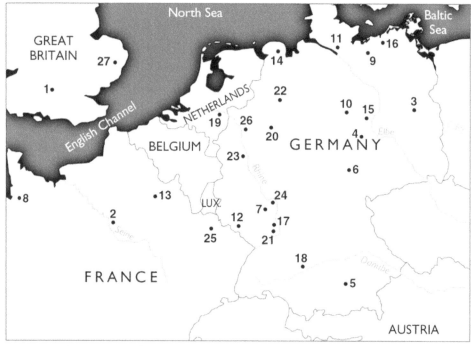

Map locations (all locations in Germany unless otherwise noted)

1. London, England
2. Paris, France
3. Berlin
4. Aschersleben
5. Munich
6. Erfurt
7. Kempten
8. St. Lo, France
9. Wismar
10. Brunswick
11. Hamburg
12. Saarbrucken
13. Laon, France
14. Wittmundhafen
15. Magdeburg
16. Rostock
17. Ludwigshafen
18. Ulm
19. Nijmegen, Netherlands
20. Hamm
21. Lachen-Speyerdorf
22. Osnabruck
23. Cologne
24. Mainz
25. Metz, France
26. Sterkrade
27. Halesworth, England

Introduction

The two years and eight months I was on active duty serving in the Army Air Forces during World War II were the most exciting times in my life. I also see it as a miracle that I survived the roughly thirty combat missions I flew over occupied Europe and Germany in 1944. Many other men just like me flew missions during that period and ultimately made the supreme sacrifice. I do not know why I was spared but feel blessed that I have been able to live a full life. I look back on the war with few regrets. If I ever had any concerns about the destruction of property and loss of life that might have been caused by the allied bombing campaign, they were eliminated during a trip my wife, Jean, and I took in 1983.

We returned to England that year to attend a reunion of the 2nd Air Division of the Eighth Air Force. After a wonderful time visiting with old friends, we decided to visit Switzerland for a few days. One morning we took an all day tour that included a stop in Bern. The driver parked the bus and told us we would have an hour to walk around and visit the city. Jean and I had only walked about two blocks when a gentleman who was also on our tour approached us and said, "I believe you are Americans," in very broken English. He asked if we had visited any other places in Europe, and I told him we had just visited England for a few days, where I had attended a reunion of my World War II Air Force unit. He then asked if I had flown over Europe during the war, and I told him that I had been a B-24 pilot. He immediately took my hand, embraced me, and told me he owed his life to me and the others who had flown over Europe on bombing missions. He said I was the first pilot he had met and that he had always looked forward to meeting someone who flew those planes.

He then explained that he had been a young Jewish boy of sixteen living in Poland when the Germans invaded. All of his family had been killed in the Holocaust, and the only reason he was not killed was that he was young and valuable to the Germans as slave labor. With tears in his eyes he said the only thing that gave the Jewish prisoners enough courage to survive the last years of the war was the fact that every day or every few days, they could hear and sometimes see the bombers go over. Hearing the bombers would give them that little bit of hope that maybe, just maybe, they would some day be freed. He told us he was so indebted to me and the other airplane crews that he wanted us to come to Israel to visit him and his family.

He pulled out his billfold as we were talking and showed us the pictures of his family. One of the pictures was of his daughter's wedding. He pointed out the guests in the picture, including the head of the government, the defense minister, many cabinet ministers, and other high government officials. He told us if we would visit Israel, they would lay out the red carpet, and we would be treated as royalty. He begged and pleaded for us to come. We told him we could not at this time but would look forward to visiting sometime in the future.

I planned on writing him after returning home to thank him for the visit we had and to tell him that some day we hoped to visit Israel. Unfortunately, I lost his name and address. However, our visit with him that day made all of my combat tour well worth the effort and sacrifice. It also encouraged me to ponder my life's experiences. I turned 62 in 1983 and knew retirement was not too far in my future. As I thought about my life, I realized that I had indeed seen and participated in a lot, including the Great Depression,

World War II, and the baby boom. I soon recognized that I had been blessed with loving parents, dedicated comrades, and a wonderful wife. Looking back to when I was a boy, I never imagined that my life would have unfolded as it had.

*   *   *

Prior to the war I lived on a ranch near Abilene, Texas, with my parents, sister, and brother. I was born in 1921 and was the youngest in the family. Life in central Texas was difficult in the 1920s and especially so during the Depression years of the 1930s. My earliest memories are of helping out around the farm. My chores varied and increased as I got older, but they included gathering wood, collecting turkey and chicken eggs, looking after the livestock, growing cotton, and hunting. I remember many 4:00 a.m. wake-up calls and being desperately cold in the winter and oppressively hot in the summer. We did not have electricity until the end of the 1930s and never had indoor plumbing.

During the Great Depression years, life was difficult at best. Few people had any money, and for most, it was a time of simple survival. Thankfully, my family always had enough to eat because we had water to irrigate a large garden. We spent all summer working the garden, and mother was seemingly always canning vegetables. About the only things we bought were salt, pepper, vanilla flavoring, baking powder and soda, coffee, sugar, and cocoa. Mother made cheese from our cow's milk, and we grew enough wheat to make flour. We also kept a couple of beehives for honey. Besides vegetables, we ate a lot of chicken and occasionally some beef, fish, and pork.

While we did not want for food, we had little extra spending money. Airplanes had always been my favorite toys. Before the Depression, when I was seven, my parents gave me a large toy plane that had wheels, wings, a propeller, and a seat where I could actually sit and peddle the aircraft. If the wind was blowing enough, it would turn the propeller, and I really believed I was flying. After I wore out the plane in the early 1930s, there was no way my family could afford to replace it. However, my parents never forgot how much I loved airplanes. For Christmas in 1933, my parents gave me an apple, an orange, a few nuts, and a small tin airplane. Since I had not expected anything in these difficult times, I was thrilled. The plane was only about eight inches long and probably did not cost more than ten cents, but I was as proud of that gift as any I had ever received. I realized that my mother and father had really sacrificed to even give me that.

Despite the hard times I was still able to go to school and have numerous friends. In the little free time we had, we swam in the local quarry, explored the countryside, and whenever possible, went to the local airport in Abilene. Fortunately, my mother sometimes supplied the airport's manager with milk and butter, and I would go with her whenever she made deliveries. The manager let me go out to the planes and look them over. I was really fascinated by them and would spend every minute walking and feeling all over the planes. After I got older I would walk or ride my horse over to the airport whenever I had a little time to spare. In the late 1930s, the Army Air Corps started using the airport as a stop on aviation cadets' cross-country training flights. They would land at Abilene and stay about thirty minutes. I considered those cadets to be the luckiest people on earth. I knew that I would never be able to realize my dream of being a cadet, since I was too scrawny and most likely would not be able to get enough education to even try. To me, it was an impossible dream.

High school proved to be a very important time in my life as it presented many different challenges. I had to leave my local community school after the tenth grade because it did not offer classes beyond that level, and I transferred to a high school seven miles away in Abilene. Just getting there posed a problem, and I typically had to either walk or hitchhike. Furthermore, I had always been a small boy and probably never topped 125 pounds before I graduated. My lack of stature made me an easy victim for the local bully. However, I was able to persevere through these years and did particularly well in my agricultural classes. With the help of my agricultural teacher, I even made plans to attend Texas A&M University after I graduated. My teacher arranged for me to milk cows at A&M in exchange for room and board. My only expenses were going to be for books, uniforms, and other miscellaneous items. Unfortunately, I was unable to find steady work in the summer of 1940 after I graduated and make enough money to cover my expenses.

I faced a real dilemma at this point as I did not know exactly what to do. Thankfully, my sister and brother knew of opportunities in Abilene, and I was able to land a job at Camp Barkeley, an army camp being built there.[1] I began work at the most opportune time as the camp was being expanded to accommodate more than 50,000 troops for training. I started as an errand boy but very quickly earned promotions to perform other duties. It did not take long before I was making more than $100 a month and felt like I was rich. In 1941 I was able to buy my first car, a used 1937 Chevrolet four-door sedan, and I even seriously considered dating for the first time in my life. Unfortunately, there seemed to be no girls available. Since Abilene had a population of only about 30,000 and there were 50,000 troops stationed at the base, I did not have much hope.

My work at Camp Barkeley did convince me that I did not want to be in the infantry, or for that matter in any of the ground forces. The only type of service that really interested me was being a pilot, but that was not possible because you had to complete two years of college before you were eligible to apply to the Aviation Cadet Training program. At that time my first choice was the Air Corps with the Navy a distant second. I was certain, however, that I would have to make a decision before too long because of Japan and Germany's aggression. I suspected that at some point the United States would be drawn into the war, and since I was twenty years old, I

[1] The War Department began construction on Camp Barkeley in 1940 and finished it in July 1941. During the war, it served as a base for infantry training, as a Medical Administrative Officer Candidate School, and starting in 1944 as a German prisoner of war camp. For more information, see John J. Hatcher, "Camp Barkeley: Abilene, Texas," *Texas Military History* 3 (Winter 1963); and http://www.hispanicabilene.com/barkeley.htm, accessed on June 29, 2005.

would be expected to serve. Little did I know that events thousands of miles away in the Pacific would change my life forever.

This is the story of my experiences from December 7, 1941, to my discharge from active service in the Army Air Forces in September 1945. From the time I saw my first airplane I had a burning desire to fly but did not have much hope that it would ever happen. However, while the war brought many unspeakable horrors, it also provided me with new adventures, challenges, and opportunities.

IN HOSTILE SKIES

CHAPTER 1

The Dream

IT WAS FOUR O'CLOCK in the morning on December 7, 1941, when the alarm sounded. Dr. C.L. Prichard, a close personal friend and our family doctor, and I had driven from Abilene to Harper, Texas, to spend the weekend with my sister Frances and hunt deer and turkey on a ranch north of town. We decided we would get up early on Sunday morning and hunt for a couple of hours before we returned. After hunting and deciding the turkeys were too smart for us, we put our guns in the car and drove to my home, which was about five miles east of Abilene. As soon as we arrived, my parents met us and asked if we had heard about the Japanese bombing Pearl Harbor. We had not. They said that several of our warships had been sunk and thousands had been killed. While I had never heard of Pearl Harbor, the news impacted my life significantly. This event meant there was no longer any question about whether I would have to go into the service. I had registered for the draft after Congress had passed the bill requiring all young men to register at the age of eighteen.[1] Now, it was no longer a matter of if, but when and where I would serve.

[1] In September 1940, Congress passed the Selective Service and Training Act initiating the first peacetime draft in American history. See J. Garry Clifford and Samuel R. Spencer, Jr., *The First Peacetime Draft* (Lawrence: University of Kansas Press, 1986).

I had been working at the Quartermasters office at Camp Barkeley since September 1940. Colonel E. C. Adkins, the quartermaster, and H. M. Bauer, his assistant, had both said they would like to have me continue to work for them and would help me join the service and get assigned to their office. I appreciated the fact that they wanted me to work for them, and it would have been an excellent situation for me since I could have continued in the same job and served my military duty at home. However, after giving it serious consideration, I decided it would be best to delay my military career. My parents were building a new home on the north side of our farm, and since dad was not in good health, I felt it would be best for me to help them until they could move into the new house. I had also recently bought some steers and had them in the feedlot. I feared I would not break even financially if I sold them. Additionally, I believed I was already doing my part for the war effort with my current work at Barkeley.

I had worked at Camp Barkeley long enough to know that I did not want to serve in the infantry or artillery. The one thing I really wanted to do was join the aviation cadet pilot training program. All my life I had loved airplanes. Ever since I saw my first one, there was hardly a week that went by when I did not build some type of plane. The planes, when mixed with my desire and imagination, would take me soaring through the clouds. I felt being an aviation cadet and an officer with silver wings on my chest would be the greatest achievement a man could attain. However, I realized my chances of becoming a pilot were slim at best—you had to complete two years of college just to apply. Since I had not been to college, I had little hope.

The months after the bombing of Pearl Harbor were a real challenge. I did not want to be drafted, but I knew that unless I enlisted, it was inevitable since I was twenty years old at the time.[2] I had made up my mind that the U.S. Army Air Forces would be the best place for me. Before I could enlist, I had to help my parents finish their house and then sell the steers I had recently purchased.

[2] Davis was born on April 9, 1921.

It was during this time that a surprising and exciting development occurred. The Army Air Forces eased its requirements for applying for aviation cadet training. Anyone who had completed high school and could pass a test based on a two-year college level would be accepted for cadet training.[3] That was great news for me. After about a day of excitement, the reality hit that I would have to pass the test. I knew it would be difficult, because at best I was an average high school student. In spite of the odds, I intended to make the attempt as soon as possible. I went to the Army Air Forces recruiting office and signed up to take the test. The list of applicants was long, and the office only had facilities to handle about thirty a day. I was told I would have to wait ten days. I was afraid that I might get my draft notice before I could take the test.

The day I was scheduled to take the test finally arrived. I got to the recruiting office early that morning and joined a large group of young men who were standing out front. We all went in and took a seat. Finally, they announced that we were to report to a sergeant who briefed us on what to expect. As soon as I started, my confidence vanished. I had absolutely no hope of passing. Several hours later, we completed the last section. The recruiting officer excused us for lunch and told us to return to have our papers graded. I was so discouraged that I thought about just going home. Changing my mind, at one o'clock I returned. Finally, one of the sergeants called my name, and I sat across from him while he graded my test. I began to think that I had probably made the lowest score ever recorded. It did not take him long to check all the answers and to add the score. I could not see the totals, but after he completed the grading, he started back through the test, grading it again. I wondered if I had gotten any of the questions right since he was taking so long and doing so much checking. He apologized for taking so much time, but he wanted to re-grade the test since I had scored a seventy-nine and a grade of eighty was passing.

[3] See Wesley Frank Craven and James Lea Cate, eds., *The Army Air Forces in World War II, Volume 6—Men and Planes* (University of Chicago Press, 1955), 435 and 549.

I was pleased that I had scored so high but disappointed that I had not gotten one more answer correct. There were a number of questions that could have gone either way. As I left I felt fortunate to have come so close to passing. I also learned while there that I might have one more chance. The Army Air Forces was going to change the test and when it did, I would be eligible to take it. Unfortunately, no one knew when it would be offered, and I was afraid I would receive my draft notice any day.

There was one person who was glad I failed the test. My mother was not excited about seeing her son become a pilot. She believed flying would be the most dangerous thing I could do. While she never did tell me that she did not want me to join the Army Air Forces, I could tell she wanted me to choose some other branch of the military.

I decided to wait and hoped the new exam would arrive before my draft notice. I knew that as a last resort I could try to take the Navy flight test. I went by the Navy recruiting office, but just inside the door was a large picture showing an airplane landing on an aircraft carrier. All the water and such a small place to land had no appeal to me, so I turned around and left the building. I gambled that I would get to take the new Army Air Forces exam and plotted a strategy to do better than the first time. I had thought a lot about the test I had taken, and knew that if I were able to take another test, I would do it differently. Each part of the test had a time limit, and I tried to answer the questions in sequence. On my next attempt, I would skip the more difficult questions and come back to them if I had time. That would give me an advantage of answering more questions.

It was during this period that something unexpected happened. Each spring and summer I played softball with various teams in the local league as a pitcher and third baseman. I was playing on the base team with Leonard Antilley, a young man I had grown up with. We were both working for the Quartermaster's office when on one of our afternoon breaks we decided to go outside and sit on the front steps to drink a Coke. While we were sitting, two young ladies who worked in our office also decided to come out to drink their

Cokes. We were passing the time of day when Leonard and I suggested they come out to see us play in the ballgame that afternoon. Since neither one of them had a car, we also agreed to take them.

That afternoon Leonard and I picked them up. After visiting a while on the front porch, we went to the car and faced a small dilemma—where would everyone sit? Since we were in my car, Leonard said he would sit in the back. The young ladies, Jean Ellis and Margaret Hester, asked where we wanted them to sit. We suggested that one sit up front with me and the other sit in the back seat with Leonard. They hesitated a minute and finally Jean said she would sit in the front with Davis. Everyone at the office called me "Davis." We were hungry after the game, and I suggested that we go to the drive-in and get a sandwich and a milk shake. We had a lot of fun that evening driving around town, even though gasoline was very scarce.

It had not officially been a date, but we really had a great time. A few days later, I summoned my courage and called Jean to ask her for a date. She said she could not go because she already had plans. Undeterred, the next week I tried again and almost fainted when she said yes. It was not long before we were going steady. It was great having something other than going into the service to think about.

Each day I would go by the recruiting office and check to see if a new test had been received. Each day I would get the same answer. I was beginning to think they would never get a new test. One day when I got home in August 1942, I had an envelope that I knew was a notice to report for a physical for the draft. It was, and now I was really desperate about what to do. If the Army Air Forces did not get the new exam within a week, I decided to take the Navy test. If I failed that, I would join the Army Air Forces as a private. On the last possible day, I went by the Army Air Forces office to check on the new exam. I had no reason to believe it would have arrived. When I asked and they said they had received a new exam that day, I did not believe them. However, it was true, and they told me that I could take it the next day.

I was there early the next morning ready to take the test. I gave the test my best effort, but I ended up with the same feeling I had before. I did not think I had done well and was really discouraged. We finished about noon and returned after lunch to have our tests graded. It was a long wait. Finally my name was called, and I went up and sat across the table from the sergeant as he checked each answer. It seemed to take forever. As he added the score I could not stand to look. Finally he said "Congratulations. You have scored an 87." At first I thought he was kidding, but he assured me I had passed. Only three of us out of the thirty who took the exam passed. We were asked to report in the morning for our physical, and if all went well, we would be sworn into the Army Air Forces.

I could hardly wait to tell Jean. I could not believe that I had passed the first hurdle to becoming an aviation cadet. Everyone was happy except my mother. She claimed she was, but I knew she had reservations. Jean and I celebrated that night. Even after the thrill of passing the exam, I thought this was too good to be true and was afraid that they would find something that would disqualify me during my physical exam. I was not aware of any physical problem, but I still worried about what they might find.

Once again I was in front of the recruiting station before it opened on August 19, 1942.[4] I was anxious to take the physical. It took a lot longer than I had thought because it was very thorough. They were especially interested in your heart and eyes. Finally I was told that I passed the physical and would be sworn in that afternoon. It is impossible to describe my feeling as I left the recruiting office after being sworn in. We were told we would be put on ready reserve status and would be called to active duty before long, perhaps in two or three months. What a change my life had taken. At last now I knew the direction my military service would take me.

Not knowing how long it might be before I would be called to active duty, I continued to work. Late that summer, Jean planned to take her vacation and visit her mother in Tyler, Texas. She asked me to come down and meet her family. Since I had never been to the

[4] Enlisted Record of Davis, August 19, 1942, in author's possession.

piney woods of east Texas, it sounded like a great idea. I spent two nights visiting Jean's family and had a great time.

Jean actually grew up in Edom, a small community about eighteen miles west of Tyler. Her father died when she was fifteen years old and her brother was ten. She had to transfer to Van, Texas, since Edom did not have a high school. She graduated as valedictorian of her high school class, but finding enough money to go to college was almost impossible. Somehow she managed, and enrolled at Texas Woman's University in Denton, Texas, in the fall of 1940. During her second year in college she received a call from her uncle living in Abilene who told her that there was an opening for a secretary at Camp Barkeley. Since her family was poor and she wanted to serve her country, she decided to leave college. She boarded a bus to Abilene and got a job at the Quartermasters office. That is how we became acquainted.

Although Jean and I worked in the same office, we did not see much of each other, and because everything was rationed, we were not able to date very often. Gasoline was really hard to get.[5] We would usually go to the movie on Saturday night and on Sunday we would sit on the front porch and visit. Occasionally, we could rake up enough money and gas to visit a local park.

By late fall I still had not received orders to report for active duty, and it seemed as if I was the only young man remaining in civilian clothes. I was a little embarrassed, because I believed people were wondering what was wrong with me and why I was not in a uniform of some kind. Thanksgiving and Christmas came and went, and there were still no orders. I dropped by the recruiting office to see why I had not received them, and the recruiting officer assured me that my time was coming soon.[6] Finally, on February 4, 1943, I

[5] The U.S. Office of Price Administration managed efforts at conservation and rationing. The United States rationed many products including gasoline, tires, meat, coffee, and sugar. For more information see William L. O'Neill, *A Democracy at War: America's Fight at Home and Abroad in World War II* (Cambridge, MA: Harvard University Press, 1993), 136 and 248-9.

[6] It was not unusual for men who joined the Army Air Forces to have to wait several months to a year to actually begin training because of shortages of instructors, airfields, barracks, and equipment. See Stephen E. Ambrose, *The*

received my orders to report for active duty at the Army Air Forces recruiting office in downtown Dallas on February 17.

The night before I left, Jean and I ate out and went to a movie. I did not get home until after midnight. I do not think I went to sleep at all because of the excitement of what the future might hold. I did not pack a very large bag because whatever I took with me would have to be returned. This was the day I was leaving home, perhaps never to return. We got to the train station about nine that morning after I had picked up Jean. My parents, my brother Richard, and his wife Fern went to the train station to see me off. At this point, even though I was excited to go, I dreaded seeing the train come in. I was glad to see four young men I knew also taking the train to Dallas to report for active duty.

My friends and I found a place where we could sit together and spent most of the day talking about what we might expect and what we wanted to do. I enjoyed the train ride to Dallas, and after we arrived about 3:00 p.m., we walked to the federal building where we were to report. We were not by ourselves, as there were perhaps 250 other young men who had reported that day. We had to sign a number of papers and complete several forms. For the most part, I did not know what they were. We were also given short physical exams and asked to drop our pants and bend over seven different times that evening.

There was no question we were in the military now. We received a meal ticket that allowed us to go across the street to a small cafe and eat dinner. At this point we had no idea where we would be sent, but we knew the Army Air Forces had training centers in Georgia, California, and Texas. About ten o'clock that evening we were advised that we would be sent to the San Antonio Aviation Cadet Classification Center. Trucks took us to the train station that night, and we boarded the train about 2:00 a.m. Once on the train, we rode on day coaches, so sleeping during the trip was difficult. This was the second night in a row that I had not been able to sleep,

---

Wild Blue: The Men and Boys Who Flew the B-24s over Germany (New York: Simon and Schuster, 2001), 45.

and I was feeling the effects. We arrived at the train station late in the morning and traveled in a convoy of trucks to the base.

For the next three weeks we took every kind of test you could imagine. We were interviewed and analyzed time and time again. There were a number of physical exams. The doctors and nurses were especially concerned about our hearts, and they gave us complete heart exams several times. I was amazed at how the tests revealed many young men to have some kind of heart defect. Few knew that they had heart trouble prior to the exam. We lost young men not only to heart problems, but also to other physical disabilities. It seemed as if heart, eye, and back problems were the most prevalent disqualifying conditions. It was sad to see so many fine young men who had dreamed of flying suddenly be told they were assigned to ground duty. After all the tests, we received the usual military uniforms and had our hair cut so close that it looked almost like you had been shaved.

In addition to all the tests, interviews, and physical exams, the doctors and nurses gave us our shots and vaccinations. We also spent a lot of time in a theatre being briefed, watching various films, and listening to all types of lectures. We did physical training, practiced marching, and worked kitchen and guard duty. Our days and nights were very busy. Most of us were afraid of the possibility that we would be cut from the aviation program. The most difficult thing to control was the terrible case of homesickness. At times it was so bad that you would think, "What the hell. I wish they would wash me out." I wrote letters to Jean and the folks almost every day. However, there were some days when I did not have time to get a letter or card off.

While a few of the trainees had entered the cadet program to become bombardiers or navigators, most of us had enlisted hoping to become pilots. I had developed the mentality of taking it one day at a time. Because I did not want to be a navigator or bombardier, I was really concerned that I would fail some part that would disqualify me from pilot's school. After three weeks of testing, we were anxious for the day to come when we would receive orders telling us which school, if any, we would be assigned.[7] Finally, we were advised that assignments would be posted at four the next afternoon.

I dreaded going down to see if I had qualified for pilot training, or if I had been assigned to some other duty. When the orders were posted, there was such a large crowd around the board that I could not get close enough to see. People exhibited various emotions when they found their name on the orders.[8] Some would shout for joy, and others would express disappointment at the assignment they had been given. Finally, the crowd cleared, and I was able to check the board. I found the "D" section and ran down it to Davis. There were a lot of Davis's. I found my name and could not believe it when I saw that I had been assigned to pilot training. For the first time since I had left home I had something to be really happy about. I could hardly wait to call home to tell Jean that I had qualified. The phones were busy for hours because of all the cadets calling home to tell loved ones how they had been classified. I finally got through and told Jean that I had qualified for pilot training and would be assigned to preflight school in San Antonio.[9]

My cadet class would be Class 43-K.[10] The day for us to move across the road to preflight finally came. After a brief speech from the commanding officer we started the march four abreast. Our uniforms were pressed, our shoes were shined, and we made every effort to look as good as we could. Long before we got to the gate to enter the preflight training area, we could hear calls coming from all directions, "You will be sorry." The closer we got to the gate the

---

[7] Craven and Cate, *Army Air Forces in World War II, Volume 6*, 549-54.

[8] The cadets who did qualify as pilots were sent to other schools for instruction. Cadets who did not pass all the tests, but still did well, were generally sent to bombardier training or navigation school. Those who did not qualify as pilots, navigators, or bombardiers were assigned as enlisted men to different schools for training as gunners, radio operators, mechanics, and other jobs.

[9] Craven and Cate, *Army Air Forces in World War II, Volume 6*, 559-62. Preflight training involved both academic and physical exercises. Besides the initial tests, this was the first place where cadets could wash out of the program.

[10] The 43-K refers to the year, 1943, and the specific class Jim was in, K-class.

louder the calls were, and they seemed to be coming from every direction. This was a welcome that I could have done without.

We marched to an area in front of some two-story barracks. As we stood at attention an officer briefed us on what we could expect during our stay. For example, from this day forward there would be no walking except while in formation. Everything else would be running. Finally, he told us we were to pick up our bags and go to the barracks assigned to us. When he called my name I ran to the pile of bags and searched until I found mine and carried it to the building that would be my home for the next two and a half months. Inside, our upperclassmen were waiting. Each building would have fifty cadets in it, twenty-five lowerclassmen and twenty-five upperclassmen. The upperclassmen occupied the upstairs and we stayed on the lower floor, where we were assigned a bunk. Each upperclassman was assigned to and became personally responsible for a specific underclassman. Our seniors instructed that everything had a specific place and had to be in that place or else, so get everything put up on the double.

As we were going through the process they ordered us to stop, get our pen and paper, and write a letter home. I was glad to have the opportunity because I needed to write home anyway, but before I could get one line written, orders came to fall out and get in formation. It was two weeks before I ever finished that letter. We ran outside leaving everything in a mess. We stood at attention for a personal inspection. We were screamed at, shouted at, and degraded in every possible way. We were then ordered to pick up all the rocks around our barracks area and put them in a neat pile. We broke ranks in a mad dash to start picking up rocks. There were a million rocks, and no one could pick them up fast enough, stack them neatly enough, or do anything that would please the upperclassmen. We had not had lunch and were about to starve, but no one dared mention that. This went on for hours. We were the dirtiest, most exhausted group of men you have ever seen.

Late that afternoon our upperclassmen told us to clean up for dinner by a certain time. With twenty-five men trying to use one bathroom at double speed, it was interesting. Once we were inside the cafeteria, we heard the rules for eating. We would sit at attention at all times on the front four inches of our chair. We could not be seated until all upperclassmen had been seated, and we were told to take our seats. Each of us would sit between upperclassmen. We could not take any food until all upperclassmen had taken what food they wanted. We were also required to eat what they called a square meal, which meant eyes straight ahead, with food lifted vertically from the plate until level with the mouth, and then brought to the mouth. All the food from the serving dishes had to be eaten while you were at attention with eyes rigid and straight ahead. There is no way you can eat like that. When we were ordered to rise and leave the mess hall, we were still starving because none of us were able to take more than three or four bites.

We marched back to our barracks in double time. Once there, it got worse. We stood at attention for hours while being screamed at, lectured, and in general, given hell on earth. When taps sounded we knew the lights had to be turned out, which we thought would finally give us some peace. We were wrong. We were given a brief period to use the bathroom—nowhere near enough time for everyone to use it. We then had to get in bed and lay at attention. We lay in our bunks at attention for four and a half hours longer while being lectured to. The upperclassmen would take turns walking the aisle. At 2:30 a.m. they told us they were all going upstairs and that under no circumstance were we to get out of our bunks for anything, not even to go to the bathroom. We were dying to use the bathroom. We finally heard the last upperclassman walk up the wooden stairs and across the squeaking floor to his bunk. No one said a word, but we were all thinking the same thing.

After about ten minutes everyone started to ease out of bed at the same time. We were all trying to be quiet so we would not be heard. Our footlockers were at the foot of our bunks, which did not leave much room in the aisle. We were all in our underwear and barefoot creeping to the bathroom, trying not to make any noise. Suddenly we heard feet hit the floor upstairs. We all tried to leave the bathroom at the same time in total darkness in order to get back to our bunks before the upperclassmen could catch us. It was a mad house. Not only did we have twenty-five men trying to get through the bathroom door at the same time, but those who were able to clear the bathroom door had an even bigger problem. The first ones out stumbled over a footlocker and fell in the middle of the floor. Others coming behind them kept falling over them into one heap of human bodies. As a result of our disobedience, we had to get back into our beds at attention and were lectured until reveille, which came at 5:00 a.m. This was a day we would never forget. It had started off bad; it went downhill from there.

We began our classes and other scheduled activities. We took courses in several different areas, some of which we could not spell let alone understand. It took a lot of effort and dedication to pass them. I learned about math, theory of flight, and ground activities. I especially enjoyed the classes on weather. We also took courses in navigation, airplane identification, sending and receiving Morse code, physics, and many other subjects. The most difficult subjects for me were physics and Morse code. I had never had physics and really did not know what it was all about. Morse code was particularly hard since I do not have much rhythm or musical aptitude.

Every second of the day was obligated from five in the morning until at least midnight. Our study period was from 7:00 until 9:00 p.m. I needed more time to study than that, and had to do some at night, usually after the upperclassmen went upstairs about midnight. The rules prohibited us from studying after midnight, but I would get a flashlight and crawl under the covers and study about two hours. I never got more than two or three hours of sleep a night. Thankfully, a young man who slept next to me and had been to medical school helped out a lot. I doubt that I would have survived tests if it had not been for his help.

The physical training was as tough as our academic classes. We had to meet rigid standards in every type of physical fitness. In addition to meeting minimum standards in all track events—the 100-yard dash, broad jump, high jump, and hurdles—we had to meet a certain time in the cross-country course. I found pushups and pull-ups difficult because of my long arms.

We also drilled in military training, including marching and weapons training. One of the toughest drills we had was on a Saturday evening. We were required to drill for two hours in our gas masks. We were either running from one end of the parade field to the other, or if not running, we would be on our hands and knees crawling. To do that for two hours without a break left us exhausted. The amazing thing about preflight was that I gained fifteen pounds, despite the tremendous physical exertion, never having enough to eat, and functioning on little sleep.

Our first Sunday we were allowed to go to morning church services. We all went if for no other reason than to get away from the upperclassmen. Before the services started, the cadet sitting next to me noticed a door in the front of the church that led to a hall and a back door. He suggested we go out the back door to the edge of a hill that was covered with brush and trees, and there we could hide for an hour and hopefully take a nap. We were acquainted with the terrain in the rear of the church because it was part of our cross-country course. The more we thought about it the more we believed it was a great idea, and so we escaped. That was the first peaceful hour we had experienced for a week. When the services were over, we returned to our barracks.

The second week we experienced a tragedy. One evening during inspection an upperclassman told me and my bunkmate that our floor was filthy and to get a bucket, soap, and water and clean it. The floor was as clean as it could be, but we knew there was nothing to do but scrub it. I had had a typhoid shot that morning and felt terrible. My arm was so sore I could hardly move it, and I had a high fever. My bunkmate had a terrible cold and should have gone to the doctor that morning, but we all knew if we missed any time due to sickness we might not be able to make it up, so we would have to be in terrible shape to report to sick call. We scrubbed the floor for two hours. The next morning I felt better, but my bunkmate was worse. I told the upperclassman in charge that my mate was too sick to go to breakfast and should go to the hospital. He agreed and called for an ambulance. The next day we were told he had developed bronchial pneumonia and had died. As sad as we were, we were still required to continue our schedule. It had a sobering effect on everyone for the next few days—especially me.

Regularly, the upperclassmen would have each of us perform some song, read a poem, perform a dance, or whatever. They were all humorous, but we were not allowed to laugh. Each morning and evening we would have to do our thing. They required me to stand on my footlocker at attention, hold out my right arm with my fingers hanging down and my thumb folded in. This would represent a cow's udder and they would ask someone to go in the latrine, get a bucket, and return. They would go through the procedure of milking the cow by pulling on my fingers. This could last a minute or an hour. Since most of the cadets were from the midwest or northeast, they thought of me as a cowboy from the Wild West. One member of our class had been in the army for some time as an enlisted man and was at one time stationed in the South Pacific. He had a palm tree tattooed on his arm and every morning and every evening someone would have to go to the latrine, get a bucket of water, and water his palm tree. Every act was created to be humorous, but we were not allowed to laugh, which made it that much more humorous.

Ernie Davis, one of my friends, was always in trouble. When something funny happened, which occurred often, he could not help but giggle. He stayed in trouble all the time. One day the seat on one of our bathroom commodes was broken in half and Ernie made a large sign and put it on the commode that said "Reserved for Half Ass Upperclassmen." We were all in trouble until he finally admitted doing it so that the rest of us would not be punished. They made him go to the bathroom, stand in front of the mirror in a rigid brace and laugh as loud as he could for what seemed like hours. His voice got weaker and weaker until he could not make a sound.

Two things happened to really help boost my confidence. I always had wanted to play football, but my first two years in high school were at a small rural school with only three boys in the eighth and ninth grade classes. Because I had to transfer to Abilene High School for my last few years of school, and I often had to walk the seven miles to my home, I did not have time to play football in high school. Now, as part of our training, we were allowed to play tag football. In fact, each unit had a team and we competed with other units for the championship. One of the cadets on the team with me was a graduate of Cornell. He played football for them, and upon graduation continued as an assistant coach. He was very impressed with my ability to play quarterback and how well I could pass. We did not win the championship, but he told me if I wanted to play football after the war, to come to Cornell University and he assured me I could make the team.

The other big boost I received was in the cross-country race. Out of the thousands of cadets, I finished second. The young man who beat me by less than a hundred feet was a top runner from the Big Ten Conference, hailing from Ohio State University. I had needed more confidence, and those two events helped.

I heard that we would be given day passes on Sunday, April 4, at the end of our fourth week in preflight. I called Jean as soon as I could and told her. We decided she would catch the bus to San Antonio, and we could spend the day together. I would have off from 10 a.m. to 8 p.m. Through the cadet service club, I made a reservation for her at the Gunter Hotel. I could hardly wait. I had been on base now for over two months without leave. Finally, I would have a chance to spend the day with Jean.

The day finally came, and I was one of the first in line to board the bus to town. We arrived downtown, and I rushed to the hotel. I checked with the front desk, and they told me they did not have a Jean Ellis registered as a guest. I was disappointed and could imagine all kinds of things that might have happened to her. I felt like she would have called me if something had happened to keep her from coming. I was aware that all the buses were full and it was difficult to get on them. As it turned out Jean had arrived about midnight the night before, and when she tried to check in they said they had no reservation for her and no vacancy. She had to spend the night in a lounge chair on the second floor balcony.

We spent that day walking around downtown and sitting in the lobbies of the Gunter and St. Anthony hotels. It was a great day in a lot of ways. Before I entered the service we had been going together for about a year. At that time, the war looked as if it would last for years and there was no way to know what the future might hold for us. We often had talked about when we might marry. That day in San Antonio we decided that we would marry as soon as I was stationed at a base and had enough time. At this point I felt I had accomplished a lot, but I realized how much more it was going to take to successfully complete my cadet training. If by chance I did finish preflight and was sent to primary flight school, maybe we could marry while I was in primary. To me that was a big "if." All too soon the day passed and Jean got on the bus to go back to Abilene, and I headed back to the base. It had been a good day. At least I felt like a human again instead of a robot.

Preflight was almost halfway through and some of my buddies could hardly wait for us to graduate. At last, our final day as underclassmen arrived. The class system went out the door and for one day we were together for one big party. Even looking back on all the hell the upperclassmen had put us through, we really hated to see them go. We also envied them because they were shipping out the next day to primary training. To think, in a few days, they would be flying airplanes. It was going to be exciting for us as well, since we were now the upperclassmen. We were going to be the big dogs and could holler "You will be sorry" to the new arrivals. As it grew later and later and we still had no underclassmen, we really did not think much about it until a captain came by and gave us the sad news that the group we were to receive had been on a train when three of the cadets had gotten sick. Because they were diagnosed with a contagious disease, all the cadets were quarantined, and so we would not have an underclass to discipline.

Although everyone was disappointed that we would not have an underclass to get even with for all the hell we went through, it was, at least for me, a real blessing since it would allow more time to study. I needed every minute I could get. By far the most difficult course I had was a two-week physics class. It was a two-year college course and had three tests. To pass required an average grade of seventy-five on the three tests. The first test was a disaster for me and the second test was not much better. I had to score ninety-five on the final test to pass the course. The night before the final exam I studied all night and was so tired the next morning that I could hardly stay awake. I did not think there was any way I could get the grade I needed. After I took the test I felt I had done poorly and was hoping that they would wash me back one class rather than dropping me from the cadet program entirely, which they had the option to do. That evening I was reluctant to check the test scores. I could not believe my eyes when I saw my final test score of ninety-seven. To say I was happy would be an understatement. Because this was my last problem course, for the first time I felt confident I would graduate from preflight. We had lost several from our class by this time. Some had failed a course; others had developed physical problems; a certain number could not, or would not, adjust to the intense demands of training; a few were dropped because of bad attitudes; and others resigned or were washed out for unknown reasons. Our ranks were beginning to be depleted.

Until now, I had not really thought about the next phase of training, which would be primary training. Now I was anxious and was looking forward to actually getting into the flying part. There were various rumors as to where we would be sent for primary. The most persistent one was to California. Naturally I was hoping it would be somewhere in the southwest, but the fact that I was going to graduate from preflight was the most important thing. The day before we were to leave we heard that we would be sent to Hicks Field, an air base about twenty miles north of Fort Worth. I was thrilled, because it was not far from my home in Abilene.

It was now late May 1943. We were excited when it came time to board the train to Fort Worth. As the trucks pulled out of preflight I looked over the base we were leaving and the classification center. I offered a prayer of thanks for having been chosen to join the aviation cadet program, passing the entrance exam, having qualified for pilot training, and surviving preflight. At this time it seemed everything had gone my way. I felt like I had overachieved and I was wondering when my bubble would burst. It was an unbelievable dream that had come true so far. Perhaps the most exciting thing was the real possibility that maybe, just maybe, things would work out for Jean and me to get married while I was in primary training.[11]

[11] Preflight was only the initial stage of training for aviation cadets. Assuming the cadet passed this stage, he then entered a four-part training cycle to become a pilot. The four parts were primary, basic, advanced, and phase training. For a good description of the training cycles, see John C. McManus, *Deadly Sky: The American Combat Airman in World War II* (Novato, CA: Presidio Press, 2000).

CHAPTER 2

Training

WHEN WE ARRIVED AT the Fort Worth train station, several army trucks were there to take us to Hicks Field. While waiting to leave the train, word spread that our upperclassmen at Hicks Field consisted entirely of West Point graduates. Remembering our preflight experience and knowing the discipline required of West Point cadets, we were all a little nervous. The ride to the base took about an hour. None of us had ever seen Hicks Field, so we did not know what to expect.

Upon arriving we were given our barracks number and instructed to pick up our bags and report. We discovered that all the buildings looked rather old, and most were built with corrugated iron. They were not like most army buildings, as they were one story and accommodated about forty people each. The big surprise, and I might add a very pleasant one, was the reception we received from our upperclassmen. They were very polite and helped us with our bags. They quickly relieved our fears of being underclassmen. They assured us that there would be none of the discipline we had in preflight. They helped us in every way possible.

We assembled and heard what we could expect while at Hicks Field. While we would not be allowed off the base during the week, we received the welcome news that we would have a pass each weekend from noon Saturday until eight o'clock Sunday evening.

That meant that Jean could come down on the weekends. I called her as quickly as I could, and we made plans for her to come to Fort Worth the next weekend.

We were awakened at 5:00 a.m. to eat breakfast. Some days we would go to ground school in the morning and fly in the afternoon. Other days would be reversed. As always there would be physical training. The fact that it was a relaxed atmosphere with little harassment from the upperclassman was a welcome change.

Finally, the day came that we had all been anticipating. We were to report to the flight line to meet our instructors and start our flying lessons. I did not know how fortunate I was to be assigned to Donald A. McDonnel. He was a civilian under contract to the Army Air Forces as an instructor. He was a great person and pilot—I could not have had a better teacher. He was an older person and had flown the mail in addition to being a bush pilot in Alaska. Each flight instructor had four students. The other three cadets that I flew with were Francis L. Creighton, Frank D. Caple, and Louis H. Daugherty.

We gathered at the flight line at 1:00 p.m., and McDonnel took us out to the planes we would be flying. They were PT-19's.[1] It was a low-wing plane with an inline engine and two open cockpits. When we first approached them, they looked like monsters. He explained all the various parts and in general acquainted us with the plane. After about an hour he told us he would take two of us up that afternoon for an orientation ride and would take the other two up the next morning. Francis and Frank got the first flight while Louis and I waited on the flight line. McDonnel left with Francis and was gone about thirty minutes and then he took Frank. When they returned he told Frank to have me come out. It turned out he had enough time to give me a ride. I had not expected to go, and as a result I had consumed two or three Cokes. I hurried to the plane and crawled

[1] The PT-19 "Cornell" was a single-engine trainer built by Fairchild. It had an open cockpit with seats for an instructor and a cadet. For more information see Ambrose, *The Wild Blue*, 57; and United States Air Forces Museum, Fairchild PT-19A, http://www.wpafb.af.mil/museum/ac/pg000040.htm, accessed on June 30, 2005.

into the front seat. Since I had only been up in an airplane one time previously, I was quite nervous.

We took off, and he put the plane through a number of maneuvers. After he had shown me several different moves, he asked me to put my hand on the controls and follow him. He told me that he was turning loose the controls and asked me to fly the plane. He instructed me to turn left, then right, and was reminding me to keep the plane straight and level. Because of the Cokes I had consumed, however, my stomach became very upset. He realized I had a problem and called me over the intercom and asked if I was sick. I could not even talk at that time so I shook my head that I was. When he took the controls, I grabbed my paper sack and upchucked. I was so sick that I did not care what happened. As gently as he could he flew back to the field and landed. Once we had stopped and cut the engine, I began to feel better. He got out of the rear seat and came up to see how I felt. I was terribly embarrassed and was afraid I had blown it. He assured me that a lot of cadets got sick and not to worry about it, but I was still disappointed. That was the first time (and also the last time) that I ever got sick in an airplane.

Jean rode the bus to Fort Worth on Saturday morning and I met her that afternoon. I do not remember ever proposing to her. I guess we had simply assumed for a long time that we would get married, so all that was left was to make the plans as to when and where. We decided the wedding would be on Saturday, June 19, 1943, and be held at her uncle's home in the small town of Handley. It joined Fort Worth on the east and would be convenient for everyone. Because my time was so restricted, Jean had to take care of all the arrangements.

As far as I knew, my flying was satisfactory. We were all aware that the washout rate was high in primary.[2] In some cases as much

---

[2] Close to forty percent of all cadets failed to finish their training. From July 1939 to August 1945, a little more than 193,000 cadets finished flight training out of more than 317,000 who started. See Craven and Cate, *Army Air Forces in World War II, Volume 6*, 577-78.

Morse code training for cadets (courtesy of the Air Force Historical Research Agency, Maxwell Air Force Base, Montgomery, Alabama)

Aviation cadets in weather class (courtesy of the Air Force Historical Research Agency, Maxwell Air Force Base, Montgomery, Alabama)

as fifty percent of the class would be washed out. Cadets dropped out or were removed for many different reasons. Some just could not keep up with the heavy academic and physical demands. Others were so homesick that they could not concentrate on their studies. Finally, a few simply decided they would prefer ground duty or that it would be easier just to be an enlisted man. With this in mind, we knew every day might be our last. After about a week our numbers started dropping. In the evening when we would come to the barracks after a busy day, we would see a cot that had been stripped and all of the cadet's belongings were gone. For some reason if a cadet washed out, they would remove him from the base immediately. As a result we had a lot of friends leave without being able to say goodbye. All of the cadets were really great young men, and many friendships developed only to suddenly end. It would be true as long as we were in the military. Nothing was certain and we all lived from day to day. I know that Jean and my parents got tired of me writing about my fears of being washed out. The first month had taken its toll and at least thirty-five percent of our class had been sent to other assignments.

McDonnel was the nicest person when we were on the ground, but he became anything but that after we took off. He would scream, yell, and chew on you from the time you left the ground. The first time I ever got really scared was the day we were doing aerobatics. My instructor told me to roll the plane, and I really thought I might die. When we were bottom side up, the microphone fell down and hit me in the face, trash and wrappers fell out, and I was hanging by my safety belt. After that I was not sure if I wanted to be a pilot. That day was by far the worst ride I had experienced up to that point, and McDonnel was making that clear. Eventually he told me this was the worst flying he had ever seen, gave me a list of things to do, and told me when I completed them to return to the field. He had told me to do so many things so fast that I could not remember what to do or in what order. I was too scared to ask him to repeat it, so I started doing whatever I could. He had never been this loud and demanding.

On my next flight, everything I did was horrible. Partly because I felt McDonnel might tell me it was over when we returned to the field, I dreaded going back. To make the situation worse, I made the worst landing I had ever made. I must have leveled off twenty feet above the runway and dropped it in. We hit the ground hard and bounced a couple of times. I taxied up to the flight line and had to wait a couple of minutes for the jeep to lead me to a parking place. I put the plane in the proper place, cut the engine, and filled in the logbook. I was in no hurry to get out of the plane to meet McDonnel at the tail to discuss the flight. I delayed it as long as I could. Finally I had no choice, and I crawled out and walked to the rear of the plane.

I did not see McDonnel. I looked everywhere, but he was not in sight. I got back on the wing and looked in every direction but did not see him. He was nowhere around, and he could not have gotten far enough away that I could not see him. The only thing that could have happened was that he fell out of the plane while I was doing a slow roll. I ran across the ramp and through the airplanes as fast as I could to operations and told them I had lost my instructor. I explained what happened. To be sure that he was not in operations they paged him—was I ever relieved when he walked through the door. He apologized for getting out of the plane while we were waiting on the parking jeep. What a day but at least I did not get dismissed from the cadets, for now.

Two days later, we practiced landings at an auxiliary field about fifteen miles north of Hicks Field. It was similar to Hicks in that it did not have paved runways. In reality it was just a smooth cow pasture. I had made three landings and was taxiing around to take off again when McDonnel told me to stop. He got out of the rear cockpit, walked up the wing, and told me he wanted me to take it up alone and shoot a few landings. It all happened so fast I really did not have time to get nervous. I taxied out and headed into the wind and shoved the throttle forward. I guess I was a little disappointed that I was not as scared as I thought I would be. As I pushed the throttle forward, the engine began to roar, and soon I was rolling down the runway. The tail lifted and I started pulling back on the stick. Being a grass field it was a little bumpy but it was not long before I could feel the plane lift off and smooth out. The PT-19, being a low-wing open cockpit plane, was one of the finest and most enjoyable planes you could ever hope to fly. I climbed to traffic pattern altitude and turned to the right, then to my right again to the downwind leg. I found it strange to be alone and not have any fear. I have to give credit to my instructor.

At the proper time I made another right turn to the base leg of the pattern and then to the final approach for a landing. Everything was just right as I settled in to a good landing. I taxied around to where McDonnel was and he motioned for me to go again. I made five takeoffs and landings by myself that morning and after the fifth he motioned for me to stop. He got into the rear seat and told me to carry him back to the field. That was one of the greatest thrills of my life. When we met for our after-flight talk, he told me I had done a very good job. That evening when the word got out I had soloed, my buddies picked me up and threw me in the shower with my clothes on.

On the weekend of June 12 Jean came to Fort Worth, and we selected our rings and made as many of the final arrangements as we could for our wedding the next weekend. As usual I did not have a lot of time to think about the wedding because they kept us so busy. That week the weather had been cloudy and rainy. Finally, Saturday June 19 arrived. When we woke up that morning the rain was pelting our tin roof. We got to the flight line and met for the morning briefing. The first words that were spoken put me into shock. Our instructors told us that because we had missed some flying time during the week and because it was raining now, all passes would be cancelled for the weekend so we could make up for the lost time, no exceptions. Our wedding was scheduled at 8 p.m. that night, and now I could not even get to a phone to tell Jean I would not be there.

The instructors told us to remain in the briefing room until advised as to what the schedule would be. We had been in the room about thirty minutes when the rain stopped. I was anxious to get to a phone to tell Jean that I was confined to the base, and there was no way to get out. I was thinking about everything but flying that morning, and I am sure it was reflected in my performance. The skies cleared at about 11 a.m., and it turned out to be a beautiful day. After all planes returned, we met back in the briefing room and heard that we would be given weekend passes after all, because we got in a good morning of flying. It was now 12:30 p.m. When we were dismissed, one of my buddies told me that I had been given two tours for something. That meant that I would have to go to the parade ground and walk with a parachute for an hour before I could go on pass. I had no choice. It was now about 1:00 p.m. I walked my tour and rushed back, took a shower, and dressed as quickly as I could. It was now a little after 2:00 p.m., and I had to get a cab to town, stop at the jewelry store to pick up Jean's ring, and go to the courthouse to get the marriage license. I had plenty of time but not much to spare. I rushed to the main gate and discovered there were no taxis available. There was no other way to get to town except going to the highway and hitching a ride.

About the time I got to the highway, a taxi showed up and carried me to the jewelry store so I could get the ring. It was only about four blocks to the courthouse where I would have to get the marriage license. When I got to the courthouse, I found all the offices closed. I walked all over the first floor and could find no one. As I was walking up the stairs, I heard a door close and rushed down the hall in the direction of the noise until I found a janitor emptying trash. He said the courthouse closed at noon on Saturdays. I told him that I wanted to get a marriage license and asked him who I should see and where. He explained the he did not know who issued licenses. We walked up to the first floor and I told him I was being married at 8 p.m. and had to find someone to issue a license. He was very sympathetic and said he would call someone who might know. He made a call and talked to someone who referred him to someone else. He finally told me the county clerk issued the license and gave me his home phone number. I called the number and a gentleman answered. I told him my problem as best as I could. He said he was just leaving to go on a fishing trip, but that if I could come out immediately that he would fill out a license for me. After a great deal of effort, I finally found a cab to take me to the address he had given me.

He invited me in and I asked the cab to wait for me. He started filling out the marriage license and asked for the certificate of my blood test. I did not know what he was talking about. He explained that you had to have a blood test three days before you applied for a license. I said I was in the military as a cadet and stationed at Hicks Field. He explained that there were no exceptions, but he really wanted to help me out. He gave me the name of a doctor who I then called and told my sad story. After a pause the doctor said he would give me a certificate, but he would have to go to his office, which was downtown. I told him I would be there as fast as I could. I got there first and waited. I did not know if I would be in time for my wedding or not. By now I wondered what else could go wrong. The doctor soon arrived and filled out the proper papers. I thanked him and had the cab carry me back out to the county clerk's home. In filling out the form the clerk discovered that he needed something from his office. I released the cab and rode to the courthouse with him. Finally I had the marriage license in hand. I thanked him and rushed out the door to catch a cab to get to Handley, where the wedding would be. This was Saturday afternoon in Fort Worth and everybody was downtown. I ran from street to street trying to find a cab, but none were available. I was about ready to give up when someone blew a car horn, and I heard a voice call my name. I stopped, turned around and to my utter surprise, saw my brother and his wife who were on the way to the wedding. I was never so glad to see anyone in my life. I jumped in their car, and we got to the wedding just as it was about to start. I came in the back door and Jean said, "Where have you been? It's time for you to get in the living room for the ceremony."

In spite of all that happened that day we did get married. After the wedding, we drove to a restaurant and had dinner. I had not eaten since breakfast that morning. We spent our one-day honeymoon at the Blackstone Hotel in downtown Fort Worth. Then, I guess as a last swipe, fate did deal us one more surprise. When we checked into the hotel and were shown our room, we discovered it had very small single beds.

The next day after breakfast we drove to the motel that my aunt owned, which was across the street from the Fort Worth stockyards. We had lunch with my parents and the rest of my family. All too soon the day was over and the sad reality dawned that I would have to go back to Hicks Field and Jean would have to return to Abilene. As we kissed and bid each other goodbye late that afternoon, we made plans for Jean to come back next weekend. Little did we know that it would be two months before we would see each other again.

That next Thursday we were restricted to the base indefinitely because of an outbreak of polio. I had to call Jean and tell her the bad news. During the remaining weeks we were at primary, morale was not very good, mainly because there were no weekend passes and nothing to break the routine. About the only thing we could do was play baseball and feed Cokes to Rosie, a donkey who was considered the mascot of Hicks Field. She loved Cokes and would drink every one you gave her. Cokes came only in bottles in those days, and after you took the cap off, she would take the mouth of the bottle between her teeth, hold her head up, and let the Coke drain into her mouth.

As we got further along the number of washouts dropped off. We had lost about 50 percent of our class by the end. One of my close friends was washed out near the end because he returned from a solo flight with telephone wire hanging from the landing gear of his plane. The only way he could have gotten it was by buzzing, definitely a no-no, so he was out. We had been told many times that we would be eliminated from cadet training if we were ever caught flying too low. I was also learning that tragedy could occur. Another close friend of mine, Fred Donahue, was flying solo one day, and either lost power from engine failure or was buzzing. He failed to clear a power line and plowed into the ground. They hauled the plane back to the base and piled it behind one of the hangars. Perhaps it was put there to impress on us what could happen. It made you sick to see the twisted wreckage with blood all over it.

As the final weeks of primary passed, those of us who were left became confident that we would make the grade and graduate to basic flight training. The last week of primary we began to get anxious as to where we would be sent. Rumors were plentiful. Finally, orders were posted that we would be sent to Enid Army Air Force Base in Oklahoma. At least it was in the southwest but still too far for Jean to make the trips on the weekends.

It is difficult to explain the exhilaration I felt after having passed another phase of training on the way to earning the silver wings of an Army Air Forces pilot. We would be flying BT-13s in basic training.[3] It was one of the planes I had watched as a boy as aviation cadets made cross-country flights into Abilene. I had watched them as they flew overhead and thought that some day I would love to fly one, never dreaming that it would ever be possible. Now I would live that impossible dream.

We also realized that the BT-13 would not be as easy or as forgiving as the PT-19. The BT-13 was an all-metal trainer with a huge radial engine. The thing I really remembered about it was the loud noise it made as you changed the propeller pitch. Learning to fly the plane was a challenge. It was thought that if you got as far as basic flight training, then you were over the hump. The washout rate in basic and advanced was much less than in primary. We were also aware that we would be back at a military base, whereas primary was a contract flying school. As a result, basic would be much stricter. Once again, we packed our bags, boarded the train, and moved on to Enid.

At the time it was named Enid Air Force Base, but in later years the name was changed to Vance Air Force Base in honor of Col.

---

[3] The BT-13 "Valiant" was a single-engine trainer built by Vultee, with two seats—one for the instructor and one for the cadet. For more information see Craven and Cate, *Army Air Forces in World War II, Volume 6,* 226; and United States Air Forces Museum, Vultee BT-13B "Valient," http://www.wpafb.af.mil/museum/early_years/ey17.htm, accessed on June 30, 2005.

Leon Vance, the deputy commander of the 489th Bomb Group during the war. I served in the 489th in England, and it was there that Colonel Vance won the Medal of Honor. He spent several weeks in the hospital as a result of an air crash. After leaving the hospital and on the way home to the United States, the plane he was on disappeared over the Atlantic Ocean.

While the civilian facilities at Hicks Field had spoiled us a little, Enid Air Base, located in the open rolling hills of north central Oklahoma, was still a nice place to train. Our barracks at Enid were the same type of two-story buildings we had experienced in San Antonio. Our time would be spent participating in ground school, physical training, and flying. Our classes were similar to the ones we took in primary, but I did not find them quite as difficult because the new material built on what we had studied earlier.

Physical and flight training began almost immediately. It was now late July and very hot. In short order, we were scheduled to meet our instructor at the flight line. That was always an exciting event because each of us was hoping to be assigned to a good instructor—we needed all the help we could get. Once again I was fortunate to be assigned to an instructor who was really a nice person and a great teacher, Lt. William Genre.

The day we went out to the BT-13 for our first time was exciting, and in a way, intimidating. This plane was a great deal larger than I expected. We were shown all the procedures on how to start and fly the plane, and the next day we were scheduled to start flying. At the time the BT-13 seemed so large and powerful and, to a degree, scary. On the morning of one of my first training flights, I was at the end of the runway waiting for the BT-13 in front of me to take off. I do not know what happened but as it left the runway it made a loop backward and landed off to the side at a 45 degree angle. The student released his safety belt and fell head first out of the cockpit. He was not hurt, but it scared me.

It was a thrill to get in the plane, start the engine, and taxi out for takeoff. Everything went well on the first flight. With the teaching of a fine instructor, I had done well, and I could feel it. There was only one thing missing. Jean was still in Abilene, and I could not share the joy of my progress with her. Up to this point I had not had any close calls. Primary had been easy for me and now basic was going great. In fact it had been too easy. Soon, I would learn a hard lesson because of that.

My first solo flight in the BT-13 was uneventful. We were half-way through basic training, and Jean was coming up the next week-end. It was the first time we had seen each other since we married on June 19. One night we were assigned to go to an auxiliary field to shoot night landings. The field was about thirty miles west of Enid. It was a great night—the moon was full, the air was stable, and everything was perfect for flying. The thrill of Jean's visit combined with the perfect night made it a wonderful time to be in the air. It was one of those times when no matter what you did it turned out perfect. Every takeoff and landing was excellent. After the twelfth landing, the control ship called and told me I had scored excellent on my flight, and as a reward I could go back to the base and would not have to complete the rest of my required landings. I was the only one who got to go back to the base early that night.

When I got back I found a lot of planes were shooting landings. I decided to not let down to traffic pattern altitude immediately, but to go south of Enid instead so I could enjoy the beautiful night and savor the reward of returning early. I could still see the lights of Enid and the base when I started to lose altitude. The canopy was cracked about an inch and I had the lights turned down low. For some reason, the lights of Enid disappeared, which seemed odd but I gave it no serious thought. Then, the air base's lights disappeared. That shook me up and I realized that something must be wrong, but I could not figure out what it might be. I rolled back the canopy and as I did, I saw some trees go by. The moon was so bright there was no doubt they were trees. It scared me to death. I immediately pulled the stick back, pushed the throttle forward, put the prop in low pitch and was climbing as fast as I could, still not knowing what was wrong. Soon the lights of the base appeared, along with the lights of Enid. I tried to figure out what had happened and finally

Jim Davis during Primary Flight School Training, June 1943 (courtesy of Jim Davis)

PT-19 training plane (courtesy of the Air Force Historical Research Agency, Maxwell Air Force Base, Montgomery, Alabama)

realized that I had misread the altimeter. After that I would always remember that when you are flying an airplane you have to be alert every second. It was the best lesson I could have learned, even if it did almost kill me. On the way back to the base I realized how fortunate I had been. If I had been only a few feet to my left I would have hit the trees. I missed a crash and probably death by only a few inches and a few seconds. I got weak thinking about it. I never told anyone what happened because I was too ashamed of how stupid and careless I had been.

Our training now involved more advanced flying, including aerobatics. I enjoyed it but not like many of the other cadets. It seemed that all of my classmates had a burning desire to be fighter pilots. I had never given any serious thought to what I would like to fly if and when I became a pilot. I remember the first time I tried to do a loop solo. Either I did not have enough airspeed or I did not pull it up fast enough. Just as I was reaching the top, the plane stalled and I thought it was going to come apart. It fell into a spin. I do not remember how much altitude I lost but at times I thought I was a goner. I finally got enough airspeed to get the plane under control. During that spin, I recalled all the stories about how easy it was to snap the tail off of a BT-13. That experience made me think less about flying fighters.

Jean's visit was great but far too short. We started making plans about what we would do if I completed basic and advanced. If by chance I made it through advanced flight school, she would take a leave of absence and would spend the last week of my advanced training with me and then would go with me to wherever I might be stationed. Those were really big "ifs" because I still had a long way to go and a lot could happen.

Although we had lost some classmates, it was nothing compared to the percentage that we lost in primary training. Things were going well for me, and I really felt like I had it made. We reached the point of training where we would take a course in instrument flying. This phase of training would require a different instructor. The day we reported to instrument instruction was the beginning of a very difficult period for me.

For some reason, my instructor was irritated with me from the moment we met. I never could figure out why. The first time we went up he literally gave me hell. After the third flight he told me he did not know how I had gotten this far because I was a terrible pilot. At the end of the next flight he told me that he was giving me a pink slip. A pink slip usually meant the end. Of course there would be a check ride by a check pilot, but most of the time that was a formality. I never expected anything like this. I was scheduled to fly with a check pilot the next day. I was totally demoralized and for all practical purposes had resigned myself to this being the end of my flying career. I was even thinking of my transfer options. I thought that at least I had gone much further than I ever thought I would. With that kind of attitude, I really did not need to even take a check ride.

My check pilot was a captain, and we sat down and had a visit before the flight. He interviewed me and then explained what we would do on the flight. He made me feel better, but I still felt like the end was near. We took off and went through all the procedures that he told me to do. We then shot some landings, and I was told to go back to the field and land. I knew this would be my final landing. It had been so good and now I would be filling out the log sheet for the last time. I took a little longer filling out the log because I wanted to make it last as long as I could. I dreaded getting out of the plane and going to the debriefing. We went into operations and into his office. He asked me to sit down and looked over some notes he had made during the flight. Finally, he looked up and said, "Mr. Davis, I could not find anything wrong with any phase of your flying. In fact, I thought it was an excellent flight." I almost fell out of the chair. He explained that he would clear me to return to my instructor.

I was excited about everything except going back to my instructor. The next day was as bad, and worse. After two days he gave me another pink slip. The following day I rode with a major for a check ride. At this point I did not know what to expect. My emotions had been on a roller coaster for several days. After the flight with the major, the same thing happened. He told me I should go back to my instructor. I did, and after two days he gave me a third pink slip. The next day I flew with the commander of the base, who was a colonel. After the check flight he told me the same thing the other check pilots had told me, that my flight had been good. How relieved I was when he told me I would not have to go back to my old instructor but would report to someone else. Everything went fine from there, and I finished my instrument training on time with the other students. I did have to double up on my flights for several days. I still do not know how I ever survived three check rides.

At this point in our training I had to fill out a form to select the type of advanced training that I preferred. We had a choice of single engine or twin engine. It was a preference and did not necessarily mean we would get it. I signed up for single engine. It really did not matter because my true goal was to win my silver wings. When the orders came out, I was ordered to Victoria, Texas, for single-engine advanced training. One of my good friends was a large person about six feet tall, who weighed over two hundred pounds. He badly wanted to be a fighter pilot, but because of his size they ordered him to go to twin-engine advanced training in Frederick, Oklahoma. He was crushed. That evening we were visiting, and he asked me if I would object if he went down to headquarters the next morning to see if he could get them to swap our assignments. I really did not give it much thought because I did not care what I got to fly. I had forgotten about it until that afternoon when he told me that headquarters had agreed to make the change. Suddenly, I was not going to Victoria after all, but instead would go to Frederick, Oklahoma, for twin-engine advanced training. There was one good thing about it—Frederick was a lot closer to Abilene than Victoria.

It was late September when we arrived at Frederick Army Air Force Base. There was a different attitude about advanced than we experienced in primary and basic flight training. We had weathered the storm and felt like we would graduate unless something drastic happened. We were not as excited about flying the AT-17 and the UC-78.[4] These were twin-engine trainers manufactured by Cessna, and were commonly referred to as the Bamboo Bombers because they were constructed primarily from wood. The only difference between them was that the AT-17's propeller was wooden and the UC-78 had steel variable speed props. They were very light for twin-engine airplanes because fabric covered their body and wings.

Once again I was fortunate to be assigned to an excellent teacher and pilot. Multi-engine training was not as difficult as we had thought it would be. We had the usual ground school and physical training, which, along with flying, made our days very busy. Our classes continued to build on what we studied in primary and basic, and most of us did not find them overly difficult. In our flight training, we did a lot of landings, formation flying, night flying, and cross-country exercises. December 5, 1943, was graduation day. Because we expected to be able to live off base during the last week of advanced training, like the previous classes, Jean made plans to spend the last week in Frederick.

We learned to enjoy flying the Bamboo Bomber, and the training went well until the last part. We were scheduled to make a cross-country flight to Shreveport, Louisiana. It was called a day-night cross country since we would leave Frederick after lunch and fly over Wichita Falls, then over Fort Worth and Dallas, over Marshall, and land in Shreveport late in the afternoon. We would eat dinner in Shreveport and leave after dark to return to Frederick by the same route. It was a beautiful, clear November day. There was no wind and not a cloud in the sky—a perfect day to fly. We had our briefing and prepared for takeoff. There were twenty-seven planes making the flight.

[4] Both the AT-17 "Bobcat" and UC-78 "Bamboo Bomber" were two-engine trainer and light transport planes built by Cessna. For more information see Craven and Cate, *Army Air Forces in World War II, Volume 6*, 577; United States Air Force Museum, Advanced Flying School, http://www.wpafb.af.mil/museum/history/wwii/afs.htm, accessed on June 30, 2005; and United States Air Force Museum, Cessna UC-78 "Bobcat," http://www.wpafb.af.mil/museum/modern_flight/mf5.htm, accessed on June 30, 2005.

As it turned out, only eight planes ended up landing at Shreveport. My copilot and I flew one of the eight. The other nineteen planes all either made emergency or crash landings along the way. If we had not made an error in going through our checklist before we took off, we would probably have been among them. The emergency landings were caused by carburetor ice. We failed to check our carburetor heater, which should always be in the off position. Whoever flew the plane that morning had evidently used the heater and not turned it off. For some reason we failed to notice it being on before we took off. Because it was on, we did not have any trouble. Many of the planes who did not make it to Shreveport had an engine lose power and quit. As a result they had to make emergency landings along the way. One of my friends lost power in both engines and landed in the middle of a huge ammunition storage facility near Marshall, Texas. Neither he nor anyone else could understand how he safely landed between rows of ammunition and was able to slip under the electrical wires.

We were told to be especially careful on our return flight. If we detected a drop in RPMs or loss of power, we were to quickly turn on our carburetor heater. For some reason the AT-17 was affected often by carburetor icing. To the best of my knowledge all the other eight that successfully landed in Shreveport had made the same error that we had going through the checklist. Otherwise, we all would have had the same problem. After it got dark we took off for the return flight to Frederick and made it back to the base without any problems. We did not take off with our heaters on, but we turned them on as soon as we reached cruising altitude.

On another occasion I was assigned to fly a night training mission as a copilot. The pilot and I were supposed to practice blind field landings at an auxiliary field. The field was equipped with landing lights that you could only see if you were landing from one certain direction and approaching the field at the proper landing angle. These types of airfields were used in combat areas so the enemy could not locate the landing area at night. Our first landing was going fine until the lights disappeared. It was a dark night, and we were close to the ground when the lights vanished. When the lights disappeared we did not know if we were too high or too low on the approach. As an emergency procedure, I turned the landing lights up to see how high we were. To our surprise we were just about ready to touch ground. The pilot pulled the throttles back and set it on the ground. Although the grass was tall and the ground was rough, there were fortunately no trees. Then, a barbed wire fence appeared immediately in front of us. We had just touched down and were still rolling fast. The only thing we could do was push the throttles forward and try to pull the plane over the fence. The plane left the ground and barely cleared the fence, only to stall out and fall to the ground again. We bounced a couple of times and suddenly we could see the runway where we were supposed to land.

Soon after this flight, we were all issued $300 each to buy our officers' uniforms. For the first time, I realized I had it made. A tailor came to the base to take our sizes and order our uniforms. I do not remember all the clothes we ordered, but I do remember the most exciting things were the "hot pilots" hat and the trench coat.

The last week of advanced training was really a ball. Our officers' uniforms had arrived, and it was a thrill to try them on. My brother had driven with Jean to Frederick so we could spend the last week of advanced training together and have a car to drive to Abilene after I graduated. He returned by bus. We rented a room in a house. We had been told that we would be given seven days leave after graduation before we reported to our next assignment.

I had finished all my requirements a week before we were to graduate and was enjoying being through. Other cadets used the last week to finish any or all of the required flights they might have missed because of sickness, bad weather, or equipment failure. During that week I was not scheduled to fly, but one day my name was on the list to report to the flight line that evening. In the briefing they assigned me to sand bag for a cadet who had not completed his required night flying time. Actually it was a night cross-country flight. Sand bagging was the term used when you had to fill in as a copilot.

During the briefing we were told that we had been scheduled to fly to Abilene, but because a front had developed over north Texas that afternoon, the flight would be made to Amarillo instead. We were briefed that the weather would be good and since it was a shorter flight than he needed to get his required time in, we were to circle Amarillo three times and return. When we got back to the area, we were to call the tower and ask for instructions to land or to fly a while longer so he would have enough time. Since I would be copilot, I would do all the navigation. We sat down and worked out the route we planned on flying. After getting everything planned we went out to the plane, made our preflight inspection, started our engines, taxied to the runway, and took off on what would be nothing but a routine flight. We took the heading to Amarillo and were on our way.

There was no moon and the air was a little bumpy at times. We arrived at Amarillo, circled the city three times, and headed back to Frederick. When we were near the field I called in, gave them our location, and asked for instructions. After a couple of minutes the

Jim and Jean the day after
they got married, June 1943
(courtesy of Jim Davis)

tower called back and told us to fly to Snyder and back and to call the tower again when we were over the field. That did not sound right, so I asked the tower to repeat. The only Snyder I knew about was about fifty miles northwest of Abilene. Since they had told us a front had built up in that area and storms were developing, it did not sound logical that they would send us there. Although I had never heard of a Snyder, Oklahoma, I decided to check the area fifty to one hundred miles around Frederick to see if there was one. I could not find another Snyder on the map.

We did not have any time to waste because I had to work out a heading to Snyder, Texas. I gave him a heading and started some fast checking. My concern now was how much gas we had. I did not think we had enough to make it all the way there and back. Frederick's lights had long since disappeared behind us, and I had never seen such a dark night. There were stars but the area we were over now was ranch land with very few houses. It was not long before we started seeing clouds, and finally they blocked out the stars. The cadet I was sandbagging for was from Wisconsin. I do not remem-

BT-13 training plane (courtesy of the Air Force Historical Research Agency, Maxwell Air Force Base, Montgomery, Alabama)

ber his name and I am sure he would rather forget mine. After we left Frederick he was very uneasy, but I assured him I knew west Texas like a book and not to worry because I knew where we were. Soon there were clouds all around us. My friend really got excited as we started seeing some lightning flash to the west and east of us. The air had grown very bumpy. At this point I had no idea where we were and was concerned not only about the weather, but also by our fuel situation.

Our gas was not holding up as well as I had expected. My pilot, whom I will call Bill, wanted to turn back. I was ready to, but I was hoping to find something on the ground to give me an idea of where we were. As we passed through the frontal system we got thrown all over the sky. Bill told me we were lost and going to run out of gas, and if we did not find a place to land, he was going to bail out. We made a hundred and eighty degree turn and started back through the frontal system. The turbulence was terrible. Every red light on the instrument panel was now glowing. Rain was pounding the windshield. Bill suddenly announced that he was going to bail out since we were lost and going to crash. He got out of his seat and moved to the back.

While he was checking his chute, I crawled over to the pilot seat—I was more comfortable flying from there. The multitude of red lights on the instrument panel was very annoying. I buckled myself into the seat and heard Bill shuffling around in the back preparing to bail out. He called out that he was bailing out and I heard the door latch as he opened it. I heard the wind whistling and then I heard the door close. As quickly as the door opened and closed I thought he either left in a hurry or had decided to wait a while.

I heard a noise, glanced back, and saw Bill on the floor. I asked him if he was going to jump and he replied he would in a minute. Then I heard him throwing up. I was not in a position to help him—I had no idea where we were or how much fuel we had left, was annoyed with all the red lights, and was almost nauseated myself from the smell of Bill's vomit. I was flying on instinct hoping that I would get lucky and find Frederick. Bill again announced he was bailing out and again I heard the door open and close. I looked back, and once again he was down. He tried to leave several times but would always back out. I finally saw what I thought might be some ground lights in the distance. The closer we got the more certain I was that they were the lights of Vernon, Texas. I wanted to keep my altitude so that if the engines died, we would have plenty of room to bail out. Frederick was not far from Vernon and I knew the direction because we had flown in the area many times. As we left Vernon I was able to contact the Frederick tower. They called our plane number, and I immediately answered. For a long time I received no answer so I called again. After a pause they called and wanted to know my location. They asked me to call when we reached the traffic pattern.

Because all the red lights had been burning for the longest time, I knew we should not chance trying to fly the regular traffic pattern, and so I received permission from the tower to land immediately because we were virtually out of gas. As we approached the field I called Bill. He came to and crawled into the copilot seat as we made our final approach. As we settled in for the landing, I could not have been happier. Because the AT-17 had a tail wheel and sat on the ground at a very steep angle, I felt I should taxi as fast as I could to keep the tail up as high as possible. If I had let the tail down, the gas would have settled in the rear of the tanks and the engines would probably have died. A jeep intercepted us, and I had to slow down and follow him to our parking place.

The tower told us to report to operations as soon as we parked the plane. That scared me because I felt like something was wrong but I had no idea what it could be. The jeep driver led us to a parking place and motioned for us to stop. When he motioned for us to cut our engines, we did not have to since they died all by themselves. We ran out of gas at the exact second that we were to stop them. How lucky could we be? We filled out all our forms, got our gear together, and started the long walk to operations. I felt lucky to be on the ground but scared that we were in trouble. We entered operations and a sergeant asked us to be seated because some officers wanted to see us. They were behind closed doors, and it was after midnight. That could mean nothing but trouble. After waiting for perhaps ten minutes, the officers asked us to enter. There were six or seven officers seated around a table, all colonels and majors.

After the formalities of introductions, they ordered us to sit and submit records, logs, and maps of our flight. They gathered around and reviewed them for several minutes. Finally they asked us where we had been and what we had done that evening. I described the flight as best as I could, telling them exactly what happened. They asked us where we had landed that night. We told them that we did not land anywhere. One officer spoke up and said that we had to have landed some place, because we could not have stayed in the air that long without being refueled. One of the officers asked me where my hometown was, and I told him Abilene. Once again he asked me if we landed in Abilene or some airstrip near Abilene. I told him we did not get to Snyder because of a thunderstorm in the area and we were getting low on fuel. They asked why our log was not filled out after we turned around. I explained that Bill got sick and had to lie down in the back. I added that it was impossible to fly, navigate, and keep the log without help. They questioned us a long time and finally asked us to leave the room and wait in the hall. As we left the room I still did not know what the problem was. Bill was as white as a sheet, and I was scared that I might be washed out even though I had completed all of my requirements.

After several minutes they asked us to return. A colonel asked us if we had ever heard of Snyder, Oklahoma. We told them we had not. The colonel said they had not heard of Snyder, Texas, either, so he guessed we would have to call it a draw. They pointed out where Snyder was in Oklahoma, only a few miles north of Frederick! I explained that we searched all over our maps just in case there was a Snyder, Oklahoma, but we did not look that close to Frederick. They told us that they had checked every place we might have landed but found nothing that indicated we had been on the ground, so they would have to accept our story. However, the thing they could not understand was how we could stay in the air as long as we did on the fuel we had. They said they had maintenance dip our tanks and there was no gas left in them. The meeting broke up with everyone shaking hands and laughing about what happened that evening. As we were walking down the hall I heard one of the officers saying, "I know they are lying. They have to be. There is no way they could stay in the air that long without refueling."

Orders were posted and I was given a commission as a second lieutenant. Our class was divided into different groups and sent in many directions. I had to report to Tarrant Field, near Fort Worth, for B-24 training. Some of the cadets were assigned as instructors, some went to pilot pools, and others were sent to various locations for specialized training in different types of aircraft.

At last the day came. What started out as a fantasy as a small boy later became a dream, and now a reality—the day I was to receive my wings as a U.S. Army Air Forces pilot. In a ceremony, we were awarded our wings, given our orders, and sent away with a blessing. Jean had already loaded the car, and we left about 8 p.m. for Abilene. The thrill of graduation dominated me for the next few days of leave. I had to report to Tarrant Field on December 12. Jean and I left on the 10th to try and find an apartment in Fort Worth. We drove slowly because our tires were paper-thin. We were within twenty miles of Fort Worth when our right rear tire blew out. It could not have happened at a worse place. The shoulder of the road was very narrow and rocky. I finally got the tire removed and the spare on. The spare tire was also in bad shape and made a bumpy ride.

We got to Weatherford and went to the rationing office to get a coupon for a tire, but the board refused to give me one. After much hassle and convincing, they finally gave me a coupon to buy a used tire. It was now dark and I soon discovered used tires were difficult to find even with a coupon. The first two places we went did not have a tire that would fit my car. Finally, the last place had one but it was not much better than the spare I had on. I bought the tire and they mounted it and we were on our way to Fort Worth. We spent the night in a motel and early the next morning we started looking for an apartment. Everything we looked at was awful. We finally decided on a small hut in the backyard of a house. It looked more like a chicken house than an apartment. It had a small bedroom that was only slightly larger than the bed. It did have a small bathroom and a small cabinet with a hot plate on it. We paid the lady a month's rent. Later that day we met one of my classmates, and he told us that he had found a nice garage apartment not far from the base. The lady had another apartment that some people were moving out of that day, so we hurried over and looked at it. It was much nicer and closer to the base; so, we told the lady that we would like to rent it if we could get our money back on the one we had just paid for. We went back and told the first landlord that we found a place closer to the base, and she generously returned our money. We loaded up our belongings and moved. We could carry everything we owned at the time in a suitcase and a couple of military duffle bags.

CHAPTER 3

Flying the Beast

THE NEXT MORNING WE reported to Tarrant Field to be processed. I filled out all the forms that were required and took several physical exams. After I had gone through all the examinations, a sergeant told me that the flight surgeon wanted to see me in his office. I knew that was not routine, and it had never happened to me before. After I got dressed, I went to his office and had to wait about thirty minutes. As I sat there, I wondered what could be wrong. I was finally asked to go in. I sat down while he went through my papers. He looked up and asked "Who sent you here?" I was speechless. I said, "Sir, my orders directed me to report here." He told me he did not know why they sent me because to qualify for four-engine training a student had to weigh at least 140 pounds and I only weighed 134. This was such a surprise to me I really did not know what to say.

I did not want to leave B-24 training because Fort Worth felt like home, we had a nice place to live, and many of my good friends were in this class. After the initial shock, I explained that I usually weighed from145 to 160. Then I really started trying to build my case. I told him the loss of weight had occurred in the last three weeks and that I would be back over 140 in a few days. I also explained that many of my friends were here, and I had already paid for an apartment for a month. I told him I did not want to be sent to a pilot pool to be assigned to no telling what kind of duty. I

AT-17 training plane (courtesy of the Air Force Historical Research Agency, Maxwell Air Force Base, Montgomery, Alabama)

was all but crying and begging to stay at Tarrant. He finally said, "I really believe you want to stay here." After pausing for some time he said that if I wanted to stay in four-engine training, to come back the next morning at 10 a.m. to be weighed again. He told me in order for me to get my weight up, I should not go to the restroom for any reason. In addition, I should go by the grocery store, get a sack of bananas, and eat as many as I could before tomorrow morning.

I did exactly as he told me. By the next morning I was very uncomfortable. I had eaten a whole sack of bananas overnight and felt I would clear 140. The next morning I reported to him and only weighed 137. We sat down, and he asked me again if I really wanted to stay in four-engine training. I assured him I did. He went through my records again and said that he felt like he was making a mistake but that he was going to list me as weighing 140. I could have hugged his neck. Later I would understand why they required the weight restriction. Actually, I think it should have been higher than 140. To fly a four-engine plane such as the B-24 took a lot of strength and endurance.

The first day or so is usually spent in briefings and orientations. As always there was ground school and physical training. Once again I got a really nice and capable instructor. Each instructor taught four students, and besides me, the others were W. L. Dyer, E. C. Eanes, and L. H. Daugherty. The time finally came for our introduction to the B-24.[1] After being briefed on the plane's characteristics, we went to the flight line to see the airplane and to take a short flight. As we approached the airplane it looked huge and got larger as we got closer. This was the first time any of us had been near one. I could not believe anything that large could fly. To walk around and crawl into it was frightening, and it got worse as the engines were started. As we taxied out for takeoff, the noise, beating, and banging were terrifying. It was at this point that I thought back to training and how I let a friend get my orders changed from single engine to multi-engine. I also remembered three days ago when I was almost disqualified for being too light for four-engine planes.

I had never realized the B-24 was so massive and so complicated, but I had made my choice. Good or bad, I was going to give it the best I could. The B-24 was many things to many people. You could not call it pretty. When I first walked up to one it was anything but a beauty. However, on each flight after that, the great old airplane made a believer out of me and most other pilots who flew it. Its Pratt-Whitney engines were great and

---

[1] The B-24 "Liberator" was a four-engine bomber built by Consolidated to hold a crew of ten. It had a maximum speed of around 300 mph, a cruising speed of 175 mph, and a range of more than 2,000 miles when fully loaded with munitions. Along with the B-17, it was the primary bomber used by the Army Air Forces in the European Theatre. See Steve Birdsall, *Log of the Liberators: An Illustrated History of the B-24* (Garden City, NY: Doubleday, 1973); William Carigan, *Ad Lib: Flying the B-24 Liberator in World War II* (Manhattan, KS: Sunflower University Press, 1988); William Carigan, "The B-24 Liberator—A Man's Airplane," *Aerospace Historian* Spring (March 1988): 11-24; Roger A. Freeman, *B-24 Liberator at War* (London: Ian Allan, 1983); Frederick A. Johnsen, *B-24 Liberator: Rugged but Right* (New York: McGraw Hill, 1999); and Michael O'Leary, *Consolidated B-24 Liberator* (Oxford, Great Britain: Osprey Press, 2002).

very dependable, and it could carry a heavy load. As the plane moved into position on the runway for my first takeoff, and the pilot pushed the throttles forward, I heard a tremendous roar. As the plane picked up speed, I could not believe the bumping and thundering noise. I thought there was no way you could fly this plane very long without a disaster. As the plane lifted off the runway, the bumping noise stopped, but the engines still roared. After we reached cruising speed and power was reduced, it was not quite as bad, but we soon found out that large planes bounce around like the smaller ones do. We flew about an hour that first afternoon. Each of us sat about fifteen minutes in the pilot's seat, took the controls, and made a few turns. Upon landing we all felt the same way. This was going to be a very exciting two and a half months of learning to fly this monster.

Each time we flew the B-24 it became a little less complicated and not quite as large. Things progressed very well, and although we had learned a lot, we were still not really comfortable with the plane yet and certainly not ready to solo. Usually the instructor would fly with two students one day and then fly with the other two the next day. Sometimes he would take us all up together. On the night of January 27, 1944, we reported to the flight line for some night flying, specifically to practice landings. Our instructor told us that he would take Dyer and Daugherty up that night and for Eanes and me to do our studying. It was a marginal night for flying with low clouds and light rain. We had thought all day that it was too bad to fly, but they were flying anyway. As our instructor left with the other two he said that he had checked with maintenance and they had told him that they would not have any planes ready for flying other than the ones already assigned, but if by chance they did get a plane ready, for Eanes and I to take it up and shoot a few landings. We laughed because we knew he was joking. In the first place we did not have the required hours for soloing in the daytime and one of the strict policies was that you had to solo in the day before you were allowed to solo at night. We still needed about five hours of day qualified pilot time before we would be eligible to solo in the daytime, and even more for night solos. Besides, this was not a night to solo—the rain and wet runways made it much more dangerous.

The standard rules were that we had to stay until 10 p.m. and then we were free to go home. About 9:50 Eanes and I were getting ready to leave when a sergeant came in and told us we would have to put our flying clothes back on because maintenance had just called and told him they had a ship ready to fly. He informed us that our instructor had told him if they did get one ready, to tell us to take it out for some landings. We laughed and went back to changing to our uniforms. As we left the locker room and started out, the sergeant told us he was not teasing. We were to shoot some landings. We laughed again and told him that we had not soloed in the daytime yet because we did not have enough hours, so we certainly could not solo at night. He finally convinced us he was not kidding.

We did not know what to do except to go back to the locker room and put on our flying clothes. I kept saying to myself that I would not dare take a plane up solo tonight. After we got our clothes on we told the sergeant to get in touch with our instructor if possible and get this cleared up because there had to be a mistake somewhere by somebody. He tried to get in touch with our instructor but was unsuccessful. In the meantime a truck had pulled up to the door to carry us to the airplane. We told the sergeant to keep checking with everyone to see why this had happened and to call us when he got this mess cleared up.

It was an eerie feeling when we arrived at the plane. The flight engineer was not aware of the situation, and I am sure if he had been aware of our incompetence, he would have run and hidden. We went through the procedure of preflight as best we could, still thinking that this was a terrible mistake and someone would tell us to cancel and return to the flight line—no such call came. It was now critical because it was time to board the plane. I told Eanes that he could sit in the pilot seat and I would fly as copilot. He said he did not want to; therefore, we decided to flip a coin to see who would have to be the lead pilot. I lost the coin flip and had to try to take this thing off.

By this time this plane was looking bigger and bigger. To get into a B-24 you had to get down on your knees and enter through the bomb bay. Once inside the bomb bay you had to climb a ladder to reach the door to the flight deck. I made my way into the left seat, fastened the seatbelt, and started the preflight checklist. If it had not been for the flight engineer, who would fly with us, we would not have been able to get the engines started. But we did and now it was time for me to call the tower to ask for taxi and takeoff instructions. At this point I was so scared that I do not know how I was able to remember what the aircraft controllers said. I did not know then nor do I know now how I ever got to the right runway because we were not familiar with taxiways or runways. The rain was no help because it made the lights twinkle and the reflections on the wet runway and taxiways were very confusing. Somehow we got to the right runway and set our brakes to check our engines. It was at this point that I finally realized that this was no dream. This was real, and even though someone had goofed, we were going to have to try to fly this monster. We ran up each engine, and they all checked out okay. I was hoping at least one would have a problem. I called the tower and told them we were ready for takeoff.

We had to wait a few minutes for a couple of planes to land. Finally, the tower cleared us for takeoff and told us to shoot touch and go landings. There is no way I could describe the feeling I had as I released the brakes and slowly moved the throttle forward. The plane started rolling down the runway faster and faster. The copilot called out the airspeed because the pilot did not have time for anything but keeping the plane going down the runway straight and getting it into the air. The copilot called out the speed—twenty, thirty, forty, fifty, sixty, seventy miles an hour. Seventy is a critical time because you are committed to take off and would have little chance of cutting power and stopping the plane before it crashed into something.

As he read off eighty miles an hour, the tower called and told me my number four engine was torching real bad.[2] It really scared me because I had never heard of torching. I thought maybe he meant it was on fire. I hollered to the flight engineer who was standing just back of the pilot and copilot's seats and told him number four was torching real bad. By this time we were almost to takeoff speed and I was pulling the wheel back in an effort to get off the ground. I had to get in the air no matter what was wrong with number four. I could feel the plane getting lighter and lighter and finally I could feel it clear the runway. We were in the air and climbing. The engineer suggested I call the tower and ask for permission to leave the traffic pattern to work with the number four engine. After some hesitation the tower agreed and sent me to an area about twenty miles west of Tarrant field where we could correct our problem. We climbed to about five thousand feet just under the clouds. The flight engineer was on his knees between the pilots' seats, working with the controls and hoping to fix the engine problem. At this time I was feeling a little more relaxed. We had successfully made a takeoff and that gave me some confidence. I was hoping that we could get number four running right so we could return and land. The one thing that worried me was the possibility that number four might catch on fire or that we might have to shut down the prop.

Those concerns were quickly forgotten when the engineer suddenly said, "I smell smoke." He immediately made his way to the rear of the flight deck and opened the door to the bomb bay. He virtually disappeared from sight as the smoke engulfed him. He hollered out, "The bomb bay is on fire!" On a B-24 the worst thing you can hear is that there is a fire in the bomb bay because of the gas fumes there. When you have a fire, it is time to bail out. Because I was pilot as a result of the coin toss, it was my decision to make. I told him to open the doors and bail out. I also told Eanes to get out of his seat and be ready to leave the plane as soon as there was enough room to jump. At this time the smoke in the cockpit

[2] A bad fuel mixture caused torching, the emission of smoke, sparks, and occasionally fire from the exhaust.

was very bad. I did not think things could get any worse, but they did. I called the tower and told them there was a fire in the bomb bay and we were bailing out. I gave them our location. It was then I heard the terrible words, "the doors won't open." The engineer and Eanes were desperately trying to open them manually. They were successful in getting the bomb bay doors cracked enough that the slipstream started pulling the smoke out. As the smoke cleared, they could see the fire was on the right side of the bomb bay. Eanes decided to continue cranking the doors, and the engineer got a fire extinguisher, climbed on the catwalk in the bay, and put out the fire. Because the fire was out, there was no need to jump now. I told the tower what happened and that we were coming back to land.

Under any other circumstances, I would have dreaded the landing but after all that had happened, landing the plane seemed like no problem at all. As we came in on the final approach, all the fire trucks and ambulances were along the runway with their red lights flashing. In the rain, the reflections off the wet runways made it look like Las Vegas at night. We landed with no further problems and taxied back to our parking place. The strangest thing about the whole incident was that no one ever said anything about the flight, not even our instructor. I am sure there was a lot said, but not to us. It was as if the flight never happened. Looking back on that evening and all that happened, I gained some of the confidence that a person has to have to make a successful flying career.

Because we were now officers, we could enjoy the officers' club. For the first time since we married, Jean and I were enjoying life. Although I was on duty much of the time, we were still able to do a lot of things together. Jean's family never owned a car so she did not know how to drive very well, especially in a large city like Fort Worth. We spent a great deal of time driving around so she could become familiar with the city. She soon learned to drive easily all over Fort Worth. However, I did find out it is not easy for a husband to teach his wife how to drive.

B-24 training progressed to the point that I respected the plane and had a lot of confidence in it. We were on a training mission one day and upon returning to the base we found the weather had closed in. The ceiling was only a few hundred feet. I did not know where the tops of the clouds were because we were instructed to fly at 21,000 feet, and even at that altitude the clouds were heavy and dense. The tower asked us how much fuel we had because it would take a long time to work all the planes in that were stacked up. They advised us the weather was bad all over the southwest. The only fields that were open and would probably stay open were in far west Texas. We were given the option of going west or waiting our turn to land. We had enough fuel to stay in the air about three hours, so I decided to stay and make an instrument landing. I felt like we could work our way down in an hour or so. It did not work that way because planes came in short on fuel, and the tower gave them priority.

It took three hours and fifteen minutes before I was cleared to land, and it was the first instrument landing I had ever attempted. It was hair-raising coming in on the final approach in clouds so dense you could not see the wing tips. Fortunately when we broke out of

Jim Davis after graduation
from flight school,
December 1943
(courtesy of Jim Davis)

the clouds we were about three hundred feet above and about four hundred feet short of the runway. We only had enough time to cut the power and touch down. I was glad to be on the ground. One of the other trainees was not so lucky that day. He and his crew elected to fly west in an effort to find a clear field or at least one that was not as cloudy as Fort Worth. It was never determined what happened, but the plane was located southeast of Big Spring, Texas, on the side of a mountain. Apparently they had developed a problem, and in bad weather they tried to or had been forced to land on a ranch. The plane landed and rolled about two hundred feet before it fell off a cliff, killing everyone on board.

One day we were scheduled to shoot landings at Tarrant and we told our wives to come out and watch us. Everything went well for the first few landings. We made a good approach and touched down at the right place on the runway. I had the nose wheel on the runway and the throttles pulled back. Suddenly my seat broke and slid all the way back. I was trying to slow the plane down, but because the brake pedals were on the top part of the rudders, I could not reach them unless I slid forward. When I did that I could not see out. Before it was over we ran off the runway and out in the grass. Finally the copilot came to my rescue. I know that did not impress Jean. That was the only time she ever came to watch me.

We were down to our last phase of training and the final thing required was a cross-country flight. The four students and their instructor would take the trip. The students could select any place they would like to go. Because none of us had ever been to Los Angeles we decided to go there. We left early one morning and flew to Tucson, Arizona, and refueled. Then it was on to Los Angeles. We could not land there due to fog, so we decided to go to Phoenix. We were taking turns between flying and navigating. I was at the controls on the flight to Phoenix. We planned to land at Luke Field, but they were busy with a class of cadets shooting landings and suggested we land at Phoenix Municipal airport. We did and were on the ground taxiing to the terminal building when the plane suddenly pulled to the right. Because I was not taxiing fast, the plane stopped.

Then for some reason the plane started leaning to the right. It ended up that the taxi strip was not capable of supporting a B-24, and the right wheel was sinking into the pavement. We hoped we could develop enough power on the right two engines to pull us out, but that did not work. Finally we walked to the terminal building and called Luke Field to send over some men and equipment to pull our plane out of the hole. It took them three days. Originally we were only going to stay overnight, but we got a mini-vacation instead.

When we got back, we received our orders to go by train to Salt Lake City for our next assignment. There we would be tested as crewmembers. This was not a happy time, as the wives could not go because we were only going to be there for two weeks—just long enough to get our crewmembers and do all the related paperwork. From there we had no idea where we would go. We also realized that the next phase of training was the last one before we would be assigned to a war zone. I did not look forward to combat. Jean and I had enjoyed Fort Worth and now it was ending. One thing I never got used to or liked was saying goodbye and having no idea when or where we would ever see each other again.

Early the next morning Jean and I said our goodbyes, and I boarded the train to Salt Lake. I arrived in February 1944 and was assigned quarters at the base. The weather was bad and it seemed like we had to walk in mud everywhere we went. Everyone's attitude had changed. It was much more reserved and serious. The past year had been exciting—first hoping to get in the cadet program, then hoping to qualify for pilot training, and finally to make the grade and become pilots. Now we realized that in a few short months we would probably be in some far off part of the world in combat. We had heard about the tremendous air battles being fought over Europe, and the large losses of planes and men sobered our thoughts.

Each of us wanted to be first pilot and airplane commander, but we were aware that some would be assigned to crews as copilots. We were anxious to get our crew assignments so we could meet the nine other men with whom we would live, fight, and maybe die (the B-24 carried a crew of ten men). The pilot was the airplane commander and in him would rest the responsibility of making all final decisions during missions. The crew would consist of a copilot, navigator, bombardier, flight engineer, radio operator, and four gunners.

Orders were posted, and I was assigned as pilot. My crew consisted of John Nowaski as copilot, Frank Morris as navigator, Ernest Mackey as bombardier, Arthur A. Siegfried as flight engineer, and Dexter Bodin as radio operator. The gunners were Robert Kluge, Herman Trego, Thornton Benson, and George Van Hooten. They were a fine group of young men. Nowaski, who was from Chicago, was a very large person and had been a flight instructor for over a year. He had a lot more hours than I did, for which I was grateful. Morris was from Dearborn, Michigan, and had been a student at the University of Michigan before entering the service. He was a person with a lot of class. His father was vice-president of the Cadillac Motor Division of General Motors.[3] Mackey was a graduate of either UCLA or USC as an engineer. Because he was older and more mature than the rest of us, we called him the old man. He had been around the block and knew the ropes about a lot of things. He loved to gamble and was what I would call a real professional gambler. He was a crapshooter.

Siegfried was a sergeant from the Bronx, and I know he was the best flight engineer ever to fly. He was a great asset to me and was a person you could depend on under any situation. I do not believe I could have ever made it without Siegfried. Bodin was from Des Moines, Iowa, and had been a student at the University of Iowa. Van Hooten was from West Point, New York. His father worked for the U.S. Military Academy, and they lived on "the base." Trego was from Maryland, and we sometimes called him our coon hunter because he was an avid outdoorsman. Kluge and Benson were from the Midwest. I was most fortunate to have each of these young men as a part of my crew. We all fit together and became a very capable crew.

[3] Frank E. Morris, "Memoirs of the War," in author's possession.

We spent almost two weeks at Salt Lake City, where it snowed every night and melted every day. Our orders sent us to Biggs Field in El Paso, Texas, for phase training.[4] This was the last period of training before we went into combat. It was supposed to be demanding and take about two and a half months. I was disappointed I had to live on base and could not bring Jean down.

Soon it was time for us to pack up and board the troop train to El Paso. It was going to be good to be back in Texas, although it would be over three hundred miles from Jean. We stopped in downtown Albuquerque and were given three hours to walk around. The bars did a booming business during those hours. We were about a hundred miles south of Albuquerque when the train stopped in the middle of the desert. Because of the sudden stop, we felt like it had to be an emergency. We were all hanging out the windows to see what the problem was. Even the poker games stopped to see what was happening. The word finally got around that the train had to stop because someone had gotten out of the train and was sitting on top of one of the cars. He was having a ball after having too much to drink while in Albuquerque. The alarming thing was that when they got the person down it turned out to be my copilot. That caused me to have some reservations about Nowaski.

When we arrived at Biggs Field, I was surprised to see mountains. They seemed too close to the base for us to be flying in the area. The barracks were typical military, like the ones we had in Enid and Frederick. For the first several days we spent most of our time being checked out and spent very little time as a crew. It took about ten days before we were scheduled to fly. Our first scheduled flight together took place on a hot day in March with strong, gusty winds. Nowaski and I had been flying together for several days and were familiar with the procedures and the field. The rest of my crew had never seen a B-24, much less ridden in one. We rode to the plane together and I took time to explain the plane as best as I could and answer any questions they had. After the briefing, we boarded the

---

[4] For more information on the various training levels, see endnote 11 in chapter 1 and the glossary.

B-24 in flight (courtesy of the Air Force Historical Research Agency, Maxwell Air Force Base, Montgomery, Alabama)

B-24s being assembled in factory in Ft. Worth, Texas (courtesy of the Air Force Historical Research Agency, Maxwell Air Force Base, Montgomery, Alabama)

Top down view of a B-24 in flight (courtesy of the Air Force Historical Research Agency, Maxwell Air Force Base, Montgomery, Alabama)

plane. The takeoff was uneventful except for the gusty wind and turbulence. I do not recall ever having experienced more severe low-level turbulence than we had that day. We were assigned an altitude of 10,000 feet. Once we reached this altitude, the plane suddenly got caught in an updraft and literally leapt for several hundred feet and then, just as suddenly, dropped back down.

It was only a few minutes into the flight when I got a call from one of the gunners in the rear that two crewmembers were throwing up. The first one was so sick they thought he was going to die. Soon everyone was sick with the exception of Nowaski, Siegfried, and me. They were lying on top of each other, having long since thrown up everything in their stomachs, and now they had dry heaves. The odor was terrible. I called the tower and requested permission to land. That was the whitest, sickest group of people I had ever seen. Fortunately, that was the last time we had a problem with airsickness.

As in Fort Worth, the planes were old, and even though they were well maintained they still had a lot of mechanical problems. During the two and a half months we were at Biggs we lost a number of planes, and forty-five people died.[5] One evening when Frank Morris and I were leaving the barracks to go to the officer's mess, we saw a huge fireball spring from Mt. Franklin. One of the B-24s taking off did not clear the mountain and flew into it. To see a plane explode and know that ten of your friends had just lost their lives made you sick, but we had become aware that it could happen to any of us at any time. Every time I go to El Paso I pause and look at the spot on Mt. Franklin where the plane hit that night and think that but for the grace of God, it could have been me.

On another occasion, one of our crews was flying night bombing missions on the range north of Alamogordo, New Mexico. The flight plan called for the bombing to be made from an altitude of 12,000 feet. Near there, but not in the bombing pattern, is a mountain named Sierra Blanca. It is 12,003 feet high. For some reason they got off course, as we all did from time to time, and came back to the base without their bomb bay doors. They had hit the top few inches or so of Sierra Blanca. They were fortunate to survive.

One night we were scheduled to fly a celestial navigational mission. The flight plan called for us to make a simulated bomb run on a target in the Pacific Ocean about a hundred miles west of San Diego. The night sky was clear, and the stars were bright. This type of flight takes a lot of preflight work and planning. We had been in the air about two and a half hours when suddenly the door to the front nose turret flew open, and as a result the wind blew through the navigator station and scattered Frank's papers all over the front of the plane. Siegfried examined the door and found he could not close it because the latch was broken, and not fixable in flight. While he was busy gathering up his papers, Frank accidentally stuck his finger in the heater fan and virtually cut the end of it off. His blood was all over his papers, and he was not able to do his work. Due to the broken door and Frank's injury, we had to return to Biggs.

[5] Over 3,500 men died in flight training exercises during the war. See Ambrose, *The Wild Blue*, 68-9.

It was well after midnight when we landed. We filled out our forms, gathered our gear, and waited for a truck to pick us up. The gunners had gathered some distance from our plane, and I did not even think anything about it until I realized there was an unusually large group. I started counting heads and discovered there were nine gunners instead of the usual four. I went over to check and found that five of my "gunners" were women. My regular gunners had smuggled five ladies from the Women's Army Corps on board that night. I was grateful it was late and none of the big brass knew about it. I made it clear that we would never again have unauthorized people aboard.

One night we were flying another navigation and bombing training mission. Once again we were to fly to a point over the Pacific. Everything had gone well that night and it was getting late. We had finished all the requirements of the mission and all we had to do was to fly back and land. There was no moon, the air was smooth, and there were what seemed like millions of stars. I had set the plane on autopilot, and we were cruising at 12,000 feet at 165 miles an hour. Suddenly the plane gave a violent jerk and nosed steeply to the left. I immediately hit the autopilot emergency cutoff switch and grabbed the controls. In that part of the country there were no ground lights at all. Without a moon in the sky, there was no way to tell where the horizon was. At times I felt like we were on our back, which you do not do with a B-24. I was sure we were in a spin because the altimeter was winding down. I wrestled with the plane for what seemed like an hour. All the gyros and instruments had tumbled and the only instrument I had that was working correctly was the needle and ball.[6] I never knew how I got the plane in a position where the needle and ball indicated I was flying straight and level again.

We had been trained that if we were ever in a situation like that, we were to forget our own feelings and instincts and rely entirely on the needle and ball. I was doing that, but my feelings were that

[6] The needle and the ball refer to a glass tube with a ball inside. When the ball was in the center of the tube, it meant you were flying level.

we were still in a screaming dive to the left. Fortunately Nowaski got his bearings back. He assured me we were flying straight and level. I told him to take over the controls because I had a severe case of vertigo.[7] When we came out of the sudden dive, we were at 5,000 feet. We had lost 7,000 feet of altitude. I did not get my bearings back until we could see the lights of Tucson. That was the only time I ever got vertigo, and I can testify it is real and almost impossible to overcome. We never figured out what happened. It is a mystery that has no logical answer.

The one thing that I missed was Jean's encouragement. It was too far for her to come on the weekends. It was probably best that she was not there because our schedule was so full, and we had practically no free time. We were getting near the end of phase training and were certain we would be given a week's leave before we went overseas. We had about two weeks left in phase training, and my crew had developed into a fine working team. Then one morning I was shocked. I received orders stating that Nowaski was leaving my crew to become a first pilot. I was happy for him, but I had come to depend on his skill. In a couple of days Edward Steeve joined my crew as the new copilot. He had just graduated from cadets and had never been close to a B-24. There was no way I could teach Ed all the things he needed to know. I protested, but it did not do any good. I had to make do with a copilot who did not know anything about a B-24.

I soon realized what a problem it really was. The first flight we had together was a simulated bombing mission on Midland, Texas. Siegfried and I showed Ed how to start the engines and what he should do on takeoff. We got off the ground that day without any problems and made our run on Midland and headed back. On the way back I tried to tell Ed all he had to do during flight and landing. At Biggs, we found ourselves in a difficult situation. A frontal system was approaching and the wind had become strong with gusts up to fifty miles per hour. When you get those conditions in El Paso, the

---

[7] Vertigo occurs when a pilot loses his equilibrium and is unable to determine where he is.

sand and dust in the air are terrible. The flight controllers instructed us to fly around the area until they decided what we should do. We were low on fuel, and the weather was getting worse. The sand was so bad you could only see the field when you were directly above it. There were three of us still in the air, and we needed to get down. We were finally instructed to land on a short, auxiliary runway.

Because we could not see the field unless we were right over it, we had to make careful landings. We all missed the landing area on the first two attempts. To the right of the landing area was what we called the boondocks. It was an area of mesquite bushes covered by drifting sand. The bushes were as much as fifteen feet wide at the base and five or six feet high. It was certain disaster if you landed there. We had a 45-degree crosswind, and the wind was variable. The third time I tried to land I came in at the right place. Because the wind was so strong and at such an angle, I really struggled to hold my heading. As we got near the ground and just before the plane touched down, I had to kick the rudder around so the nose would be more in line with the runway. At the time I kicked the rudder, a strong gust of wind hit, and we were flying again. It only took the plane a couple of seconds to drift over the boondocks. I had no choice but to give the engines full throttle and shout "gear up." The next few seconds, in fact the next few minutes, seemed like an eternity. We were barely above the ground, and between wind gusts the plane would start to settle. We could not have been more than inches above the boondocks. I was desperately trying to keep from crashing. This continued, and the end of the runway, which was off to my left, was coming up and the fence and houses beyond were getting closer.

With all that was going on during this disaster, I did not have time to think or check anything. All my attention was focused on keeping the plane in the air. I knew something was wrong because we should have had enough speed to start climbing, but the plane was still just above the ground and on the verge of stalling. We cleared the fence and now were barely over the rooftops of the houses. If there had been TV antennas as they are today, I would not have cleared them. By the time I reached downtown El Paso, I was beginning to get enough speed to get some control. We passed downtown no higher than the office buildings. We reached the mountain pass and were able to increase our speed. As soon as we got high enough to clear the mountains, I started looking to see why the plane had not responded when I had given it full power. It did not take long to figure it out. When I had called for the gear up, Ed made the mistake of raising the flaps and leaving the gear down. That had taken all our lift away and left our drag.[8]

I had to decide if I wanted to keep Ed or try and find a copilot who had experience flying a B-24. Ed was a really nice and brilliant young man, but I needed someone who could take off or land in an emergency. Not only that, but Ed had never done any formation flying and it would take a lot of time to train him to do that. Time was something that we did not have because this was the last week of phase training, and we would be going into combat within a month. One thing a pilot needed was a good copilot. However, I was afraid if I asked for another one, I might end up with an even larger problem. I do not think I slept any that night. After considering everything, I decided to keep Ed and hope for the best.

We finished the rest of our phase training and were looking forward to having a few days in transit to our next assignment. Orders were finally posted, and we left on a troop train the next day for Topeka, Kansas, where we would be assigned a new B-24. We were totally demoralized because we had been told earlier that we would have perhaps five days in transit to report to our new base. Jean and I had planned to meet in Abilene and spend a couple of days together. Before leaving, I called Jean and told her the bad news. We decided she would try to get to Topeka by the time I arrived. We knew this would be the last time we would be together for months or even years. The problem was that most buses were

[8] Lift is the force that pushes a plane up in the air and is caused by the airflow over and below the wing. Drag is any force that slows a plane down. When Jim's copilot raised the flaps, he reduced the speed of the air over the wing and consequently the lift. He further complicated the situation by leaving the landing gear down, which increased the drag.

full. It would be a hard trip for her to make, but the party was over and this would be the last dance. Every day the news gave accounts of the air war over Europe, and I would have been crazy to think my chances of surviving were great. So in reality, this was the last time for Jean and me to be together for a long time, or perhaps ever.

I was very discouraged that things had not worked out as I had hoped. Thankfully, when we arrived in Topeka, Jean was already there and had found a room in a residence. For the next ten days we were processed for our overseas assignment. I was assigned a new B-24 with only ten hours logged on it. It was one of the new "H" models, and unlike the ones we used in training that were painted olive drab, these planes were silver.[9] We were told the olive drab paint slowed the planes down by four miles an hour. I had to sign for the new plane, and I saw on the papers that it was listed as being worth one million dollars. We flew every day checking out the plane and all of the equipment. Jean and I ate at the officers' club and went to movies every night. The day we hoped would never come finally did. Although I still did not know where I was going besides either the Eighth or Fifteenth Air Forces in Europe, I had to leave the next morning.[10]

I had to report to the flight line the next morning at one o'clock, so Jean and I decided it would be best for her to leave that night. We went to the bus station at 9:00 p.m. for her to return home. It was hard to say good-bye. I watched the bus pull out and suddenly I never felt lonelier. The next morning I would start on one of the most unusual experiences that a person could ever have.

[9] The United States produced twenty-two different variations of the B-24 during the war. Altogether, it produced over nineteen thousand B-24s. See O'Leary, *Consolidated B-24 Liberator*, 37.
[10] The United States operated two air forces in the European Theatre, the Eighth and Fifteenth Air Forces. The Eighth Air Force flew out of Great Britain and the Fifteenth Air Force flew from Italy. See Robin Neillands, *The Bomber War: The Allied Air Offensive against Nazi Germany* (New York: Overlook Press, 2000), 173-4 and 293; Roger A. Freeman, *The Mighty Eighth: Units, Men and Machines (A History of the US Eighth Army Air Force)* (Garden City, NY: Doubleday, 1970); and Ambrose, *The Wild Blue*, 105-26.

CHAPTER 4

Topeka to Belfast

AFTER JEAN LEFT, I slept very little because of the thought of what tomorrow would bring. We got up about 1:00 a.m. and put our bags in front of the barracks so the truck would carry them to the flight line. As I walked out the front door I could see a continuous line of lightning from the southwest to the northeast. It was distant and did not cause any concern at the time. We went to the mess hall and had breakfast, although none of us were hungry. There was very little conversation, partly because it was early and partly because of the journey we were preparing to undertake. After breakfast we were told that we would fly to Grenier Field at Manchester, New Hampshire, and would receive instructions on the next leg of our overseas trip when we arrived. By now it was obvious we would be sent to England.

Because of the approaching storm, we hurried through our checklist. After the engines were started, I was given instructions to the runway. The wind was strong with gusts up to forty miles an hour. By this time the storm was so close that the lightning kept everything lit up. We got to the end of the runway, made a hurried check of everything, and eased the throttles forward. As the engines roared, we began to pick up airspeed quickly because of the strong head wind. Because the pilot was totally involved in getting the plane into the air, it was necessary for the copilot to call the

Jim Davis's crew in front of a B-24, 1944. *(Back row from left to right)* Ernest Mackey (bombardier), Frank Morris (navigator), Jim Davis (pilot), Edward Steeve (copilot). *(Front row from left to right)* Herman Trego (tail gunner), Arthur Siegfried (flight engineer), Thornton Benson (gunner), Robert Kluge (gunner), Dexter Bodin (radio operator), George Van Hooten (gunner). (Courtesy of Jim Davis)

airspeed aloud. We started out with an airspeed of forty-five miles per hour because of the wind. Ed called fifty, then sixty, seventy, eighty, ninety. At this point I was thrilled that we had beaten the storm. Suddenly, the airspeed Ed was calling out was decreasing. At first I thought Ed was making an error in reading the indicator, but he said that while it was crazy, we were losing airspeed rapidly. I could tell by the speed the runway lights were going by that we had terrific ground speed, but I could not understand why the air speed was suddenly dropping. I also knew from the feel of the plane that we did not have enough speed to leave the runway.

Something strange was happening and I did not know what. The red lights at the end of the runway were fast approaching. I first thought I would cut the engines and try to stop the plane with the brakes, but I knew that would not be possible because of our high ground speed—at least a hundred and fifty and probably more. There was no way I could stop this plane now. I was committed to take off, and I had to keep going and keep hoping that something good would happen. If there had been time to think, I would have been scared to death. Fortunately in those situations you do not have time to think and can only rely on instinct. The lights at the end of the runway came and went. Now we were beyond the runway and on the overrun, which is an unpaved extension of the runway designed to be available for emergencies such as this. I knew at best this overrun would be two thousand feet, and we were still nowhere near flying speed.

On previous flights, I recalled an old farmhouse off the end of the runway. The building had mostly fallen down around an old stone chimney that projected at least thirty feet into the air. We were now beyond the overrun part of the runway and on a grassy pasture. The ground was rough and the plane was reacting violently to the terrain. Suddenly the old farmhouse appeared in front of us. We were approaching it at an incredible speed. As we got closer to the rock chimney, it was evident we were going to crash. The picture that is etched in my memory of that moment is still as vivid as the day it happened. Our ground speed was high, and although the stone chimney was thirty feet high, we were so close that I had to look up to see its top. An instant before we were about to crash into it, Ed threw his arms up over his face, turned his head toward me, and let out the loudest scream a person could make. Suddenly I felt tremendous pressure on my seat. It seemed that a great force was trying to drive me through the plane's bottom. I had a strange feeling we were floating. Nothing made sense. The sudden realization that we were in the air was too much to accept.

The plane felt strange, and almost instantly we were flying almost two hundred miles an hour with our flaps and gear still down. I hollered at Ed to raise them. He looked at me with the strangest expression on his face. I am sure I looked as strange as he did. Neither of us knew or could believe what had just happened. At that time I had never heard of wind shear, or a mega-burst.[1] It was years later before those terms were properly defined. We slowly realized we had not crashed into the chimney. We finally got the plane trimmed and cruising at 160 miles an hour. The rest of the crew never realized what happened. After we settled down, I offered the best prayer I could. Today, looking back on that takeoff, I still do not believe it could have happened. Except for the grace of God, we would not have survived.

After our exciting takeoff, the rest of the flight was uneventful. We reached Grenier Field and landed without any further problems.[2] We were told that evening that our planes would be serviced, and we would leave the next day for Goose Bay, Labrador. Two days earlier thirty B-17s had attempted to leave from Newfoundland to England. The winds were thought to be favorable, but about six hundred miles out they ran into terrible storms and severe headwinds. Twelve of the planes turned around and made it safely back, but the other eighteen planes were never heard from again. Because of that, our commanders decided not to send planes directly across the Atlantic anymore. We were told that we would fly to Goose Bay, then to Bluie West One in Greenland, and finally to Prestwick, Scotland.

We enjoyed a good dinner and a good night's sleep after our day's adventure. When we were told we would land at Bluie West One, it made chills run down my back. I had heard many times that it was the toughest place to land in the world. If you made one mistake on the approach, you were a dead duck because the location of the field did not allow a second chance. At this point I did not know how many miracles I had left.[3]

[1] Wind shear is a rapid change in wind direction or velocity. It is particularly dangerous during take-offs and landings because pilots have little room to maneuver.

[2] The North Atlantic Ferrying Route typically took planes to Europe with flights from bases in New England to Newfoundland, then to Greenland, and finally to Great Britain. See Craven and Cate, eds., *The Army Air Forces in World War II, Volume 1*, 342-9.

[3] The U.S. Army Air Forces began construction on Bluie West One in 1941. It served as a major stopping point for aircraft being ferried to Europe. See William Kray, *Bluie West One, Secret Mission to Greenland, July 1941: The Building of an*

The morning was beautiful and clear as we were briefed on our flight to Goose Bay. When we got to the plane, we found everything ready for takeoff. The ground crew had also filled the bomb bay with containers of mail. We made a normal takeoff, headed over New England, and could see the Atlantic Ocean on the right. The further north we flew the denser the clouds became. Our briefing indicated that the weather was expected to be good when we reached Goose Bay. When we arrived, the tower told us we would have to circle the area for a while because they were having a heavy snowstorm and planes were having trouble getting on the ground. We flew as directed for a long time, and it began to get dark. The flight controller informed us the snow had been so heavy and deep that it had covered the runway and the runway lights. They were in the process of getting all the base's vehicles to line up along the edge of the runway with their lights on so we could see where it was. Because the nearest other airfield was beyond our range, we had no choice but to land there. Thankfully, we did so without incident.

The next day, the weather was too bad to leave, so we got a day of rest. It was the first day off I had enjoyed for several weeks. It seemed that from the time I lost my copilot, every flight had resulted in near disaster. This was not because of Ed—he had learned the duties of a copilot very rapidly and was doing an excellent job. However, Ed had not yet had the opportunity to learn to take off, land, or fly formation. That meant that if something happened to me, the crew would be in a difficult situation. No one knew that better than I did, but we simply had not had time to allow him to practice. For the crew's safety, it was imperative that Ed learned these skills.

The weather cleared the third day and we were advised to report to operations for a briefing on our flight to Greenland. It was critical that we get everything right on this flight because there was

American Air Force Base (Bennington, VT: Merriam Press, n.d.). The airfield is still in operation today and is called Narsarsuaq. For pictures and information concerning the history of the airfield, see http://iserit.greennet.gl/bgbw/contact. html, accessed on July 7, 2005.

no alternate landing base. We were told the flight would take us approximately five hours. The weather briefing indicated that because a low-pressure system was developing, we would probably encounter clouds and perhaps have to do some instrument flying. This did not sound encouraging, but we had to move out because there were other planes on the way to Goose Bay and they had to have the room.

A briefing officer told us that we would pick up a radio beacon when we got within seventy-five miles of Greenland's coast. The scary thing was that if you were off course, it would be easy to miss. If this happened, you were in a terrible mess because you would not know whether to go up or down the coast to find it. If you chose the wrong way, you could either land on the ice cap or in the ocean. Neither option was survivable. We were briefed that if you ditched into the water, you could survive approximately fifteen minutes. If you landed on the ice cap, you might last a little longer. It was critical that our navigation be accurate. With no radio aids and the prospect of several hours of instrument flying, I did not feel comfortable about the flight. We were told that until we picked up the beacon, we would fly using our radio. The beacon was located on a small island about ten miles from the coast. As we passed over the station, we would make a turn to a certain heading that would take us to a pass in the mountains. All of this sounded simple—if you made contact with the radio station.

As we approached Greenland, we were supposed to see a passage open up in the two to five thousand foot high mountains that were up to a half mile wide. In reality, we would be flying down a tunnel with towering mountains of rock covered with snow on either side. The thing that really made it difficult and dangerous was that upon entering the fjord you would have to fly the right bank until you came to a certain landmark, such as the bow of a sunken ship sticking out of the water. At that point you would immediately switch to the other bank and follow it until you came to another specific marker, such as a buoy. Then fly that bank until another designated marker appeared. Then switch to the other bank and fly it until another marker. This would require you to switch from flying one side to the other at the specified markers. The reason for that was that the fjord in which we would be flying had branches that looked the same. You could not tell the main fjord from the ones merging into it. If you made any errors, you would end up in a dead end with no way out but to crash into the side of a mountain.

The landing strip was fifty-five miles inland from the coast, so it would take about twenty minutes of flying down the tunnel to reach it. If you made the right turns, switched back and forth between the banks at the right time, and rounded the mountain properly, you would see the landing strip. It was at the mouth of a huge glacier that rose rapidly to the ice cap several thousand feet high. The runway started at the water's edge and slanted up about two hundred feet toward the other end. The moment you first saw the strip, you had to start your landing procedures because time and distance were critical at this stage. It was absolutely necessary that everything be done in the proper order or you would miss the runway and crash into the glacier or the mountain. If you did not time everything right and you came in too high or too fast, you could run over the end of the runway and fall two hundred feet off a cliff.

As the plane lifted from the ground for our flight to Greenland, the whole countryside sparkled in the bright sunlight. The sky was blue, and only a few low clouds hung along the coastline. It was not long before all signs of civilization disappeared. We were all alone. There were other planes that had taken off before we did and there were others to take off later, but we would never see any of them or be able to make radio contact.

At this point it seemed that everything was going too well. When I got that feeling, it always scared me. After an hour or so we could see cracks in the ice and at times a little water. The further we flew the more broken the ice was. Finally, we reached the beautiful Atlantic. I saw icebergs in sizes from very small to the large ones that looked like islands. Because we were over waters that were used by the German U-boats, we carried live ammunition. We flew low over the icebergs, and the gunners used them for target practice. It was like using an ice pick on a piece of ice. The icebergs were top heavy, and the piercing of the .50-cal. bullets caused them to split and roll over into the water with a tremendous splash. The sun shining on the spray made the most beautiful rainbows I have ever seen. However, we soon started to run into the clouds we had been briefed about.

After flying for two hours on instruments, we began having some breaks in the clouds. Soon we left them behind us and could see the ocean again. Then, we saw a white line on the distant horizon. At this point we began to receive a faint radio signal that we hoped would be the beacon we were searching for. It was not long before we clearly received the call signals and with great relief verified it was the beacon. It was good to see land even if it was snow and ice-covered mountains. We started losing altitude and homing in on the beacon as we had been briefed to do. To eliminate any possible error in flying the fjord, I went over the procedure with all the crewmembers. I wanted all the help I could get as an error would mean disaster. We neared the coast and by the volume of the radio signal it sounded like we were close to the station. We were now down to 1,500 feet. The mountains were getting closer. After we passed over the beacon, we took the heading that we had been told and turned toward the wall of mountains. At this point the mountains looked solid. As we got closer, we could see there was a small passage between the mountains. It was about 4:00 p.m., and the way the sun was shining on the mountains you could not see this gap until you were almost there. The fjord opened up just as briefed, and we made our way through the tunnel without difficulty. After approximately twenty minutes, the landing strip appeared.

We immediately started our landing procedure. I suppose I should have expected something unusual to happen by now, and it did. A huge iceberg had floated just in front of the runway. Two tugs were trying to pull it out of the landing pattern, but they were unable to move it. The iceberg projected over a hundred feet above the water. The high tide had also taken some of the runway length, which increased the difficulty in landing. With the iceberg in front of the runway we would have to come in high to miss it. We made our turn as we let down and arrived at the proper altitude. I came in as close as I could above the iceberg and sat the plane down as quickly as possible. We had just touched the runway when I started using my brakes. Because the B-24 had a weak landing gear, we normally did not use the brakes until the plane slowed down. If you pressed too hard on the brakes at a high speed, the nose wheel could collapse. It was either risk the collapse of the nose gear, or go over the end of the runway and fall two hundred feet. I reasoned I would be better off with a collapsed nose gear, so I rode the brakes hard. It was good that I did, because I used up the entire runway with about fifty feet remaining before the end.

It was a relief to be on the ground, even if it was Greenland. Before I could set my breaks and cut the engines, a jeep with a captain in it drove up and said he wanted to talk to me. I could not imagine what he wanted. We cut the engines and opened the bomb bay. The captain came up to the flight deck and told me that if I wanted to, they would refuel my plane immediately and we could leave for England that evening. Otherwise it might be three or four days before we could leave because a low-pressure system was building up to the southwest, and if it developed as expected, it would draw the air off the ice cap. As it came down the glacier to the air base, it would likely produce winds over one hundred miles an hour for three or four days. I did not have to think about that decision long or even consult my crew. I was in no hurry to get to England, and staying a few days in Greenland was fine with me.

The weather forecast sounded strange because it was such a beautiful day with very little wind. We got our bags and were assigned our quarters. By 10:00 p.m. the wind had increased to about thirty miles per hour and was getting stronger. The next morning it was more than one hundred miles per hour and stayed like that for two days. It was so strong that it would blow you down if you went outside. On the third day it had calmed down some, and we were told that we would probably be able to take off later that day.

That afternoon we were briefed on our flight to England. It would take at least nine hours and maybe more if the winds were not favorable. We were told that the weather was always changing over the north Atlantic and to be prepared for anything. We would be on our own with no navigational help until we got close to Scotland. We were also instructed to be very cautious about homing in on British or American radio stations because the Germans would often send up false signals. The bottom line was not to trust homing in on a radio beacon. We also only had thirty minutes fuel reserve so we had to be careful about our gas consumption. Strong headwinds could cause you to use extra fuel, and it was critical that we conserve as much gas as possible just in case of an emergency. We were told again that if we had to ditch in the waters of the north Atlantic, we could probably survive only fifteen minutes.

The winds had died down to fifteen miles an hour around 11:00 p.m., so we lined up for takeoff. It was a good thing the runway was downhill, the tide was out, and the iceberg had been blown down the fjord somewhere. Although it was the dead of the night, it was still light as we climbed to ten thousand feet. The stars were our only navigational aid, but because it was still too light to see them, we had to stay with our predetermined heading. We crossed the southern tip of Greenland as the sun set. Usually the point of no return was halfway on the trip, but in this case, thirty minutes from takeoff, we were already beyond that point because it would be dark at the field we just left, and there would be no way to find your way back down the fjord. For the next nine hours we knew we would land at Prestwick or else.

We were hoping as soon as it got dark that Frank could get a reading on the stars, so we could determine our position and make any necessary corrections. We soon gave up on that, because the clouds prevented Frank from taking his celestial readings. I decided to try to get above the clouds. That meant we would have to go on oxygen and would consume more gasoline. After climbing five thousand feet, it became evident that the clouds were much higher than I had hoped they were, so we abandoned that plan and let down to ten thousand feet again. Now we were in solid clouds. It was not long before we discovered ice was accumulating on the wings. The further we flew, the more severe the ice got. Even though it was night, we could tell we would have to do something or be in serious trouble with the ice load. The air had also become very bumpy. We discussed the problem and decided we had to go either up or down to try to clear the freezing level. We sat our navigation problem aside for the time being, because if we did not get out of the icing, it did not make any difference where we were. We decided we would try to go up first, but because the ice got worse as we went higher, we then went down.

At this point the clouds were so thick we could hardly see the lights on the end of the wings. They must have been covered with ice. The ice had built up on the plane to the point that it was affecting the plane's controls and attitude.[4] The B-24 had deicers on the leading edge of the wings, but we would not dare use them except as a last resort. The deicers were rubber and had bladders that would expand to break the ice off the leading edge.[5] The problem was that as the ice was chipped off, it would break unevenly, leaving a jagged surface on the leading edge of the wing. This would disturb the flow of air over the wing and reduce the lift. Our B-24 had the Davis wing (a long, deep, and narrow design), or what was called a high lift wing, and any interruption of the smooth airflow over the wings would seriously affect it.[6]

We descended to four thousand feet. The clouds appeared to thin some and the icing appeared to have stopped. I decided to descend a little lower, hoping to get into warmer air where maybe the ice would melt. We reached a layer of air without clouds, although

[4] Attitude refers to a plane's axis relative to a fixed point, like the horizon. Under the icing conditions that Jim is describing, he would have had a very difficult time keeping the plane level.

[5] The bladder on the wing was a hollow rubber device that when inflated could break any accumulating ice.

[6] The Davis Wing was a specially designed wing by David R. Davis for the B-24 that provided little drag and extra lift. See Birdsall, *Log of the Liberators*, 38-42.

there were clouds above and below us. For now, it seemed our icing problem had been eliminated.

Now we had to consider what to do about our navigation. Besides knowing we were over the North Atlantic, we had no idea where we were. We had selected a heading to correct for the curvature of the earth, but for the last three hours we had not been able to get a fix. We could try climbing and get on top of the clouds so Frank could get some readings on the stars, but that might get us back into the icing problems. We also would be using precious gasoline by climbing to the higher altitude. If we were going to get a fix on the stars, we would have to do it now, because soon it would be daylight and that would eliminate any hope of getting an accurate reading. We finally decided we would have to take a chance and climb on top if possible.

Before we started our climb there was one thing that I had to take care of. Because of all the tension of the last few hours, combined with drinking too much coffee, I had to use the rest room. A B-24 has no toilet facilities, only relief tubes (which were frozen), so I went to the bomb bay to relieve myself. I crawled through the bomb bay door hatch and stood on the catwalk in the center of the bomb bay. I decided that just as I would start to urinate, I would open the bomb bay doors just enough for it to go out the bottom into the slipstream—that all made sense. I started to relieve myself and hit the switch to the bomb bay doors at the same time. The opposite of what I had planned happened. As the doors opened, instead of going out the crack in the doors it blew back into me. Once I started I could not stop, so the next best thing to do was lean close to the containers filled with mail. It gave a little protection but not much.

It was now back to my seat to start our climb. We climbed to 21,000 feet but the clouds were still above us.[7] We then went back down to 10,000 feet. At least we would not be on oxygen and would

[7] While the B-24 could reach a maximum altitude of 28,000 feet, it took a lot of fuel to do so and would add to Jim's icing problems; therefore, he had little choice but to move to a lower altitude.

be using less fuel than at 20,000 feet. It was now beginning to get light and we lost any opportunity of getting a fix on the stars. We were about halfway there according to the elapsed time of four and a half hours, but we had no idea where we were—completely lost and flying on faith and hope. From time to time the gunners would call and report problems such as an oil leak, ice, and anything else of concern. We could not see the ocean below or the sky above as we were flying between cloud layers. Before long we were back in the clouds and turbulence. At least it was light and we could better see our ice accumulations. We were accumulating ice again, and without waiting for a buildup, I started down hoping to get out of it. We descended to 3,000 feet, and I decided to let down slowly to get under the clouds. We knew we could not depend on our altimeter to be accurate. At just below the 1,500 feet indicated, we cleared the clouds and could see the water. There was no doubt we were closer than the instruments showed. One thing was certain: we were too close. The ocean was a horrible sight. The swells looked like mountains and the breaking waves were sending spray high into the air. We might have been getting some mist from the waves even at our altitude. One quick look at the violent Atlantic Ocean and I immediately put the throttles forward and started to climb back into the clouds.

We were alternately in and out of the clouds, never knowing which way to go, up or down. When we were out of Greenland six hours, which meant that at best we had three more hours to go, it seemed as if we had been flying for days. At this time in our trip, all we could be sure of was that we were over the Atlantic Ocean. We had used a lot of extra fuel in our attempts to make celestial readings and escape the icing. We had no reason to think the weather would get any better. Hope and prayer were all we had left.

This had been a combination of the longest—and at the same time the shortest—night that I ever lived. It was the shortest because the latitude at which we were flying made the night only three hours long, but it was also the longest because we had no idea where we were and all night we had been battling the unrelenting clouds and ice. Time passed so slowly, with little conversation among the crew. They were all tired and well aware of our situation. We had been in the weather for over eight hours before the clouds began to thin out. Then an unusual thing happened. We not only saw the water, but we also saw a ship. It was indescribable how much seeing a ship meant. It suddenly gave us hope that just maybe we might reach land after all. It was not long before Dexter Bodin, my radio operator, called me and said he was not sure, but he thought he was getting a faint radio signal. It was only a few minutes later that he confirmed his suspicion.

I cannot describe in words the feeling we had when we got our first glimpse of land. We were not sure what land it was, but that did not make much difference at this point. We were going to head for it and not let it leave our sight. When we finally got our fix, we discovered it was Ireland, and we were only ten miles off course. It was such a relief. As best as we could determine we still had enough fuel to reach Prestwick, which was our planned destination.

Soon we were over Scotland. It was about this time that Dexter called me and said he had heard a radio report that said allied troops had made landings in France during the night.[8] The long awaited invasion of Europe had begun. But my concern now was to get this plane safely on the ground at Prestwick. Thankfully, we arrived there, got landing instructions, and touched down without any problem.

No sooner had the props stopped turning than a captain appeared on the flight deck. He signed and gave me a receipt for one B-24 in good condition. I then recalled that I had signed for the plane in Topeka. He instructed me to tell my crew to place all their belongings at the rear of the plane, to be picked up by a truck and delivered to the train station. He told me we would be fed and then carried to a train to be sent to Liverpool. I had neither planned nor hoped for this. I had expected to eat, take a shower, put on some clean clothes, and have a good night's sleep.

---

[8] Dexter Bodin was hearing the reports of D-Day, June 6, 1944.

I do not recall how long we were on the train, but we arrived late in the evening at Liverpool. The English in each of the villages and towns were excited and celebrating the allied landings. They stood by the tracks and waved at us. I was anxious to see the countryside, but I had a hard time staying awake. We arrived at Liverpool and got on trucks that took us to an old English army base. It was vacant, and from all indications the troops stationed there had just left. They were probably a part of the invasion forces. We were given some rations for dinner, two blankets, and three "biscuits." Biscuits were nothing more than hard pillows about thirty inches square that were supposed to be used as mattresses. We were told we could sleep anywhere we wanted to. There were no beds, bunks, or cots—nothing but dirt and filth. The inside of the buildings were so dark and filthy that some of us decided it would be better to sleep outside. As tired as I was, it did not make much difference where we were.

Mackey and Frank went to the village. I was too tired to go, so they disappeared and did not get back until after midnight. Ed and I decided it was time to rest. This was not what I thought it would be like. I was tired, and feeling the fear of going into combat soon made me think of all the things I missed back home. I wondered what Jean was doing and thought how much I would love to see her. I was afraid she might be mad at me for not writing more often. I also thought how I could have joined the army and been assigned to the quartermasters' office, out of the danger of combat. But I had no regrets, because I believed I was doing my part. I was suddenly awakened by rain, so we all gathered our gear and moved into the filthy barracks for the rest of the night.

The next morning we went to the airport and boarded a plane that took us to an air base a short distance from Belfast. This was our last assignment before we were sent to a bomb group in the Eighth Air Force as a replacement crew. Somehow the word "replacement" had a horrible sound. We would replace crews that had been shot down, crashed, or in a few cases had finished their tour of duty, which at that time was twenty-five missions. A lot more crews were being shot down than were finishing their tours.[9]

While at this base, each crew and each crewmember was checked and evaluated for certification as combat ready. If one of my crew was not considered qualified for combat, he would be replaced by someone who had been certified. I had no worries about losing any of my crew, because they had all performed great, and at this point we were really a close group of people. We had no weak link, and I would put them up against any group. Everyone's attitude seemed more subdued than it had been in the states. We all realized that we would be in combat soon and that changed a lot of things. After ten days, we had all cleared our tests, were certified for combat, and assigned to the 489th Bomb Group, a relatively new unit to England that had only recently started flying missions.[10] It was based near the little town of Halesworth, England, in East Anglia, and was the closest airfield to the English Channel.[11]

[9] The Army Air Forces originally required crews to fly twenty-five combat missions before they were rotated back to the states. Late in the war, Bomber Command increased the number of required combat missions to thirty-five. See McManus, *Deadly Sky*, 299-300.

[10] For the official history of the 489th Bomb Group, see Freudenthal, *A History of the 489th Bomb Group*.

[11] For a detailed map of Halesworth, see Roger A. Freeman, *Mighty Eighth War Manual* (London: Jane's Publishing, 1984), 287.

CHAPTER 5

The First Mission

WE BOARDED THE PLANE with three other replacement crews for combat duty with the 489th Bomb Group. We were all strangers and anxious to see what it would be like at our new base. I had never met the other three crews previously. When we arrived at Halesworth, we were assigned to separate squadrons, and other than the pilot on one of the planes, Lt. Claude Lovelace, I did not get to know any of the others very well. There was not a lot of conversation that morning on the two-hour flight, because we all knew that this could be our last assignment. I could not help but wonder what fate had in store for this group of four crews. The bomber losses had been very heavy for the last year, with no evidence that they would improve.[1] None of us knew quite what to expect.

Our most important concern was how we would react to combat. It was not a question of fear. I doubt that any of us did not fear entering air combat. A person learns a lot about himself and how he reacts in critical situations during air battles. At this time, none of us knew for sure what our action or reactions would be. Looking

---

[1] In the European Theatre, the U.S. Eighth and Fifteenth Air Forces, based in England and Italy respectively, suffered over 94,500 casualties (including dead, wounded, missing, and captured). See *Army Air Forces Statistical Digest: World War II* (Office of Statistical Control, 1945), 51-2.

84

back, I had no idea that my crew would be the only one from these four replacement groups not to be shot down.[2] They all were young, highly trained, and good looking, and had so much to live for. But war is cruel, and the last eighteen months of intense training had prepared us for the challenge, no matter what the personal sacrifice would be.

The plane started its descent and as the landing gear and flaps lowered we knew we would soon see our new home. As we crawled out of the plane, we looked around and did not see a lot of activity. We were in front of a large hangar, but there were few visible buildings. Scattered around the landscape we could see a few B-24s parked around clumps of trees and a few trucks and men. It did not look like the airfields back in the United States with all of the large hangars and other buildings close to the flight line. I could not see barracks or any other buildings of significant size. Soon a jeep drove up and a sergeant told us that trucks would come by in a few minutes to take us to our assigned squadron area.

Each group was made up of four squadrons. Three were squadrons of combat crews and one squadron was made up of a lead crew. On a mission, the lead squadron, led by a lead crew and the group commander for that day, flew in the center, with the second

[2] Jim believes the first replacement crew went down on its sixth mission, and the second one on its twelfth mission. The third crew went down during the Market Garden operation in September 1944. Lieutenant Lovelace was the pilot of the last crew. While he died, some of his crew did survive. Although Jim does not remember the names of the other crews besides Lieutenant Lovelace, the 489th Bomb Group lost thirteen planes between July 21 and September 18. Lovelace's plane was the last of these. The other planes were piloted by 2nd Lt. James Haas (captured), 1st Lt. Edwin Florcyk (killed), 1st Lt. John Slein (captured), 1st Lt. Arthur Bertanzetti (captured), 2nd Lt. Wallace Bishop (killed), 2nd Lt. Frank Palmer (captured), 2nd Lt. Mark Osborne (captured), 1st Lt. Maynard Kisinger (interned in Switzerland but later escaped), 2nd Lt. Walter Springer (killed), 2nd Lt. Victor Cochran (interned in Sweden), Capt. Thomas Plese (killed), and Capt. Robert White (killed). If the other replacement crews flew missions at roughly the same pace as Jim, the first crew that was lost was probably commanded by Lieutenant Slein because Jim knew the other pilots that were shot down at the time, while the second one was probably piloted by Lieutenants Osborne, Kisinger, or Springer. Freudenthal, *History of the 489th Bomb Group*, 287-91.

squadron flying high and to the right and the third one flying low and to the left.[3]

One or two crews usually were assigned to each squadron formation to fill in for any planes that might have to leave the formation because of mechanical problems or other difficulties. The usual group formation going out on a combat mission would start out with between thirty-six and forty-two planes. The Eighth Air Force was made up of three divisions. B-17s and their assigned fighter groups made up the 1st and 3rd Divisions. B-24s and their fighter squadrons, fourteen bomber and five fighter groups in all, formed the 2nd Air Division.[4] The 489th was in the 2nd Division. We were assigned to the 844th Bomb Squadron within the 489th Bomb Group.[5]

The trucks came and we boarded for a ride to our squadron area. Our truck drove down the ramp past two or three buildings and turned down a narrow paved road that was lined with trees and brush. We passed several airmen walking along the side of the road as well as several bicycles. It seemed to be all forest. Soon we came to a break in the trees, and on the left were the officers' club and mess. The truck continued and occasionally we could see roads that cut through the forest on the right. The roads would soon disappear in the trees, but we could tell that they were well used. About two hundred yards down the road from the officer's club, the truck turned into an open area. In the clearing was a group of Quonset huts and a couple of larger buildings. The truck came to a

[3] On combat missions B-24s typically flew in three-plane subgroups that made up larger formations. Within each three-plane group flew a lead plane, followed by wing men on the right and left who flew at a slightly higher altitude. See Carigan, "The B-24 Liberator—A Man's Airplane," 20-21.

[4] The Army Air Forces created the Eighth Air Force in early 1942 and assigned it to England to lead the American bombing campaign against Germany. It consisted of the 1st, 2nd, and 3rd Air Divisions. See Freeman, *The Mighty Eighth*, 4-8; and Frederick D. Worthen and Carroll A. Berner, eds., *Monty's Folly: Operation Market Garden* (Carlsbad, CA: California Aerospace Press, 1999), 18-9.

[5] Besides the 844th Bomb Squadron, the 845th, 846th, and 847th Bomb Squadrons were also in the 489th. See Freudenthal, *A History of the 489th Bomb Group*, 281.

stop in front of a larger steel building with a flagpole in front. The driver announced that this was the headquarters of the 844th Bomb Squadron. My crew waited while I reported.

We talked to some of the squadron personnel and found out all we could. The group had been sent out on a mission that morning, but had not yet returned. They were due back in an hour and a half and the activity would pick up at that time. I was anxious to talk to one of the pilots and find out what to expect—to learn what combat was like. We sat around the officer's club waiting. We heard the sounds of busy trucks and finally the noise of the returning planes. We walked outside to watch because the flight line was quite some distance away, and we still did not know the layout of the base. We saw the squadrons fly over the base and watched as the planes would pull out of formation and circle for a landing. I heard the sounds of ambulances and fire trucks. Some planes landed with engines feathered, some trailed smoke, and many circled the field firing red flares, indicating that they had serious problems aboard and needed priority in landing. There was no doubt we were in a combat zone.

As the crews started working their way back to the squadron area, we saw that they all looked so tired and decided we would not bother them about getting the details of their mission. We were anxious to get to our hut, unpack, and settle down for the night. Just before dark the sergeant came out and told us all the huts were full, and that we would have to spend the night on a concrete area behind the latrine. It was an area about fifteen feet by twenty feet and had a corrugated iron fence about six feet high around it. It had an opening in the end but no roof. We strung some wire across, unpacked some of our clothes, and hung them up. Supply brought us some cots and blankets.

I was tired but could not go to sleep. The day had not gone as I had hoped or expected. I lay there for several hours thinking about what the next few months would bring, but mostly of Jean and how I missed all the things of home and my loved ones. I wondered what they might be doing and how great it would be when the war was over and I could return. No one was more afraid of the future than I was. I lay there and thought about the very slim chance that we would survive. The odds were not in our favor. Only twenty-five or thirty percent survived. I was not one of those hot pilots who thought they were indestructible. Everyone was scared. Some put on a front and acted as if they had no fear, but deep down they knew fear like everyone else. I think that those who were not afraid to admit their fear were better off than those who tried to hide it.

The next morning we talked to as many people as possible to get a feel of what to expect, what it was like to be in combat, what a crew's chances were—anything that would help us settle in, but no one could give us much help. Most of the other crew members were so motivated, committed, dedicated, and intent on their jobs that to some degree they were in a trance. Many were too physically and emotionally exhausted to do much talking. Later, I would understand their situation.

I began to realize that we were only a number. I guess I wanted to find someone who would say that it was not as bad as you think, but it never happened. They could not tell or explain what air combat was really like. It did not take me long to realize that at this level, each of us was expendable. If you could not accept that, you really had a problem. That was the cold, cruel reality, and many of us could not accept or adjust to it.

After lunch I went back to the squadron office to ask if they had found a place for us to stay. The sergeant told me that we would be in hut so and so. I went back and told the guys, and we gathered up our gear and proceeded to the hut.[6] The outside of the hut was olive drab and the inside was dark. It had one door and a small entryway, with a small window on the other end. In the center of the hut was a small cast iron stove, surrounded by eight steel cots with wire mesh and springs to support three biscuits. Above each cot was a rod to hang your clothes on. We entered the hut to find each bed already

---

[6] Each crew was composed of four officers and six enlisted men. Generally, the officers from two crews shared a hut and the enlisted men from two crews shared a hut.

made up and clothes and personal belongings still in place. I went back to the squadron office and told the sergeant that all bunks were occupied. He apologized and explained that the crew that occupied the four cots assigned to us had been shot down and that someone would come by soon to pick up their personal belongings. If we were not demoralized before, we were now.

Because I was the plane commander, I had my choice of which cot would be mine. It did not make much difference to me, so each of us chose a cot. Soon two sergeants came by and picked up the personal belongings of the crew we were replacing. We went to the supply room and picked up our biscuits and blankets. It did not take Ed and me long to make up our bed and hang our clothes. It had been a long hard day with many surprises, and I was ready to lie down and take a nap. Frank and Mackey were somewhat slower.

Frank made up his bed and was putting his clothes up. He sat down with his .45-cal. pistol, working the bolt back and pulling the trigger. Mackey told him that he should not be playing with a gun. Frank said he was just seeing how it worked. Mackey insisted that was dangerous, because an accidental discharge was always possible. Frank responded that the pistol was not loaded, and produced the clip in order to appease Mackey. Mackey responded that an empty gun was the one that accidentally fired most often. Ed and I were stretched out trying to get a nap, but with Frank and Mackey in such a heated argument, that proved difficult. The argument was loud, but not loud enough to keep me from dozing off.

Suddenly a tremendous roar awakened me. At first I thought we were being bombed. We all jumped to our feet, except Frank, who was still sitting on his bed. The pistol in his hand had smoke still coming from the barrel. I will never forget the look on Frank's face. His eyes were as large as saucers. He sat there on the side of his bed, holding the smoking gun, and suddenly said in a loud voice, "Who fired that shot?" It seemed like an eternity before we could get our wits back.

Mackey was furious. "Hell Frank! You just shot that empty gun!" It turned out that during their argument Frank had unconsciously put the clip back into the gun and pulled the trigger. He finally realized what had happened. The gun going off nearly burst my eardrums because the noise and concussion in such a small, tin building was terrible. The bullet struck the floor about three feet from my cot and scattered pieces of concrete all over the hut. What worried us was where the bullet went after it hit the floor. The other four occupants of our hut were all officers who were on a mission, and we had yet to meet them. To our dismay we finally found the bullet. After striking the floor, it angled up and struck another officer's clothes. His clothes were neatly hanging over his cot, and the bullet went through every garment he owned. The last one was a new, expensive coat that he had bought in London. By the time the bullet got through the other clothes, it had lost much of its momentum and was only able to go halfway through the sleeve. We found the bullet on the floor just below his coat. This was a problem out of my realm of experience. I could only imagine what he would think after enduring a long mission that day to come home and find a large hole in the concrete, four roommates he had never seen, and his expensive custom-made Cashmere coat with a hole in it.

About this time, Mackey realized that the discharge of the pistol was probably heard all over the squadron area and the military police (MP) would probably arrive soon to investigate. In a combat area, everyone is sensitive to unusual and loud noises. We decided it would be a good idea to get out of the area as soon as possible. Because Frank and Mackey still had on their clothes, they hurried out the door while Ed and I finished dressing. We went out the door just in time to see the MPs put Frank and Mackey in a jeep and drive off. We decided to go back in the hut and wait until we had a plan about what to do.

It had been one hell of a day. Ed and I sat there trying to review the situation and evaluate our options. I could not decide what my biggest problem was: having Frank and Mackey locked up, or trying to find a diplomatic way of telling our new roommate about his clothes. An MP knocked on the door and asked me if I would go with him to base security to discuss a problem they had. When I inquired about what the problem was, he told me the captain would explain it.

At that time I did not know that when Frank and Mackey left the hut the MPs had driven up and stopped them. The MPs asked if they had heard a gunshot in the area. Mackey said "Hell yes, this SOB tried to shoot me." The MPs were not amused. It took me about an hour to get it all straightened out and get Frank and Mackey out of the slammer. By the time we got back to the hut, the other crew had returned. I told them what had happened and explained that we would either pay for or repair the damage.

That afternoon we received notice that the four new crews would have a briefing and orientation the next day at 2:00 p.m. Right on schedule, the forty airmen who made up the new crews were waiting in the briefing room. Maj. Lewis Tanner conducted the briefing. He spared no words in telling us what was expected. He did not tell us what we wanted to hear, but left no doubt that we had a very difficult tour ahead, and much would be demanded of us. He closed by saying that if we successfully completed twenty-five missions we would be given the Distinguished Flying Cross and sent back to the United States. He scared the heck out of me. Finally he said, "Gentlemen, are there any questions?" Before any one could ask anything he said thank you and left.

I had never seen Major Tanner prior to that. All I knew was that he was one of the squadron commanders. (Thirteen years later I moved to Midland, Texas, and discovered that he was living there and working as a dentist. I called him up one day and we visited for a long time. He was my dentist for almost thirty years, and we became close friends. I often told him if I ever got big enough I would give him a boot in the seat for scaring us that day.) I would find out that he told us the truth.

For the next few days we were busy learning all the procedures that we needed to know before we could fly our first mission. The most important thing was to be able to fly in close formation. I guess they felt like if you crashed on takeoff or landing you would only kill yourself and your crew, but any mistakes you made flying formation would endanger everyone else. Good formation flying was absolutely a must, and our commanders accepted nothing else. If you could not measure up, you were quickly replaced. Unfortunately, the biggest weakness in the flight training program before a crew was sent into combat was with formation flying. While we did some of it in Advanced Training and a little more while stationed at Biggs Field, it was still inadequate. We had to learn a lot on the fly after we arrived overseas. Generally, this made the first combat mission you flew very exciting and dangerous. Adding to training deficiencies in formation flying, new crews were usually assigned the most worn out and beat-up B-24 and given the worst position in the formation. Gradually, as you gained more experience, you would be assigned a better plane and better position in the group formation. I eventually moved up to the best flying position, just to the left of the lead plane.[7]

They say a cat has nine lives. I felt like a cat that had lost the first eight, and the big fight was about to start. I do not know how much luck I had when I started flying, but I had used up a lot in cadets, B-24 transition, phase training, and the flight overseas. I wondered how much longer it would hold out. But given a choice, even though our chances of survival were not good, I would not have traded places with anyone. I knew that somehow the war had to be won, and I was willing to pay the price—even if it was the supreme sacrifice.

When I say I had fear, I do not mean just the fear of being killed in combat. I am sure we all had that. Of all my fears, the fear of failure was foremost in my mind. It was the fear of not performing as expected, making the wrong decision at a critical time, and letting my crew down. At this stage you had to perform as though you were fearless and at the highest level.

It was July 6, 1944. For the last ten days we had been given all the procedures we needed to fly in combat, and we were finally

---

[7] The worst position while in formation flying was the last aircraft in the formation. In this position, the pilot had to react to the movements of all of the planes in front of him and was in the most vulnerable spot if attacked by enemy aircraft.

cleared for combat duty. The standard procedure for a new crew was for the pilot to fly as copilot with an experienced crew to learn the things you could only learn from experience. Only after his baptism of fire on that first mission would the pilot be trusted with his own crew.

It was 4:00 p.m. when Siegfried and Trego came to my hut and told me that I had been put on alert for tomorrow's mission. I hurried over to the bulletin board, and sure enough, my name was listed to report for the briefing the next morning. That was the first of fifty or sixty times over the next five months that I would see my name on that list. Few things will get your attention any faster than to see your name on that bulletin board. It is impossible to describe the feelings that go through your mind—they are so mixed. For sixteen months I had been training for this moment. So many thoughts were whirling through my head. The one that dominated was about home—Jean and my family—and what they were doing. I wondered where our mission was going. I hoped it would not be a long one to some place deep in Germany.

I returned to the hut and lay down to relax but it was impossible. The other crew came in, and I told them I was alerted for the next day, July 7, 1944. They had completed five missions and tried to tell me what to expect, but they could not. The only way to know what it was like was to experience it. I went to the mess hall for dinner, but I was not really hungry. After dinner I went to the officer's club and stayed a while listening to the music. A lot of laughter was coming out of the bar, and a group of officers gathered there to exchange stories about their last mission. About 10:00 p.m. I returned to the hut and lay down. Ed was the only one there so it was quiet and peaceful. While I knew that wake-up call would be between midnight and 3:00 a.m., I found getting to sleep nearly impossible.

If you were on the alert list, an enlisted man would come around to wake you up. When 1:00 a.m. passed, I was concerned they had somehow missed me, but I knew that often the time of the mission was changed. They would get you, one way or the other. The still and quiet of the night was broken about 1:30 a.m. In the distance, I heard trucks starting their engines, and traffic started picking up on the road. Everything kept picking up until about 2:30, when I heard footsteps outside.

I heard the door open and someone with a flashlight came to my bunk. "Lt. Davis. Sir, it's time to get up." He stayed there until I got out of bed and assured him I was awake. I hurriedly put on my clothes, got my flashlight, and started out the door. Everyone wished me well as I left. The night air was cold. It was foggy and a light rain was falling. As I looked at the sky, I wondered how it was possible to fly in this weather, but as time went by I learned that this was the norm. Once outside the hut I heard others making their way down the road. It was so dark that you could not see the people—only the flashlights bobbing. The heavy cold damp air carried sound forever, and I could hear the drone of the engines as the mechanics worked on them. The airfield was abuzz with noise—the planes, the trucks carrying bombs and gasoline, and the pilots and crews fumbling in the darkness.

I made my way out to the road and down to the mess hall. There was little conversation. Perhaps it was too early, but I think most of us were thinking about what the day would bring. Even on mission days, there was the usual griping about the food. I do not think anyone was hungry, but you had to eat. No one knew how long the day would be, and we could not eat until we returned. Our usual breakfast was powdered eggs, potatoes, ham, pancakes, syrup, toast, and jelly. The toast had a texture and taste as if it was made from sawdust. The jelly was orange marmalade. It was always covered with bees that looked more like wasps. You had to use one hand to fight the bees off while you got a spoonful. I have never enjoyed orange marmalade since then. There was always hot coffee and tea to drink. I never enjoyed coffee before then, but it was hot and seemed to break the early morning chill.

After breakfast I took the long walk to the briefing room. Even though we could have used bicycles and trucks, many of us walked. Once in the briefing room, I visited with some friends to speculate about where this day's mission would take us. The location of each day's target was one of the best-kept secrets during the war. It was not long before the room was almost full of anxious airmen. I heard some conversation, but because of the early hour, about 3:30 a.m., and the mystery of the target, it was fairly subdued.

We all stood when the group commander and his entourage (a briefing officer, chaplain, weatherman, and three other officers) entered the briefing room. The chaplain started with a prayer; the group commander followed with a few words; and then the briefing officer took over. In the front of the briefing room was a small stage. Behind it was a screen where the day's targets and the courses were written. A curtain always covered the screen until the briefing officer started. The moment he pulled the rope to draw back the curtain and expose the target for the day, the room went from dead silence to all kinds of groans and comments.

I do not think anyone in the room had ever been to the target area before because it was deep inside Germany. The target area for today was a JU-88 airplane factory in Aschersleben, Germany.[8] I would later learn that this target, in my estimation, was one of the most heavily defended targets in Germany. It did not look good. It would take about seven and a half hours to complete the mission. That is a long mission in any airplane, but especially in a B-24.

For every mission, the briefing officer went into great detail about the flight plan to the target and/or targets that each squadron or unit would have in the area. The route was always broken with many legs at different angles to try to keep us away from heavy antiaircraft fire (flak). The routes were also designed to confuse the Germans as to what our real target was for the day. There were always secondary targets if for some reason the primary target could not be bombed because of clouds, smoke, haze, or other conditions. The flight plan was also designed to have all groups fly the same course until the last minute, when each would branch off to their specific targets. This was necessary for the safety of all groups as it allowed the fighter escort to provide better protection. They

[8] The Germans initially designed the JU-88 as a medium bomber, but eventually turned it into its principle night-fighter plane.

could fly up and down the bomber line and be available to protect any group in case of an enemy attack. We were told what we might expect along the route as far as fighter attacks and flak. The weatherman briefed us on the expected weather, not only in the target areas but also along the course. Because bad weather was such a constant factor in England, he briefed us on what we might expect on takeoff, assembly, and landing. The weather people were good, but the weather changed so often that they frequently missed the forecast completely.

After all the general information was given on the target, the group leader, Lt. Col. Byron Webb, gave a summary of what he expected from us as well as what he did not expect. Colonel Webb was a very aggressive person. He gave us a pep talk, and after the talk all the crewmembers, except the pilot and copilots, departed the room to attend their own sub-briefing for each position on the plane. After the rest of the crew left, we were given all the necessary information that pertained to the pilots such as the time to start engines, what plane we would follow on takeoff, what course we would fly, our place in the formation, the area and pattern in which our group would form, and the altitude for the flight.[9] We also learned the exact time we would complete assembly, what place we would be in the bomber line, what time we would leave the English coast, what plane we would fly off of and what plane would be our wing man, how much fuel we would carry, what type of bombs we would use, what would our secondary target be in case of bad weather, and what crews would move up in a formation if a plane had to leave. On many missions, the Eighth Air Force would send in a few planes for replacement reasons because there would always be planes that could not complete their mission due to engine difficulties or other problems.

[9] If a pilot could not find his group after takeoff, he had to return to base. It was too dangerous to join another group as the Germans had captured many allied planes and would sometimes try to use these to infiltrate a group. When they were able to do this, the infiltrator could relay information to German defenders on the ground and fighters in the air concerning formation size, altitude, and heading.

Finally, we learned the call words for the group, squadron, and fighter escort. Every event, time, and place had a special word that was different for every mission. If we took off and for some reason the mission was aborted, there was a word sent out for that. We would be given an altitude that was called a reference, and any radio communication related to altitude would be in terms of plus or minus so many thousand feet. Everything had a code name, letter, or some other identification. In effect you had to learn a new language for every mission, and you had to have it right. Looking back I do not see how it was humanly possible to receive, digest, and use all the data that every mission required. It demanded total and complete concentration.

After all the crewmembers left, I met the pilot I would be accompanying as copilot. I am not sure he appreciated having a new copilot, because it is a lot easier to work with someone you are familiar with, but if he had any reservations he did not show it. After the briefing was over, we went to our locker room and dressed.

Dressing is a physical challenge in itself. If we were going over any part of Germany, we would not carry anything except our dog tags. If our mission was to an occupied country such as France and did not involve flying over any German territory, we would carry a packet that included false identification, pictures made in civilian clothes, and a .45-cal. pistol in a holster strapped around your shoulder. If you had to bail out and landed in Germany, it was important to try to hide and surrender to the military rather than civilians, because your chance of being killed by the military in Germany was much less than if you surrendered to civilians. This was especially true if you landed in the target area that you had just bombed. If you bailed out over France, the civilians would do most anything to protect, hide, and in many cases smuggle you out to England.

In dressing for the mission, first you put on thermal underwear and then an electric flying suit, which was a four-part uniform consisting of a jacket, pants, socks, and gloves.[10] Snap fasteners

[10] The electric flight suit had wires running through it. When a crewmember was at his station in the plane, he could plug the suit into the plane's electrical system and the wires would produce heat.

would join them together. Your regular flying suit went over that; followed by your heavy flying boots and heavy gloves; then would come your flak jacket; and finally your Mae West jacket.[11] I never could find a good place to strap on the .45-cal. pistol. We wore a leather helmet, and a steel helmet like the ground forces wore. The pilots had to wear a backpack parachute over all of that. Much of the time we would be subjected to temperatures of fifty to sixty degrees below zero for many hours. As a result, any skin exposed to the air would be frostbitten in a short time. Many of the gunners and other crewmembers would carry pieces of steel plate to sit on during times we were exposed to antiaircraft fire. They did not want a piece of flak to come from below and strike them in the rear. In addition to that, many would carry Bibles or other items such as good luck charms.

After getting dressed we boarded trucks that carried us to our plane. The rest of the crew was already doing their preflight checks. It was dark that morning, and the air was damp. The rain had stopped, and fortunately the fog had lifted. I was riding on this first mission as copilot in the lead plane for the squadron. I assume every crewmember had a certain amount of anxiety and fear over what might happen. I had plenty because it was my first mission. Although I had imagined what it might be like, you never know exactly what to expect. I had never met any of the crewmembers before, and I was not sure they were thrilled to see a rookie copilot. After each crewmember had completed his preflight check, we gathered in front of the left wing and made sure everything was ready for the mission. It was about 4:30 a.m. and still dark. The breakfast I had eaten two hours ago was in the same place it was when I got through eating—just too much excitement to digest. We spent the last few minutes before boarding the plane shooting the bull—a few jokes, a little laughter, and a few brags from the gunners about how many planes they would shoot down if the German Air Force was to challenge us today. This crew had completed several missions,

[11] Davis's navigator, Frank Morris, estimated that all of the clothing weighed in excess of sixty pounds. See Morris, "Memoirs of the War," 31.

so I considered them veterans. I soon found out that one mission made you a veteran.

After we settled into our positions on the plane, we started the long checklist in preparation for starting the engines. The crew chief would stand behind the pilot and copilot during the rundown on the check list and would help get the engines started. Everything was done by the clock from now on. We would start our engines precisely at the designated time, which was 4:45 a.m. Engines were started in a special order. The engines were numbered one through four, starting with the outboard engine on the left. Engine three was always started first because it had the only hydraulic pumps on it. Also by starting the inboard engine on each side first, it would allow the crew chief to stand close to the engine being started with the fire extinguisher and would not expose him to the possibility of walking through or toward a moving propeller.

After number three was started and running smoothly, the copilot would then go through the same procedure in starting number four. After it was started and running smoothly, number two engine would be started and then number one. After all the engines had warmed up, the instruments would have to be checked to see that the hydraulic, vacuum, and other pressures were within the required limits. There were many other things that had to be tested and checked before taxiing out for takeoff.[12]

At a precise time we would move out, and as we would pass other parked planes they would follow us to the end of the runway in exact order. The line of planes would move up as each plane took off at thirty-second intervals. As we got close to the end of the runway, we would run up each engine separately to check that everything was operating properly. Then we would lower the flaps, close the cowl flaps, set the prop pitch, and be ready to move out onto the runway as soon as the plane in front of us had started his takeoff. The flight engineer would usually sit at the top forward hatch during the time we were taxiing to watch the engines and

[12] For a detailed description of the procedures for a B-24 takeoff, see Carigan, *Ad Lib*, 25-38.

give any necessary directions the pilots needed. After the plane in front of us released its brakes and started rolling down the runway, we prepared for our turn.

We started moving the throttles forward and the engines responded with a loud roar. After the throttles were pushed full forward and the engines were at full power, we released the brakes and the plane started rolling down the dark runway. We were taking off with a full load of bombs and gas, which meant we would use almost all the runway. I started calling off the airspeed as we picked up momentum. The red runway lights marking the end of the runway were getting closer and closer when finally we lifted off. Soon the bumping and vibration began to disappear until a quiet smooth feel indicated we were airborne.

The lead squadron formed, then the high squadron, and finally the low squadron. Each ship had a specific place in the formation. We passed through four layers of clouds before we reached the assembly altitude. I could now understand why it was important for a new pilot to fly as copilot the first mission, because there was so much you had to know and so many things to remember. At this point I wondered if I could remember all the things and still fly the plane. How the planning of the mission and the execution were ever accomplished is remarkable. That they were able to select the targets and work out the details as fast as they did was unbelievable.

As impossible as it seemed to me, the group formed in perfect order and moved into the bomber stream. As we took our place in the stream, we passed the English coast and flew over the English Channel. As we reached 10,000 feet, the pilot called the crew and advised them to put on their oxygen masks. We would be on oxygen for the next five hours. It was now time for the bombardier to go to the bomb bay and pull the pins on the bombs. By pulling the pins the bombs would be "armed." If for some reason you had to break formation and return to your base, the bombardier could replace the pins, and it would be reasonably safe to land with them. As we flew over the English Channel, the pilot asked the gunners to test fire their guns while we climbed to an altitude of 23,000 feet. A B-24 fully loaded with gas and bombs at this altitude is a challenge to fly in tight formation. Some planes flew better than others, but all were sluggish. Because of that, it was important to anticipate problems such as prop wash from the group in front. It was especially critical in areas where there was antiaircraft fire and another ship might get hit and explode, requiring quick maneuvering to miss the debris. Many planes were lost due to operational accidents such as slapping wings or one plane losing control and sliding into another one.

From the time we got close to the coast of Holland, we could expect to see flak or enemy fighters. I was looking for flak, and I did not have to wait long. As we crossed the coast, we started seeing bursts just out of range. It was then I saw something leave the ground about a mile from the coast. At first it took off at an angle and was trailing a large tail of smoke. It then seemed to turn straight up until it reached our altitude a little to our right and exploded with a large ball of fire. I never knew what it was. It may have been a phosphorous bomb of some kind. It scared me, but at this point anything visible would do that.

There was some communication inside the plane, but radio communication between planes or groups was strictly prohibited except in case of an emergency, such as a fighter attack. One plane in each group communicated with the fighter escort. If all one thousand bombers and seven hundred fighters were trying to talk at the same time, it would have been a disaster.

As the groups wound their way down the bomber line across Holland and into Germany, we flew through areas of moderate flak. Because this was my first mission, even the small barrages looked like monsters to me. Everything seemed to be going fine. The engines were all running well and did not show any signs of problems. We saw no heavy cloud formations, although there were some cirrus clouds at our elevation. It was hazy, which limited visibility. We had progressed to the point that we were not far from the initial point (IP) where we would start our bomb run. The bomb

run usually lasted from ten to fifteen minutes. I was scanning the
skies hoping to locate our escort of fighters. To the right and above
us, at a distance too far to identify their nationality, was a group of
perhaps two hundred planes. They were obviously fighters, because
they were moving too fast to be bombers. I took comfort in knowing
that our fighters were close.

As I looked in the direction of the target I started seeing flashes
in the haze in front of us. First there was a flash, then a large orange
ball would form, and then it would turn into a ball of smoke. I saw
several flashes, and I was not sure what they were, but I doubted
they were anything good. Then, I looked back in the direction of
what I had decided was our fighter escort. They suddenly got closer
and as the first one zoomed through our formation, I could see they
were not what I had thought. It was the German Air Force, or Luftwaffe. I suddenly realized that we were in an air battle. The planes
were German FW-190s and they appeared to be firing 20-mm can-
nons as well as smaller caliber machine guns.[13] I saw one make a
pass just to our right. The top turret gunner in the plane that was
flying off our right wing fired at the German FW-190, and suddenly
there was no top turret—in a flash the turret disappeared. I could
still see the gunner, but he had been decapitated and blood was
streaming back along the plane.[14]

Several planes came straight at us. The closest one was a FW-
190, its guns flashing. It appeared to be on a direct collision course
for us. There is too much going on at a time like this to be scared.
I was just trying to survive. I was concentrating on the incoming

[13] The German FW-190 was one of the best fighter planes of World War II.

[14] The gunner's name was Sgt. Paul Redden. See Freudenthal, *A History of
the 489th Bomb Group*, 86. Redden's death made an impact on others as well.
Davis's regular crew watched the planes land after the mission and saw Redden's plane arrive. Frank Morris later recalled, "We witnessed up close the most
bloody sight of the whole war. A plane landed with all of its rear fuselage covered with blood. A shell from a fighter or a piece of flak had torn off the top gun
turret and decapitated the gunner. His body had remained strapped in the seat,
while the wind pressure had sucked all of the blood out of his body. We looked at
the terrible sight and prayed that none of us would end up that way." See Morris,
"Memories of the War," 25.

fighter plane and his flashing guns. Suddenly I saw a flash, and a huge red ball of fire filled the sky where the German plane had been. All that remained were two tips of the wings and part of the tail section. An instant after the explosion we flew through the debris and somehow avoided hitting it. Shortly after the plane exploded, two P-38s zoomed just in front of us.[15] Apparently they had been above us and had come down and shot the FW-190 out of the sky. They were the most beautiful sight I had ever seen.

The Eighth Air Force's fighter escorts were great. With our fighters in the area, we felt much better. When the German fighters did attack the bomb group, P-51s, and sometimes P-38s and P-47s, would suddenly appear to defend us. The fighters usually flew at some distance from the bombers. I have little doubt that if it were not for the fighters, especially on this first mission, I probably would not be here today.

When the first enemy planes came through our formation, our plane was hit in several places. There were holes six inches behind my seat. Our engineer was standing just behind the pilot and copilot seats. One of the bullets went through his flight suit legs. It made two big holes but did not hit him. The attack came so quickly and was such a surprise that he was not in the top turret. After the first planes came through, he crawled up into the turret and started firing the twin .50-cal. machine guns. Adding the noise of the guns firing to the usual sounds of the B-24 made it really loud. It got even worse because the sack that usually caught the ejected shell casings either was not attached or had come loose. As he rotated the turret around, firing at the incoming planes, the shell casings were being slung all over the flight deck. It was fortunate that we had on our steel helmets to protect us from the empty casings. The enemy fighters changed course, apparently to get away from our fighter escort. Most went to our right and hit the group just behind us and

---

[15] The P-38 "Lightning" was a twin-engine fighter built by Lockheed that, when fitted with external fuel tanks, provided a valuable escort for bombers. See U.S. Air Forces Museum, Lockheed P-38, http://www.wpafb.af.mil/museum/research/p38.htm, accessed on July 5, 2005.

shot down all twelve of the B-24s that made up the low squadron. Fortunately, our squadron only lost one plane to the fighters.

We had now reached the IP where we would start our bomb run. It required that we hold our altitude, course, and airspeed for the next ten to twelve minutes. As we turned to the proper course and straightened out, we noticed a dark, black cloud in front of us that was being made by exploding antiaircraft fire. To know you had to go through that cloud and be subjected to all the exploding flak takes all the courage a person can muster. You had to run the gauntlet, because that was the only way you could reach the target. As we got closer, we could see the shells exploding. The group preceding us had lost two ships and others had dropped from the formation because of damage. We were now entering the cloud of flak. It was bursting all around us. We could smell the cordite of the bursting shells and often feel the concussion from the explosions. Sometimes you could hear fragments of the exploding shells strike the plane. It sounded like someone might be throwing a load of gravel. I could not help but flinch as the shells burst. Our bomb bay doors had been open for some time, and it was a real relief to hear the bombardier start calling out the seconds until the bombs dropped. All the planes dropped their bombs when the lead plane dropped its bomb load. As soon as our bombs fell, the plane seemed to leap in the air. We closed our bomb bay doors and retrimmed the plane because the attitude and flying characteristics had changed. It was now a great deal easier to maneuver and a relief to now turn and head for home. Even though we knew there possibly would be fighter attacks and areas of flak, the fact we had bombed our target felt wonderful.[16] We did not need a navigator that day to find our way home. There were enough burning aircraft to guide us.[17]

[16] Altogether thirty-four planes from Davis' 489th Bomb Group dropped bombs on the target. See 489th Bombardment Group, July 7, 1944, National Archives of the United States, College Park, MD [hereafter NA], Record Group [hereafter RG] 18: Records of the Army Air Forces, World War II Combat Operations Reports, Eighth Air Force, 489th BG, Box 1634, Folder--489th and 491st Visual, July 7, 1944; and Gunnery Report, July 8, 1944, ibid.

[17] More than 1,100 bombers participated in this attack, including 370 B-24s and more than 750 B-17s. The B-24s attacked an oil plant and a series of

After clearing the coast and safely getting out of range of the coastal flak, then and only then could you relax. When we got down to about 12,000 feet, we yanked off our oxygen masks. We had been on oxygen for over five hours by that time, and the mask had left its impression on my face. It felt great to be free of it.

Because our base was the closest to the Channel, we often had planes from other groups landing when, for some reason, they had to get on the ground quickly. Any plane that had a mechanical problem or casualties aboard had priority in landing. We stayed in formation and circled the field until all planes firing red flares were on the ground, and then each plane would peel off, enter the traffic pattern, and land. This was not an average day. Many planes were attempting to make priority landings. They were landing on opposite ends of the same runways as well as the cross runways. Every runway was being used. I saw some planes that had landed and veered off the runway. Some were on fire. Ambulances and fire trucks were everywhere.

It was close to noon when we finally saw a break and decided to land. The landing gear, flaps, and everything came down. We were going to have to hurry, because a plane was approaching the runway that crossed the one we were landing on. We did not want to meet him at the intersection. Another plane was close behind us, so we came in a little hot for the landing. Everything was fine until we touched down on the runway. We were not aware that our right tire had been shot out. Immediately the plane started veering to the right and we could not keep it on the runway. We ran off the runway out of control and headed for two planes that had also ended up off the runway. A lot of ambulances and fire trucks, as well as people, were around those planes, and when they saw us coming, obviously out of control, they scattered in all directions. Fortunately, we cleared the two planes and ended up doing a couple of turns before stopping.

---

factories. For a summary of the mission, including losses, see Intops Summary, No. 68, July 7, 1944, NA RG 18; and Freudenthal, *A History of the 489th Bomb Group,* 86.

We waited as a crew until our name was called to go to debriefing. It was a tradition that after a particularly tough mission, the pilot would be given a bottle of whiskey as we entered the debriefing room. We would all sit down around the table with the debriefing officer to tell him about everything that happened that day. First, it was the custom for the pilot to pour each crewmember a shot of whiskey. We would all wait until each had his glass and then we would toast our good fortune of surviving that day. Then it was bottoms up. I had only drunk a few mixed drinks before, and I had never drunk whiskey straight. But because I was glad to be back and it was a custom, I turned the glass up like everyone else and down it went. I was not quite prepared for the results. It was like drinking fire. It took my breath away and I got choked. After I recovered, the crew had a huge laugh at my expense. I never tried that again. I guess you could say that if the day's mission did not kill you, the bottoms up liquor would.

We spent about thirty minutes with the debriefing officer, went to change clothes, and then headed for the combat crew mess hall to have lunch. My crew met me at the mess hall and wanted to know what happened and what it was like. I could not really describe it any better to them that day than I can describe it now. So many incredible things happened in such a brief time that it is impossible to accurately describe the event—especially the emotional roller coaster ride you take.

CHAPTER 6

Our Early Missions

IT WAS ABOUT 4:45 P.M. when Frank and Mackey returned to the hut and told me that we were on the alert list for tomorrow's mission. I thought they were joking, but they were not. I put on my clothes and went over to the bulletin board to see for myself, and sure enough my name was there. I continued to have the feeling that we were just a number.

My spirits were as low as they could get. It had now been six weeks since I kissed Jean and said goodbye. I had been on the move ever since and, as a result, had not received any mail. Not having any letters from Jean or any of my family was very discouraging. Later that day I attended mail call, hoping that maybe I would get at least one letter, but no such luck. I returned to our hut and my crew gathered and we talked about the next day's mission. We all tried to joke and see the lighter side, but there was not much to laugh about—at least for me. I still had fresh memories of the mission I flew earlier that day and how lucky I was to survive. I could not concentrate too much on tomorrow's mission for thinking of the one I just finished. Because the mission would be the first for my crew, they were excited.

I was busy thinking of what happened this morning and what might happen tomorrow. I would be responsible for all the details from the briefing, going through preflight, starting the engines, taxiing out, taking off, and finding our place in the formation. All of this had to be done in precise sequence and timing. I was unsure whether I could keep all of the information in my head. I was also concerned that I would have to fly the entire mission, because we had not had the time or opportunity to teach Ed formation flying. I had thought about discussing this problem with my squadron commander but hesitated because he probably would have taken Ed from my crew and given me someone else. Ed was such a fine person and a good pilot that I did not want to lose him; so, I decided to keep my mouth shut. It was tough enough to learn in the training program, but to learn it while flying combat was even more difficult. In fact, he had not even had the opportunity to learn to take off or land the plane. I was aware of that, but I always felt if something happened to me he could get it safely on the ground.

Not having slept last night, the events of the previous mission should have been enough to make me sleep. However, after I learned that we were scheduled to fly tomorrow, I forgot all about being exhausted and had difficulty sleeping. About two o'clock the next morning I heard the sound of trucks being started, and I knew it would not be long until I would get my wake-up call. Soon I heard footsteps outside, the door opened, and the private with his flashlight came to my cot and gently touched my arm and told me it was time to get up. I got dressed, and before I left I made sure Ed, Frank, and Mackey were ready to go. I was afraid Mackey would go back to sleep because he went to bed about an hour before wake-up time. We all walked out the door and as usual found the weather chilly and misty. With the help of the flashlight, we found our way to the road and made the long walk to the mess hall. Following breakfast, most of us caught a truck to the briefing room. After an opening prayer, the briefing officer drew the curtains back, and the large map of England and Europe indicated our target was near Paris.

No matter where the target was there were always groans and moans. Today they were real and loud. Some of the crews remembered a recent mission to Paris, and from what I had been told it was hell. Floyd Harville, the pilot of the other crew that shared our

P-47 "Thunderbolt" in flight (courtesy of the Air Force Historical Research Agency, Maxwell Air Force Base, Montgomery, Alabama)

P-38 "Lightning" on the ground (courtesy of the Air Force Historical Research Agency, Maxwell Air Force Base, Montgomery, Alabama)

P-51 "Mustang" (courtesy of the Air Force Historical Research Agency, Maxwell Air Force Base, Montgomery, Alabama)

hut, had been hit badly over Paris. Although they survived and re-turned safely, they had a very difficult time—so difficult that he had been placed on reserve for a few days to shake off the mission's effects. I recalled his account of what had happened to them and as a result I suddenly felt this would be a very long day. I found little consolation in the fact that it would be probably two hours shorter than yesterday's mission. After all the details and instructions were given to the crewmembers, they went to their respective position meetings and the pilots remained for our instructions.

I left the briefing and dressed. Because we were attacking a target in France, we carried our escape packet, wore our .45-cal. pistol, and slung a pair of French shoes around our necks. I never understood why we carried the shoes because if we had to bail out, the moment the parachute opened the shoes would have kept on going. Maybe they thought you might crash and could use them but I do not think if anyone survived a crash they would be aware enough to pick up their shoes. We gathered our gear and caught a truck to the plane we were assigned to fly today. By then, the rest of the crew had arrived and were going through their preflight checks. If Siegfried, my flight engineer, was not too busy, I always tried to have my preflight check with Ed, Siegfried, and the ground crew chief. We wanted to find out everything we could about the plane and the condition it was in. The engines were the most important item. I will say, with one or two exceptions, the ground crews and especially the crew chief were exceptionally dedicated and committed. They would do anything for you and worked under difficult conditions to keep the planes in as good a condition as possible.

After completing our preflight check we gathered near the left wing. I checked with each crewmember to see if he was ready and had all his equipment. I especially wanted all of the parachutes to be inspected for damage. I never had to tell or try to impress my crewmembers that I was the airplane commander and my decisions were final. Every crew that I knew looked to the pilot with respect and as the final authority. My crew called me "Skip," and I felt they had confidence in me. They were a great group of young men, and I was privileged to serve with them.

After boarding and completing our checklist, we started our engines so that they would be warmed up properly. This morning, like most of our missions, was dark as pitch with a light mist and fog. I always thought it was too bad to fly, but seldom did they scratch a mission, and somehow we usually got off the ground. Soon the ship we were to follow in takeoff order came by and we pulled out to follow. One by one the planes took off, and as fate would have it we were the last to take off, which meant we had to hurry to find our place in the formation. As was normal for any new crew, we inherited the worst plane and the worst position in the formation—the tail end Charlie or coffin corner slot. In this position, every plane that makes a move in front of you is magnified by the time it gets to you, and as a result you are always wallowing around at the rear of the formation, constantly changing direction and power settings. This was also the most vulnerable position during fighter attacks. New crews also inherited the plane that no one else wanted to fly because of excessive fuel consumption, poor flying characteristics, the possible jinx that the plane might have, and many other reasons. It is no wonder that a new crew's first six missions were the most critical. The chance that a crew might complete a tour of combat duty improved a great deal after that point. This was not only because the operational accidents that plagued new crews decreased, but also it seemed like the new crews caught the worst flak, the worst damage from fighters, and in general, had bad luck.

Every B-24 flew differently because each had its own special characteristics. Col. Ezekiel Napier, the commanding officer of the 489th Bomb Group, felt you should be able to fly any of the planes. He was a graduate of West Point and was very demanding. We flew whatever plane we were assigned. The plane I was flying on this mission to Paris was one usually assigned to new crews. Many of the older crews considered the plane to be jinxed. It would always get back, but many times it would return with wounded or dead. Further, it had a number of mechanical problems and was a gas guzzler. The older crews who knew the plane had requested others; so, it was generally used as a new crew plane.

Although the fog and mist were so heavy you could not see the red lights at the far end of the runway, the takeoff was uneventful. We found the group and our place in the formation without any problem. As we climbed over the English Channel, I had the gunners test their guns by firing a few rounds and had Mackey remove the arming pins from the bombs. At 12,000 feet I called the crew to put on their oxygen masks. The group was now well out over the English Channel and climbing to 22,000 feet. The temperature was dropping fast, making us thankful for the electric flying suits.

We received the usual welcome of several bursts of flak as we crossed the French coast. The weather was bad. There were clouds at all levels and each plane was leaving a vapor trail (contrail), which made flying formation more difficult. Not only that, but with contrails, the enemy had a way to locate you without any trouble.

From time to time we would receive moderate antiaircraft fire, but the weather was probably too bad for the enemy fighters because we did not encounter any. We changed course several times and approached the IP, which was just southeast of Paris. Our primary targets were some rail and highway bridges just east of Paris. As we passed Paris, the clouds broke briefly, enough for us to get a good view of the city, including the Eiffel Tower. We were now receiving heavy flak, but fortunately, there were so many clouds you could not see most of it. We were, however, smelling and feeling the concussion of bursting shells. The bomb run seemed longer than it actually was. It lasted about fifteen minutes, but even one minute when flak is bursting all around you seems like an eternity. We reached the target, dropped our bombs, started a slow turn, and headed back to England. We cleared the heavy flak area and as far as we knew had not received any serious damage. We reached our base without any problem. We had just completed our first mission together and we were a proud and happy group of people.[1]

It was now and only now that I could relax. As I filled out the forms I began to feel the fatigue set in. The crew started inspecting the plane for flak holes and helping the ground crew by briefing them on what might not have worked up to standard. I always visited with the crew chief and explained any problems we might have had. When we had finished all of the post flight duties we gathered under the plane's wing and waited for a truck to pick us up. After the truck came, we piled all of our gear aboard and rode it to the operations building. This was a most refreshing time because as we unloaded, a Red Cross wagon was waiting with usually two or three very fine ladies handing out refreshments. It was something that everyone appreciated and looked forward to. We waited our turn to go into a

[1] The mission took place on Saturday, July 8, and the targets were railway and highway bridges near Paris at Nanteuil Sur Marne. Altogether, more than one thousand bombers—568 B-17s and 461 B-24s—took off for the mission. While Jim's group was able to drop its bombs, most planes that day could not. See Freudenthal, *A History of the 489th Bomb Group*, 87; and Headquarters Eighth Air Force, INTOPS Summary No. 69, July 8, 1944, NA, RG 18, World War II Combat Operations Reports, Eighth Air Force, 489th BG, Box 1640, Folder – 489th P.F.F. & 491st, 1.

room and sit down with an officer to be debriefed. We went over the entire mission with him, telling him everything that happened, what we saw, what did not work and what did, how much damage we had to the plane, and in general everything about the mission. After debriefing we were free to do what we wanted to.

The last two days had taken a lot out of me and I did not know if I could fly again tomorrow. Fortunately we did not fly for the next two days because the weather over Europe had become so bad that to fly a mission was almost impossible.[2] I received some letters from home on July 9, and I read them over and over again. A word from home was the greatest thing that could happen. It also meant that hopefully I would get mail on a regular basis now.

By July 10 the weather had improved, and because the Eighth Air Force had not flown any bombing missions the last two days, we all expected one the next day. Late that afternoon the alert list was posted, and as expected, my crew was included. Automatically your attitude changes after you have been placed on the alert list. Perhaps it is a wake-up call to mentally prepare for what is coming. During my tour I was alerted at least fifty times, and it always had the same effect. Some of the missions were cancelled after the list was posted. Sometimes we would go through everything, take off, and assemble only for the mission to be scrubbed. Other times a plane you were assigned to fly was not mechanically ready.[3] There were other reasons you might not fly, but when your name appeared on an alert list, it always got your attention.

I returned to the hut after the evening meal and wrote some letters home. That might not have been a good time to write a letter, but when you are alerted for a mission, you try to think of the good things in life. I lay down on the cot and wished I could go to sleep, but found it impossible. My thoughts would vacillate from

[2] It was not unusual for bad weather to either prevent or alter missions. See Ambrose, *The Wild Blue*, 137.

[3] The standing policy in Davis's bomb group was that you would fly whatever plane you were assigned; therefore, you seldom, if ever, flew the same plane on consecutive missions.

loved ones, home, and what everyone might be doing. I was always aware that tomorrow might end up in disaster, and of all my
thoughts, I guess that ever-present fear of failure was the most
dominating. I entered combat flying with the reality we might not
survive a tour, but I always thought it would not be today. I had a
one-day-at-a-time mentality. If you tried to think of a longer period
of time, it would scare you to death. Just making it through today
was the important thing.

In the dark of night I lay there wide awake, thoughts rushing
through my mind. Suddenly, I recognized the sounds that were
present almost every night—the patter of raindrops as they struck
the tin roof. You then began to wonder if you would have to take off
in bad weather in the morning. The night remained dark and still,
except for the noise from an occasional truck, airplane, or crewman
returning to his hut. However, the sounds that always got my attention were the trucks starting at the motor pool. By the sheer number
of trucks running you knew it would only be a few minutes until you
would hear those footsteps outside. The door would open and you
would be told it was time to go.

I had my wake-up call, got dressed, and made my way to the
briefing. The pulling of the curtain and the identification of our destination for the day was not what I had hoped for. The line indicating our route seemed to stretch from one end of the screen to the
other and took us all the way to Munich. This mission would be
close to nine hours long and was at the outer range of a B-24. The
briefing officer also told us that the weather would be a problem
today, as it usually was.

The weather conditions made takeoff and assembly very difficult. Several of our planes were unable to find our formation and
as a result I moved up to fly a wing position in the regular formation in lieu of the tail end Charlie slot. Going over the Channel, the
gunners fired their guns to make sure they were ready, and Mackey
pulled the pins on the bombs. As we flew over the enemy coast, we
got our usual barrage of flak. It seemed we would never get there,
and from time to time we encountered antiaircraft fire. Our primary

target was an airfield near Munich, but because of clouds we had to go to a secondary target, which was in the center of Munich. From the time we reached the IP and started our bomb run, we were subjected to intense and accurate antiaircraft fire.

The Germans had our course and altitude figured out, and we paid a high price. The sky was dark with smoke from exploding flak. Even though we had on oxygen masks, we could still smell the smoke from the exploding shells. We also felt the concussion of the flak bursts and heard the fragments striking the plane. The thirty minutes of running the gauntlet of flak was almost too much to take, but we were lucky. Unlike about half of our planes, we had no serious damage.[4]

The trip home was uneventful. We had used nearly all our gas and only had a few gallons left when we landed. After we parked the plane and cut the engines, I took a long time to fill out the flight book. We took the ride to operations and to those wonderful Red Cross ladies with their coffee, tea, chocolate, and donuts. It had been twelve hours since breakfast and we were starving. We went through debriefing, changed our clothes, and headed for the mess hall. After eating, I headed to the hut, anxious to lie down for a while. This had been a very long day. Flying in a left-wing position in the formation for eight hours, at a temperature of fifty-five degrees below zero and being under oxygen, will take a lot out of you. Moreover, flying the left-wing position in a tight formation takes a lot more effort than flying the right wing, because the pilot's vision is a lot more restricted having to look across the cockpit.

Even those hard biscuits and GI blankets felt good. I dozed off the moment I lay down. I was so tired I did not even worry if I was

[4] Because of the overcast conditions and the unexpected presence of another group of B-17s over Munich, the mission failed to damage its target. Flak damaged thirteen planes. A total of 1,176 bombers, including 435 B-24s, took part in the mission. See Freudenthal, *A History of the 489th Bomb Group*, 87; Headquarters Eighth Air Force, INTOPS Summary No. 69, July 8, 1944, NA, RG 18, World War II Combat Operations Reports, Eighth Air Force, 489th BG, Box 1640, Folder – 489th P.F.F. & 491st, 1; Critique of Mission of July 11, 1944, July 13, 1944, ibid., 1-2; and 489th Bombardment Group Operational Statistics Report, July 11, 1944, ibid., 1-3.

on the next alert list. Later one of my crew came in and gave me some mail from home, which I was elated to get. Then he put a damper on my feelings by telling me we were on the alert list again for tomorrow. I read the letters over and over. As fatigued as I was, I still could not sleep that night.

The next morning we went through the same thing as the day before. The time came for the curtain to be pulled. I could not believe what I was seeing—another trip to Munich. I was hoping that something would happen to keep us from going, because I really did not think I could make another trip to Munich. Four hard missions in six days was too much to ask, but I was determined I would survive it. I had laughed at the suggestion that replacement crews were only a number and were expendable, but at this point I was about to agree with the idea.

This mission to Munich was much like the previous day except the weather was more of a problem, and as a result it was over nine hours long. When we returned that afternoon it took all the strength I could gather to get the plane on the ground and parked.[5] After I filled out the flight forms, I tried to get out of the seat but I was so exhausted I could not pull myself out. Ed and Siegfried came back to the flight deck to check on me. I told them to go on to the debriefing and I would be there in a few minutes after I rested a bit. They left the flight deck but I guess they knew something was wrong. They came back and said they did not want to go without me. I decided to go, but again I could not muster enough strength to get out of the seat. After they suggested calling an ambulance or catching a ride on one of the trucks to go to the hospital, I told them to just let me rest. They laid me down under the wing and put a parachute under my head. I convinced them to go through the debriefing and then

[5] This mission on July 12 to Munich was a little more successful, but it was still hampered by weather. A force of 512 B-24s and 759 B-17s participated in the mission. See Freudenthal, *A History of the 489th Bomb Group*, 94; and Headquarters Eighth Air Force, INTOPS Summary No. 73, July 12, 1944, NA, RG 18, World War II Combat Operations Reports, Eighth Air Force, 489th BG, Box 1640, Folder – 489th P.F.F. & 491st, 1-2; and Statistical Summary of Operation, July 12, 1944, ibid., 1.

come back, and I would be ready to go eat. When they returned an hour later, I was able to stand, although my walk was somewhat unsteady.

As I lay under the plane, I made up my mind that under no circumstances would I fly tomorrow—it would be unfair to the crew. I was hoping I would not be on the alert list, but if I was, I would go on sick call. I did not want to refuse to fly and would not unless it was absolutely necessary. Fortunately, we were not on the alert list posted that afternoon. After I ate supper, I went to bed and slept twelve hours. Almost eighteen combat hours had totally exhausted me. I recalled many times the day I reported to B-24 transition in Fort Worth and the flight surgeon told me I was too small to fly four-engine planes. I had reached the point that I might have agreed with him.

The next afternoon an orderly asked me to report to the operation's office. I did not have any idea what they wanted with me. A sergeant told me my crew had been put on a three-day pass starting tomorrow. I was elated and hurried to tell all the crewmembers. We got together and made plans to go to London. I was ready for some time off—this was my first off-duty time in about eight months. We were given a lot of advice from some of our friends who had been to London before. Some of it was good and some not so good. This had been a great day, and some letters from home made it even better.

After a good night's sleep, we could hardly wait to leave for London. We signed out and caught the truck to the train station. The squadron commander gave me two bottles of whiskey. I gave one to the enlisted men and one to the officers with instructions that it could not be opened until we were on the train to London. Neither Ed nor I drank, so that left one bottle for Mackey and Frank. There were six enlisted men but only three of them ever drank so it was divided about evenly. Once we were seated Mackey brought out the bottle, and he and Frank began their celebrating.

It was easier to find a hotel room than a short time ago because most of the ground forces were in transit to France. Most of the military personnel in London were from the Army Air Forces. It was great to go there if for no other reason than to get away from combat for a few days. From the time we arrived at the outskirts of London we could see the terrible destruction that the city had suffered in the last few years. Even the railroad station had sustained damage. The station was nothing more than a shell of a building with the entire roof gone. After we got our bags, we walked to the Great Northeastern Hotel and checked in. After we took our first warm shower in weeks, some of us decided to get a cab and go to the Piccadilly area, which was the center of most activity in London.

My enlisted men decided they wanted to go someplace else, so Frank, Mackey, Ed, and I took a cab to Piccadilly. We paid the driver the fare in English money, and I took care of the tip. None of us knew the value of the English currency, so I reached in my pocket and pulled out the largest coin I had and gave it to the driver. He was insulted and started showing his displeasure, but we did not understand why. During the discussion a couple of airmen came by that had been there for some time. They told me I had given him only a penny as a tip, and he was unhappy about it. I did not realize their largest coin was only a penny, so I got some more money out of my pocket to satisfy him.

We decided we would walk around London and visit various well-known landmarks, such as the Tower of London, Westminster Abbey, and St. Paul's Cathedral. We were amazed at the destruction as whole blocks of buildings were missing. We walked down Piccadilly to the Ritz Hotel—surprisingly it had survived the years of bombing with minimum damage. We spent most of the afternoon in shoe shops and tailor shops. Late that afternoon we decided to find a good restaurant and have a first-class dinner. We were told of a very nice hotel with a beautiful dining room. It had linen tablecloths and napkins, and the waiters were all dressed in formal uniforms. The menu was about the size of a card table and was printed in French. Because none of us could read French or understand the waiter's English very well, we decided to order different meals and share whatever we were served. When we received our meals, we all ended up with pigeon in some form or another. Because food was so scarce, perhaps pigeons were the only things available. Regardless, it was good.

It was getting dark and a lot more people were moving about. Frank and Mackey wanted to go to a club, so they took off and Ed and I walked around. Ed had something he wanted to see so we decided to meet back at the hotel at ten. It was dark now, and thousands of people bustled on the streets. London was under blackout, and with so many people crowding the streets it was difficult to move around. Even the cabs drove without lights. This had been a long day, so I started working my way back to meet Ed.

No sooner had I started to the hotel than the air raid sirens sounded. There seemed to be hundreds of sirens and the sky lit up with searchlights. People started running in all directions. I had never been in an air raid before and did not know what to expect or what to do, so I started moving down the street as fast as I could. The crowd began to thin out some, but I could not figure out where they went so fast. Finally, the only ones left on the streets were American airmen, who seemed to ignore the warnings. Soon you could hear this strange roar like nothing I had ever heard before. At first it was faint and at some distance, but soon I could hear antiaircraft guns start firing and a multitude of searchlights began sweeping the dark sky. The roar was now getting much louder. It was not long before the searchlights picked up an approaching rocket. It was now making an almost deafening roar and you could see it going at a very high speed about a hundred feet above the top of the buildings. By the glare of the searchlights you could see it clearly. It looked like a long bomb, with two vertical supports holding what looked like a long stove pipe, with a tail of fire coming out the rear. I did not know it at the time, but it was a V-1 bomb.[6] After it had passed over and gone about four blocks, the roar of the missile

---

[6] The V-1 Buzz Bomb was a surface-to-surface missile or flying bomb used by Germany against Great Britain. See Williamson Murray and Allan R. Millett, *A War to Be Won: Fighting the Second World War* (Cambridge, MA: Belknap Press of Harvard University Press, 2000), 599-600.

engine stopped suddenly. In a matter of seconds I heard a terrible blast, and then felt the concussion from the blast as debris was thrown over a wide area. Then the sirens from fire trucks, ambulances, and rescue vehicles came from every direction.

As the siren sounds began to subside, other noises could be heard in the distance. More buzz bombs were approaching, and they seemed to all be headed in my direction. I realized I should find an air raid shelter, but I had no idea where one might be. I began running down the street as fast as I could. As each buzz bomb got close I would try and find some recess in a building where I could hide. Soon there was a constant stream of buzz bombs. To say all hell had broken loose would be putting it mildly. The sound is impossible to describe. First came the loud roar of the buzz bombs, then the antiaircraft guns shooting at them, the air raid sirens whining, the exploding bombs, and finally the fire trucks, ambulances, and rescue units. I was as scared as possible. I wondered why I ever came to London. I worked my way down the street and was thrilled to find the entrance to an air raid shelter. With relief I started to go down the stairs, and then discovered there was no room. It was totally filled with people, so it was back to the street again.

I was not the only one on the streets—many American servicemen were in the same fix. I worked my way back to the Regent Palace Hotel. The lobby was so full that it was impossible to find Ed. There was a pub about a block away, so I went there to find out which bus to catch to get to my hotel. I could hardly get in the front door due to the crowd of airmen inside. I finally reached the lady at the cash register and asked if there was a bus or some means of transportation that I could take that would get me to the Great Northeastern Hotel. She explained what bus I should catch, when I should get off of it, and then gave me the directions for where to go after I got off the bus. I thought I had it down clear as I worked my way back to the street corner. Buses came and buses went, but I never saw the one she described.

It was now almost 2 a.m. I returned to the pub to get directions again. During all this time the buzz bombs were still striking in great numbers. After I explained to the lady at the register that I had not been able to find the right bus, she looked at her watch and said she would ride the bus with me after she got off work. The bus was packed, but we were able to squeeze our way on. I was amazed how many people were moving around while the buzz bombs were skimming the top of the buildings and going off in all areas. It seemed like we rode for an hour when she said that at the next stop we would get off. She told me I should walk down the street four blocks, turn right so far, go down a narrow street, and I would be at the hotel. I had it all down pat, and I wanted to pay her, but she would not take any money. She said it was her pleasure to be able to help me.

As she turned and disappeared down the street I suddenly realized no one else was around. On each side of the street were solid lines of buildings about six stories high. It gave you a feeling of being in a canyon. I soon discovered that the street was not straight and there were side streets coming into it. In fact, I got to the point that I did not know if I had gone too far or not far enough. I was totally lost. I was standing on the corner of a street wondering which way to go, when above the noise of the night I heard this faint clonk, clonk, clonk. It got louder and then a shadow of a person appeared. It turned out to be a man with a peg leg. I told him I was trying to find the Great Northeastern Hotel. I could not see the man's face for the darkness, but he started giving me directions about the same time a buzz bomb was coming just over the rooftops. He stopped giving the directions, turned, and started running down the street. I do not think I debated whether I should follow him or not but automatically I started running after him. He outran me, and I heard him turn a corner of a building, but when I got there he was gone.

More bombs kept coming, and I started looking for a place to hide. I saw what appeared to be two faint red lights about half a block down the street. Without thinking I ran as fast as I could, hoping they were the entrance to an air raid shelter. I got there quickly but discovered they were reflectors on the corner of a water trough. In England at that time they still used horse drawn delivery wagons and these troughs were placed in convenient places for the driver to water his horses. This was next to a small park, so I fell down to the ground and got as close to the trough as I could.

At times when there was a break in the buzz bombs I would wander down the street. When the bombs appeared to be coming close, I would find a place to get as much protection as I could. Usually that was in the street next to the curb. Water always ran in the gutters, so by this time I was wet and muddy. I turned a corner and to find a most welcome sight. I saw a small building about a half block down the street with a dim light and what appeared to be two men in it. It was a police station. I introduced myself and told them I was trying to find the Great Northeastern Hotel. One of the officers pointed across the street and said that was it over there. I thanked them and hurried across the street to the entrance but found it locked. I started knocking on the door but got no response. I then started pounding the door, and after a minute or so a small peep door opened and a man with a candle asked what I wanted. I told him I was a registered guest and I wanted in. After some conversation he finally opened the door. He then gave me a lecture about being out so late and that it was hotel policy that they did not let anyone in at this time of the morning.

At last I got to my room and when I opened the door I could not believe what I saw. Two of my enlisted men had come to the room to visit Ed and had piled all the pillows and covers over their heads trying to shut out the noise of the buzz bombs. Ed was asleep on the couch. I invited them back to their room and Ed and I went to bed. Frank and Mackey never did show up.

The next morning we were told that a building just two blocks down the street had been hit with a buzz bomb. We walked there and saw that the six-story building was totally destroyed. Debris blocked the streets where I had been only a few hours before. The very efficient English were already busy cleaning up the debris. We later took a cab back to Piccadilly but we came back before dark. London had experienced the largest number of buzz bombs ever that night. In fact I think it was the largest number ever in a twenty-four-hour period of time. I believe I heard every one and saw most of them.[7]

It was time for us to get back to the base, so Ed and I caught the first train back to Halesworth with two other members of my crew. I could not find the rest of the crew, and I decided they could get back on their own and check in before deadline. After our experiences in London, in a way I was glad to get back. We found everything as we had left it. Later that day the rest of the crew came in.

On July 19 we were put on the alert list for the next day's mission. As usual I did not sleep any that night, but it was not as bad as the first four missions. I had flown almost thirty hours of combat and had gained a lot of experience and confidence. We had so much to learn, so much to remember, and so much going on, that to a new crew just starting their tour, it seemed impossible to remember everything.

Our mission was to an assembly plant for ME-109 fighter planes at Erfurt, Germany, and required a long flight in difficult weather conditions. We encountered something we had never experienced—frost on the inside of our windows. It was so heavy that it was impossible to see out. Ed made a scraper from a piece of aluminum, and for over four hours he constantly kept scraping a hole about three inches in diameter for me to see the plane next to us. He was really tired when we finally got back to the Channel and out of the frosting condition. There was one benefit to the frosted windows—it restricted our vision such that we could not see all the action that was going on around us. Fortunately, we did not have any Luftwaffe planes to contend with, and as always we were glad to get back on the ground.[8]

---

[7] From mid-June to the end of August, approximately one hundred V-1 or Buzz Bombs struck London each day. See Angus Calder, *The People's War: Britain 1939-1945* (New York: Pantheon Books, 1969), 559-61.

[8] A total force of 1,280 bombers, including 460 B-24s, attacked aircraft assembly and engine plants. For a description of this mission, see Freudenthal, *A History of the 489th Bomb Group*, 106; and Headquarters Eighth Air Force, IN-TOPS Summary No. 81, July 20, 1944, NA, RG 18, World War II Combat Operations Reports, Eighth Air Force, 489th BG, Box 1640, Folder – 489th P.F.F. & 491st, 1, 4, and 7; and Statistical Summary of Operation, July 20, 1944, ibid., 1.

That afternoon the alert list was posted and we were again on it. The target for the July 21 mission was Kempten, Germany. This was a long mission into the southeastern part of Germany near Munich. We were fortunate not to encounter German planes, although they were in the area and attacked some of the groups. Each day we were being briefed that we might encounter the German ME-262 jet.[9] They were seen in the area of some of our formations but had not made any attacks. The antiaircraft fire over the target area was intense, and over half our planes received heavy battle damage. We received a few holes. A good friend and his crew were shot down over the target.[10] This mission was almost eight hours long, and because we had flown a mission yesterday we hoped to get the next day off.[11]

We did not fly on July 22 because of bad weather. I was not on the alert list for the next day but had to report to operations that afternoon and fly a training mission that lasted almost three hours. On these training missions, we would practice various skills, including low level flying and using our instruments. It seemed every day that we did not fly a mission we would have some kind of training.

The next afternoon the alert list had me listed. At the briefing that morning we were told that we would be flying a very unusual mission. Since D-Day the ground forces had been moving a tre-

---

[9] The ME-262 was the first jet to fly combat missions. The first attack by one occurred on July 25, 1944. See http://www.wpafb.af.mil/museum/air_power/ap11.htm, accessed on July 5, 2005.

[10] 2nd Lt. James Haas piloted the plane that was shot down. Nine of the ten on board were able to parachute to safety and were captured. The tenth, navigator 1st Lt. Robert McCracken, did not survive. See Freudenthal, *A History of the 489th Bomb Group*, 106-9 and 287-91.

[11] More than 580 B-17s and 530 B-24s took part in this mission against targets in southwestern Germany. Jim's plane was one of seventy-seven that struck aircraft production facilities in Kempten. For a description of this mission, see Freudenthal, *A History of the 489th Bomb Group*, 106-9; Headquarters Eighth Air Force, INTOPS Summary No. 82, July 21, 1944, NA, RG 18, World War II Combat Operations Reports, Eighth Air Force, 489th BG, Box 1640, Folder – 489th P.F.F. & 491st, 1-2; Statistical Summary of Operation, July 21, 1944, ibid., 1; and Critique of Mission on July 21, 1944, ibid., 1-5.

mendous amount of men and equipment to the beachhead they had gained. They felt like they had enough men and equipment to start an offensive and hopefully break through the German lines and out of Normandy. The first action of Operation Cobra was a concerted carpet-bombing by the entire Eighth Air Force.[12] We were advised not to drop if we could not clearly identify the target because we would be dropping just in front of our ground forces, and if we dropped short, we would hit our own guys. We were told that it would not be a long mission; we would not be on oxygen; and we would be over enemy territory only a short period of time. All of these things were more favorable than the long missions we had been flying. We all thought this might just be easy.

We got off the ground, and there were airplanes everywhere you looked—about 1,600 bombers and 700 fighters. We opened our bomb bay doors over the English Channel and started our bomb run. About the time we crossed the French coast we started getting some flak. The further we went the more intense it got. One of the planes just in front of me caught a direct burst of flak in the bomb bay. A tremendous fire erupted and swept past his tail. Because he was just in front of me, I started to pull out, thinking he would explode any second. Just as I started to maneuver away, he suddenly dropped down and out; therefore, I pulled back into formation. As soon as he cleared the formation, the plane exploded in a huge ball of fire. It had cleared the formation enough that the flying debris did not damage the other planes. Lt. Edwin Florcyk piloted the plane that blew up, and he did a great job of clearing the group so he would not be a danger to the other ships. He had to make an

---

[12] On July 24 and 25, more than 1,580 bombers participated in bombing missions at the start of Operation Cobra. Because of poor visibility, most of planes did not drop their bombs on July 24. However, most of the planes were able to complete their mission the next day. See Craven and Cate, eds., *The Army Air Forces in World War II*, Volume 3, 231-7; Murray and Millett, *A War to Be Won*, 429; and Stephen E. Ambrose, *Citizen Soldiers: The U.S. Army from the Normandy Beaches to the Bulge to the Surrender of Germany, June 7, 1944-May 7, 1945* (New York: Simon and Schuster, 1997), 80-4.

instant decision to get as much distance between his plane and the other planes as possible. Only one member of the crew survived the explosion.[13]

As we neared the target area it became apparent that we could not clearly identify it. Because it was only a few hundred feet in front of our own lines, we could not take a chance of bombing our own troops. The decision was made to hold our bombs. We alerted the groups behind us of the conditions and they were able to turn around before they reached the enemy lines. We were now the targets for all of the enemy gunners, and they did not have to worry about falling bombs. The antiaircraft fire was extremely heavy and accurate. The instant it burst in front of us we would penetrate the explosion. I think Mackey, in the nose turret, felt they were bursting in his lap. Even after we landed, Mackey was still white as a sheet.

That afternoon we were on the alert list again. The same sleepless night, early get up, breakfast, and the long walk to briefing followed. After the formalities the curtain was pulled, and the route led to Normandy again. There were several comments and I might have uttered one myself. I was not at all thrilled about a return trip.

During my preflight check the next morning it was necessary for me to go to the flight deck to check something. In order to get to the flight deck you have to crawl through the bomb bay. The B-24 is so low to the ground that for all practical purposes you have to get on your knees to get inside the bomb bay. Our bomb bay was full of clusters of antipersonnel bombs. They were tied five to a cluster and each weighed about twenty pounds. The fins on the bombs were light sheet metal and had sharp edges. As I stood up, I hit my head on one of the bomb's fins.

When I hit my head I dropped my flashlight and everything else I was carrying. I was standing there trying to get my bearings and then I felt some blood in my eye. With a great deal of caution I lowered myself down, feeling for my flashlight. I found

[13] Frank Trowbride was the only crewmember from Florcyk's plane who survived. See Freudenthal, *A History of the 489th Bomb Group*, 110.

it and pointed the light on my hand. It was covered with blood. The blood was now running down my head enough that I had to close my eye. I got out from under the plane and got a rag to try to stop the bleeding. Soon my crew discovered I had been injured and told me I had a long deep gash that was pouring blood. Some were trying to get the bleeding stopped while others searched for a truck or something to get me to the hospital. By this time my face, hands, and clothes were covered with blood. Soon a jeep came by and took me to the hospital. Dr. Leo Levine, our squadron doctor, examined the cut and said, "You sort of scratched it, didn't you?" I had been considering that maybe I would not have to go on the mission. Dr. Levine shaved part of my head so that he could pull the cut together. He said, "Son, this is going have to be sewed up, but for now I will pull it together with tape, and when you get back from the mission, if you get back, then come by and I will sew it then." He not only taped it together with a roll of tape and gauze but he wrapped it all around my head. I looked like I had a turban on. I told him that I could not fly because I could not even wear my helmet. He told me I would only be flying at 12,000 feet and would not need a helmet, and furthermore, he had orders from the group commander that there would be no excuses. Everyone would fly today no matter what condition existed. I explained that yesterday I had not worn my electric suit and my feet almost froze and that without a helmet my ears might freeze. To solve that problem, he wrapped plenty of gauze all over my head and wished me luck as he helped me out the door.

I returned to the plane just in time to start the engines. The crew had a lot of fun teasing me about my headdress. I know I looked funny. We left at our scheduled time and flew the same course as yesterday. Although the flak was there, it was not as bad because the ground support fighters had worked the German antiaircraft guns over. The fact that we were dropping our bombs today also gave the enemy something to contend with. We lost another plane just after we dropped our bombs. After we got back, I caught a truck to the hospital, and Dr. Levine sewed up my head.

He did an excellent job, because it is impossible to find the scar today.[14]

During my tour of duty I aborted only two missions. There were times, however, that I could have aborted a mission but did not. Our group commander, Colonel Napier, was very strict concerning reasons for aborting a mission, and we all understood that. He demanded 100 percent dedication and responsibility at all times. The first time I aborted a mission was the result of losing an engine over the English Channel as we went out on a mission. The engine started running rough and losing oil shortly after takeoff, and it continued to deteriorate as we moved into our place in formation. We stayed with the formation until after we joined the bomber line and were crossing the Channel. It finally got so rough and the oil pressure dropped so low that we were forced to feather the engine and leave the formation to return to the base.[15] We landed without any problem.[16] Another plane landed just after us that apparently had some problems although all his engines were running. A truck came out and carried us down to operations, and as I was walking down Colonel Napier came out the door and approached me. He wanted an explanation as to why we aborted. I went into detail as to what happened, and I guess he was satisfied that it was acceptable.

[14] For information on the missions of July 24-25, see Freudenthal, *A History of the 489th Bomb Group*, 110-20; Headquarters Eighth Air Force, INTOPS Summary No. 85, July 24, 1944, NA, RG 18, World War II Combat Operations Reports, Eighth Air Force, 489th BG, Box 1641, Folder – 489th P.F.F. & 491st, 1; Headquarters Eighth Air Force, INTOPS Summary No. 86, July 25, 1944, ibid.; Statistical Summary of Operation, July 24, 1944, ibid., 1; and Statistical Summary of Operation, July 25, 1944, ibid. The carpet-bombing proved very effective in devastating the Germany front lines and allowed allied forces to finally break out of Normandy. Unfortunately, several bombers accidentally dropped their bombs on American positions on July 24 and 25, killing 136 soldiers and leaving another 600 wounded. See Murray and Millett, *A War To Be Won*, 429.

[15] Feathering meant changing the blade angle of the propeller. It was done to prevent the propeller on a disabled engine from turning, and in the process, causing an extreme vibration.

[16] Davis's crew was one of three that had to abort on this mission. See Report of Aircraft Not Attacking, Mission of July 29, 1944, July 30, 1944, NA, RG 18, World War II Combat Operations Reports, Eighth Air Force, 489th BG, Box 1640, Folder – 489th P.F.F. & 491st, 1-2.

As I was explaining why I returned, the other pilot that had aborted arrived and was waiting his turn to explain why he returned. He was a good friend of mine. As the colonel excused me he looked at Lt. Joe Loadholtes. I remained to hear his problem because he landed with all four engines running. He saluted the colonel and said, "Sir, it was too damn cold up there this morning." I could not believe that Joe, as dynamic as he was, would ever answer the colonel in that manner. I immediately turned and headed for the door because I did not want to be around for the colonel's response. In a few minutes as I was dressing, Joe came in showing no pain. I asked him why he told the colonel what he did. He said, "Hell, that was what the problem was." He had lost his generators and as a result they could not use their electric suits. Because it was a long mission, they would have been in danger of frostbite.

The second time I had to abort it got a little more exciting. After our briefing on July 31, we went to our assigned plane. It was a plane I had never flown before in combat or on training flights. The first thing I usually did when I was assigned a plane I had never flown was to check with the ground crew chief to get his opinion on the condition of the plane and especially the engines. The sergeant assured me the plane was in good shape, and the engines were all running well. We took off and proceeded to the area where our group was forming. The number two engine seemed to be running rough and continued to develop more problems. We were about halfway across the Channel when we finally had to feather it. As we pulled out of the formation to return to base, I decided to not drop our bombs into the Channel.

As we started our descent, we discovered the number four engine was also developing some problems. I then decided to drop our bombs. With one engine out and another giving us problems, it would not have been wise to land with a full load of gas and bombs. A solid layer of clouds covered the area beneath us, and I was not sure if we were over land or water. Not wanting to drop the bombs on a populated area, I held them and hoped to get a break in the clouds to see where we were. We finally got a small break in the clouds and unfortunately we were over a populated area. About this time it became apparent that number four was going to have to be feathered. I was now pulling full power on number one and three, and the plane was losing altitude fast. I was going to have to land at the first runway I saw, because we could not go much further on two engines with a full load. I wanted to drop the bombs, but every time I saw a break in the clouds it showed a populated area beneath. I was homing in on our base and had told them our problem.

As we broke through the clouds I could see our base and the runway. It was too late to drop the bombs, so now it was a question of whether we could stay in the air until we reached the runway. It was going to be close either way. It seemed like an eternity from the time we came out of the clouds until we reached the area of the field. The runway was close, but the two engines running at full power could not hold altitude. There were some trees about two hundred yards off the end of the runway that we had to clear. To this day I am not sure how we missed them. The plane hit the ground several hundred feet in front of the runway. Even though we landed on the dirt, it was one of the best landings I ever made in a B-24.

One good thing happened later that day. We were told we would be given a three-day pass starting the next day. The last time we had a three-day pass we went to London and barely survived. After that experience, I said I would never go back, but we all changed our minds and decided to try it again. Surely, it would not be as bad as last time. The next morning we signed out and the truck carried us to Halesworth train station. Again, I received two bottles of whiskey, and I gave one to the enlisted men and one to Frank and Mackey. On the train we decided we would find a different hotel this time. When we arrived in London, we caught a cab to the Regent Palace Hotel, which was in the center of all the activities around Piccadilly. When we checked to see if we could get rooms there, they were full and did not expect any vacancies. We decided to eat in the dining room and then look for another hotel.

After we ate lunch, we were in the lobby discussing where to find a room. During the discussion, a gentleman in civilian clothes with an English tweed hat came over and said he overheard our problem and would like to invite us to spend the nights with him. He said he had a large suite of rooms and we would be welcome. The man looked familiar, but I could not recall where I had seen him. We really did not know what to say and hesitated. He once again assured us he had plenty of room and would like for us to be his guests. We told him we could find a room somewhere and did not want to interfere with any plans he might have. He insisted, so we finally told him we would be very grateful. We took the elevator to the top floor and went down the corridor to a door that opened into a beautiful suite of rooms. We were simply overcome by the beauty and size of the rooms. We sat our bags down, and he introduced himself to us. He was Fred Astaire. We hardly knew how to thank him. He told us to make ourselves at home. He indicated that he had something he needed to go do, and we never saw him again.[17]

The next day we visited St. Paul's Cathedral, the Tower of London, and Buckingham Palace. That evening Ed, Frank, Mackey, and I separated to visit different places. I walked around Piccadilly for a while. It was beginning to get late and I started looking for a place to eat before the buzz bombs started coming. It seemed like every place was full. I went to the rear of the hotel and was standing on the corner of the sidewalk leaning against a light post. A minute or so had passed, and two young ladies stopped to chat. In the late afternoon, a lot of young ladies gravitated to Piccadilly to visit American servicemen. I told them I was waiting for someone. They left, but others kept stopping. I could not believe all the attention I was getting, so I decided to see how many would stop within an hour's time. By then they were coming by in large numbers. Some were interested in making money, some wanted you to buy them dinner, and some wanted you to buy them a drink. Some wanted you to

<hr>

[17] While Fred Astaire's offer cannot be confirmed, he was in London in August 1944 for a few days before he flew to Paris. See Fred Astaire, *Steps in Time* (New York: Harper & Brothers, 1959), 272-3.

spend the night with them. Several even offered to give you break-fast in bed. I heard every kind of proposition you could imagine. Because most young Englishmen were in the military and in some far off place, American military personnel were quite popular. Army Air Forces officers wearing silver wings really drew attention. By actual count I was propositioned twenty-eight times in forty minutes. That will really build a man's ego.

When a great number of buzz bombs started coming over, I went to my room without having dinner. The next day we had to return to our base. We did not want to leave this beautiful suite of rooms. Mr. Astaire had not returned, so we left him a note thanking him for his hospitality. When we went back to base on August 3, we were immediately put on the alert list for the next day's mission.

We now had eight combat missions to our credit, but it felt like more. After completing six, we were considered veterans, even though there was still a lot to learn. Eight sounded like a lot until you thought of how many more lay in front of us. It was even more daunting now that we knew the dangers involved in completing a mission.

CHAPTER 7

Close Calls

LITTLE DID I KNOW that the next two weeks would be among the most difficult of my time in Europe. From August 4 through August 16, 1944, we flew seven combat and three long training missions. All of the combat missions were more than six hours long and were flown against heavily defended targets. The training missions were at least three hours long. That was a very tough two-week period, and it took a lot out of my crew. You were so physically exhausted and emotionally drained that you became hardened to the point of not caring what happened.

We were awakened early on August 4 and went through the usual routine of breakfast, followed by the briefing for the day's mission. The curtain was pulled and the black line stretched over the North Sea. We knew it would be a long mission because the line went almost to the edge of the map. We would bomb targets near Wismar, a city in the far north of Germany between Lubeck and Rostock. We would be over water most of the time, which meant we would not be subject to the constant fire from antiaircraft guns, but bailing out would be a problem. Compared to the other missions we had flown, this one was easy. We had the usual flak barrage over the target area, but we did not lose any planes and returned to our base intact. Some fighters were flying in the area of the North Atlantic, but they did not attack. We may have been too far out over the water for them. It was a relief to fly a mission and not have any significant problems.[1] When we returned, we were on the alert list again.

The August 5 mission took us into the heart of Germany to Brunswick. We always knew what to expect in this area. First was the usual morning fog and clouds that we had to contend with while taking off and assembling into a group formation. Then as we crossed the enemy coast we received the expected flak, but everything was going well. The group changed course often to avoid areas of flak, but from time to time, we still encountered some. This mission took about six and a half hours. Although enemy fighters were in the area, the escort did a good job and kept them from coming in. We reached the IP and began our bomb run. The ten to fifteen minutes of the bomb run seemed like an eternity as we flew through heavy flak. Finally, we opened our bomb bay doors and dropped our bombs. After I was certain that all bombs had cleared the bomb bay, I flipped the switch to close the doors.

When I hit the switch, the plane suddenly seemed to go limp. I had no rudder control and, it felt as if I had lost all controls. The elevators would respond but even they felt different. I got a call from my waist gunner who said, "Skip, I don't know what the matter is but we are covered up with loose cables." I knew then that flak, which was very intense and close, had severed some of our control cables. Because I had little control of the plane, it was a serious danger to the other planes near me; therefore, I maneuvered away from the formation. The only way I could control the direction was by constantly adjusting the power to the outboard engines.

I was flying on the left wing of the lead ship and the group would be starting a right turn at any time. I knew I had to get out of the way. I lowered the nose and pulled back number one and two

[1] More than 1,260 aircraft, including 524 B-24s, struck targets in northern German on the Baltic Sea. For a description of the mission, see Freudenthal, *A History of the 489th Bomb Group*, 130; Headquarters Eighth Air Force, INTOPS Summary No. 96, August 4, 1944, NA, RG 18, World War II Combat Operations Reports, Eighth Air Force, 489th BG, Box 1642, Folder – 489th P.F.F. & 491st Visual, 1-3; and Statistical Summary of Operation, August 4, 1944, ibid., 1.

engines; at the same time I increased the power on three and four. This allowed us to get away as the group started its right turn. I asked Siegfried to try to determine the extent of our damage, and I called the lead pilot and told him I had a serious problem. I was still trying to find out what control I had and how I could get the plane turned around to head back home. I was hoping to keep reasonably close to my group or at least to the bomber line so I could have as much protection as possible. If we fell behind, we would be a prime target for enemy fighters who loved to find a plane separated from the group and virtually out of control.

I got the plane turned around and headed west, although it cost me 2,000 feet of altitude. It was a sick feeling to not be able to see any other aircraft and to have limited control over the heart of Germany. I started looking for possible cloudbanks that I might get in and have a little protection. Siegfried returned to the cockpit and told me we had serious damage on the left side of the plane. Our rudder and the left elevator cables had been severed. The aileron cables were still good, but they are not worth much if you do not have rudder control. We still had elevator control, although it felt different because only the right cables were working.[2]

Frank was busy trying to figure out where we were and what heading we needed to take to get back to England. Our primary objective at this time was to get to the English Channel. If we got that far, we could decide whether to try to make it to the field and land, or bail out. I explained our situation to the crew and told them we would probably be attacked by the Luftwaffe because we were now outside our fighter protection. I asked them to put their parachutes on and be prepared to bail out at any time. Any loss of power on our outboard engines would be a disaster because they were the only steering we had. We would have had to jump. If flak or enemy fighters took out one of the engines, we would probably go into a spin, and I did not want to take any chances of the crew not being able to get out of the plane if that happened. In a spin, especially a

---

[2] See Glossary for more information on the operation of aileron cables and the elevators.

flat spin, the force is so great that it is virtually impossible to get to an opening and jump. We had frequently seen planes go into a flat spin, and few were able to escape.

The two and a half hours we flew before we reached the Channel seemed like an eternity, and we were greatly relieved when we saw it. As we neared the coast, I was hoping we could escape the normal flak, but I was dreaming. As we crossed over, we were given our usual barrage. Fortunately, no engine was hit. Now we were over the water and had started our descent. At 15,000 feet I took off my oxygen mask. I had to decide if I wanted to try to land at our base or land at the specially built runway near the coast designed for emergency landings. I needed to find out about the wind and if it was a crosswind. I could not communicate with my home base yet, but I had decided if at all possible, I would try and land there. Shortly after I crossed the English coast, I was able to talk to our control tower and explain the problem. They told me the winds were steady at ten to fifteen miles an hour with very little crosswind. The rest of our group had already landed, so I had the approach all to myself. As usual we were low on gas and did not have much time to waste. Fortunately, our approach was a good one. The plane responded beautifully, and we got on the runway the first time. After I cut the engines, I began to feel the fatigue. I sat in the seat and filled out the forms. I remained there a long time before I finally crawled out.[3] I was hoping I would not have to fly tomorrow.

That night we were again on the alert list. I could not believe it—the last two missions had been long ones and the crew was so tired they could hardly stand up. The following morning we were awakened around 3:00 a.m. After breakfast we went to the briefing and when they drew back the curtain, the black line indicated our route went over the North Sea and down east of the Elbe River to

[3] A total of 452 B-24s participated in the mission against tank and aircraft production facilities in Brunswick, Germany. See Freudenthal, *A History of the 489th Bomb Group*, 130; Headquarters Eighth Air Force, INTOPS Summary No. 97, August 5, 1944, NA, RG 18, World War II Combat Operations Reports, Eighth Air Force, 489th BG, Box 1642, Folder – 489th P.F.F. & 491st Visual, 1-8; and Statistical Summary of Operation, August 5, 1944, ibid., 1.

Hamburg—the second largest city in Germany. We knew it would be well defended. We finished the briefing, dressed, and took a truck to our plane. Everything appeared to be satisfactory during the pre-flight check. We started our engines, took off on time, and headed over the North Sea. When we reached the peninsula of northern Germany just below Denmark, we began having trouble with our number four engine. About the time we reached the IP, we had to feather it. I hoped we could stay with the group until we dropped our bombs, but we were flying at 22,000 feet, which was close to the maximum altitude for a fully loaded B-24. With one engine out we could not stay with the rest of the planes and were forced to leave the formation. We had to select a new target and drop our bombs because we needed to release our load to maintain altitude on three engines. As the group pulled away from us, we chose an industrial area along the docks of the Elbe River. We dropped our bombs but did not see if they hit the target, because all hell seemingly broke loose. Four shells suddenly exploded just in front of the nose and left wing of our plane. These were not the usual 88-mm antiaircraft shells. These were huge. The brightness of the burst almost blinded us and the black smoke that circled the burst was very dense.

My automatic reaction to the exploding shells was a quick and steep turn to the right. I did not have time to think about it. I turned ninety degrees and just as I was coming out of the turn, there were four more bursts just like the first ones. Normally, when you are in a group of planes and are being shelled, you feel like they are shooting at random and everyone is a target, but in this case, there were no other planes around. We were the target, and that gives you a completely different attitude. The enemy had corrected the second salvo the same amount that I had corrected. Being an emergency, I made as steep and abrupt a turn to the right as I could and also gave up a little altitude. As I straightened out the plane, four more huge balls of fire burst in virtually the same place as the last ones. Again I made a sudden correction and again four bursts of shells were virtually in the same place. I thought that maybe I should cross them up and turn left instead of right. For some reason, I could not make myself turn left so I yanked it around to the right again. This went on for what seemed like an eternity. I have no idea how many 360-degree turns I made. It seemed like this continued for at least thirty minutes, and we had lost about 4,000 feet of altitude in the process. With an engine out, those were precious feet, because I needed all the altitude I could maintain. A lone bomber with one engine out in this area was almost a dead duck, because that was exactly what the Luftwaffe sought. We had been alerted they were in the area when we reached the IP. Fortunately, we were never picked up, because we would have been easy pickings—another miracle.

Having no idea where we were, we had to make a wild guess and plan our course accordingly. It was not long before we started receiving some flak and felt it was probably coming from the North Sea coast of Germany. These flak bursts were 88-mm and nothing like the heavy fire we got into earlier. The heavy flak may have come from a German navy ship anchored in the Elbe near Hamburg. Whatever it was, I am glad I never saw it again. With an engine out we needed to conserve our altitude for the long trip over the waters of the North Sea back to base.[4]

We landed not long after the group. We were grateful things worked out well after our period of hell. We had no more problems other than our dead engine and made it to the field without incident. Once we cut the engines, total fatigue set in. The whole crew was exhausted. I was afraid to get up because I did not know if I would be able to walk. We were taking our time when a truck came up and a sergeant announced, "Hurry so you can get to the hangar and hear Glenn Miller and his band." Miller had played for the group and was just finishing when the planes started returning from the mission. He said he would perform again for those just returning. We dug a little deeper and got enough strength to go see Glenn

[4] Jim's squadron was part of a formation of 445 B-24s that hit oil refineries and fuel storage areas in Hamburg. See Freudenthal, *A History of the 489th Bomb Group*, 131; Headquarters Eighth Air Force, INTOPS Summary No. 98, August 6, 1944, NA, RG 18, World War II Combat Operations Reports, Eighth Air Force, 489th BG, Box 1642, Folder – 489th P.F.F. & 491st Visual, 1-8; and Statistical Summary of Operation, August 6, 1944, ibid., 1.

Miller perform. We appreciated his efforts. Only a few months later, in December, Glenn Miller left England on a plane to France and was never heard from again.[5]

This had been a long day. The crew was so fatigued that I do not think we could have flown another mission the next day. We had flown approximately twenty-one hours of combat the last three days, and two of them had been rough missions. We had now completed twelve missions. At the rate we were going, we thought we might finish our tour in September. Completing a tour was still a very big "if," though.

After eating I made it to the hut to lay down before I collapsed. The last three days had taken almost all my reserve strength. Today was especially tough because I had three hours of flying on our return with an engine out. Control pressures on a B-24 were some of the hardest of any plane in normal flight, but with an outboard engine out, it was even more difficult. I had to place so much pressure on the left rudder pedal that my left leg shook. When that happened, I would cross my right leg over to help relieve the tension. Ed relieved me after about fifteen minutes and then we took turns. As I lay on my cot, my legs were still quivering. I could not fly tomorrow. Fortunately when the alert list was posted we were not on it. I was relieved, because I did not want to have to get a slip from Dr. Levine saying I was not able to fly.

Over the next five days we only had to fly two training missions, but on August 10 we were back on the alert list. The mission on the next day to Saarbruecken was a particularly exciting one for me. We experienced the usual early morning briefing, takeoff, assembly,

[5] See Freudenthal, *A History of the 489th Bomb Group*, 131-3. Glenn Miller was one of the leading Big Band musicians in the late 1930s and early 1940s. At the age of 38 in 1942, he decided he wanted to serve in the military. After the navy rejected him, the army allowed him to enlist with the rank of captain. For the next two years, he performed concerts for military personnel. In the summer of 1944, he traveled with his band to England to perform more shows, and this is when Jim got to see the concert. On December 15, 1944, he left England on a plane to France and was never heard from again. See the Glenn Miller Birthplace Society, http://www.glennmiller.org/history.htm, accessed on November 17, 2005.

and trip across the Channel, to be greeted by the coastal defenses and the usual close calls by the fighters. Finally, we reached the IP. The intense antiaircraft fire lit the sky with small flashes, and occasional large ones when a bomber exploded. The heavy flak seemed impossible to fly through without serious or fatal damage. Prior to dropping our bombs, the formation was as tight as could be to obtain a better bombing pattern. Something suddenly struck my armrest with a force that knocked my arm up, and it felt like it might have bruised it. Because there were so many things going on, I did not give it much thought, and although my arm was sore I soon forgot about it.

After we returned to our base, I filled out my form, climbed out of the plane, and sat with some of the crew under the wing.[6] The gunners went over the plane to see how many holes we had and what damage they caused. Van Hooten came out of the bomb bay and said "Skip, come up on the flight deck. I want to show you something." Several of my crew and the ground crew gathered around the pilot's seat. The left armrest was gone from my seat and the left side was badly damaged. A piece of flak had come through the bottom of the plane and up through the flight deck floor, striking the left seat support and completely destroying my armrest.

I was so involved at the time that I thought my arm had struck the rest. I suddenly was aware that my arm was sore, so I pulled up my sleeves and found my arm had some swelling and a large bruise. The piece of flak was later found by one of my gunners and I still have it. It is about an inch long and half an inch wide. It made a four-inch hole in the flight deck. A cold chill swept over me to think that if it had been only a few inches to the right, I would have

[6] On this mission, twenty-three B-24s struck railroad marshalling yards in Saarbruecken, Germany. Other bombers hit other targets. See Freudenthal, *A History of the 489th Bomb Group,* 134-5; 489th Bomber Group Operational Statistical Report, Mission No. 62, August 11, 1944, NA, RG 18, World War II Combat Operations Reports, Eighth Air Force, 489th BG, Box 1642, Folder – 489th P.F.F. & 491st Visual, 1; and Tactical Bombing Mission Report, August 11, 1944, ibid., 2nd Air Division Operation Report, Box 27118, Folder – 2nd Air Division Operation Report Saarbrucken, August 11, 1944, 1.

been seriously wounded or killed. Only an inch or two would probably have taken my left arm off. I offered a prayer of thanks. After debriefing and eating, I went back to my hut and could not help but think how close a miss I had and how lucky I was to have only a sore arm from it.

One of the crew came in and told me that we were on the alert list for tomorrow's mission. By this time my arm was very sore, and I did not know if I could fly tomorrow. I contemplated letting Dr. Levine look at it, but I decided to wait until the morning to see how it felt. Because my arm felt no worse when I woke up, I did fly the mission to Laon, France. It was a long mission, but no serious problems developed.[7]

I was thankful I was not on the alert list for August 13. We had flown five long missions in the last eight days, and we all needed a rest. While we were not on the alert list, we still had to fly a training mission. We were back on the alert list for a mission on August 15 to a Luftwaffe airfield near Wittmundhafen in northwestern Germany. This mission was a little over five hours long and the shortest one we had during our tour. Although enemy fighters were in the area, our escort did an excellent job of warding them off, and we completed the mission without any significant issues.[8]

To our astonishment, we were again scheduled to fly the next day's mission. We knew as soon as the curtain was pulled at the

[7] Twenty-six B-24s from Jim's group bombed airfields near Laon, France. See Freudenthal, *A History of the 489th Bomb Group*, 135; Headquarters 2nd Bombardment Division, Tactical Mission Report, August 12, 1944, NA, RG 18, World War II Combat Operations Reports, Eighth Air Force, Box 339, Folder – A-3 Mission Rept. F.O. 1010, August 12, 1944, 1-4; and Statistical Summary of Operation, August 12, 1944, ibid., 489th BG, Box 1643, Folder – 489th P.F.F. & 491st Visual F.O. No. 431, Laon/Atheist A/F, August 12, 1944, 1.

[8] A total of 930 bombers participated in attacks on eleven airfields in Germany, Holland, and Belgium. Jim's crew was part of a formation of eighty-five planes that struck an airfield near Wittmundhafen, Germany. See Freudenthal, *A History of the 489th Bomb Group*, 139; Headquarters 2nd Bombardment Division, Tactical Mission Report, August 15, 1944, NA, RG 18, World War II Combat Operations Reports, Eighth Air Force, Box 340, Folder – A-3 Mission Rept. F.O. 1025, August 15, 1944, 1-5; and Headquarters Eighth Air Force, INTOPS Summary No. 107, August 15, 1944, ibid., 93 Bomber Group, Box 254, Folder – 15 August 1944, Wittmundhafen, 1-8.

August 16 briefing that we would be in for a rough one. The target was an oil plant at Magdeburg, Germany. It was a short distance from Berlin, right in the heart of Germany, and in an area the Luftwaffe usually defended with force. The briefing, preflight checks, takeoff, and assembly proceeded as usual. As we were crossing the Channel we began to have trouble with our propellers. They would not hold a set pitch. At first it was slow, but the further we went the more rapidly they would creep out of position. We should have aborted and returned to the base, but the problem did not get serious until we had crossed the enemy coast and were over enemy territory. Ed kept busy adjusting the pitch. Because they were always out of sync, it made flying a problem. Ed eventually did not have time for anything but adjusting the pitch on the propellers. The big question was whether they would get completely out of control. If they got any worse, we had only one choice, and that was to bail out. It was all Ed or I could do to keep the propellers balanced. Soon after we crossed the coast, enemy fighters arrived and remained nearby throughout the attack. Thanks to our fighters, most of them were unable to attack us. However, we did encounter pockets of flak along the way. As we turned on our IP we could see the huge black cloud of antiaircraft fire that stretched to the target.

It may have been a blessing that we were having trouble with the props because we did not have time to see the gauntlet of bursting shells that we experienced for the next twenty minutes. We smelled the smoke and felt the concussion of bursting flak. One of our ships exploded just in front of us, and we expected to meet the same fate any minute. The plane that was hit disappeared in one huge ball of flame, and we did not see any chutes after the explosion. The group made their turn away from the target and headed for home. After receiving our farewell burst of flak at the coastline, we started letting down. By the time we reached 15,000 feet we broke formation in order to get down as soon as possible. I pushed the speed up so we could land before the group got to the base.

When we reached the base area, I was cleared to shoot a straight-in landing. I decided we would come in high and land with as little power from the engines as possible. We were shooting red flares, and as usual under these conditions the fire trucks and ambulances were waiting. We got on the ground in good shape—to this day I do not know why we had the problem with the props. The important thing was that we returned safely. After a visit to the mess I headed to the hut and immediately fell asleep.[9]

I had a wonderful surprise when I woke up. Someone had picked up my mail, and I had two packages and several letters from home. Letters and packages from home were the things that kept you going. For hours I read and reread the letters and ate cookie crumbs from what were at one time whole cookies. It did not matter if they were crumbs. Anything from home was great, and we all shared our boxes. Tonight was going to be a good night. I had letters from home, and we were not on the alert list.

The next day we were given three-day passes, so we decided to go back to London. We needed to get away from the base, and London was the only place we knew to go. The previous times I swore I would not go back to London because of the buzz bombs. At night at the base, if we did not have anything else to do, we could always sit outside our hut and watch the antiaircraft guns and the Royal Air Force (RAF) attack the buzz bombs as they crossed the coast south and east of Halesworth. Sometimes they would get off course and fly near our base. Some even flew over the base. When the RAF or ground gunners hit one, it would explode in a tremendous orange and red ball. It was amazing how many they were able to shoot down as they flew low over the coast.

The next morning we left about ten o'clock, signed out, and got our usual two bottles of whiskey. By the time we got to London,

---

[9] A force of 1,090 bombers, including 431 B-24s, attacked a series of oil refineries and airfields in central Germany. Jim's bomb group hit an oil refinery near Magdeburg, Germany. See Freudenthal, *A History of the 489th Bomb Group*, 141; Headquarters 2nd Bombardment Division, Tactical Mission Report, August 16, 1944, NA, RG 18, World War II Combat Operations Reports, Eighth Air Force, Box 340, Folder – A-3 Mission Rept. F.O. 1029, August 16, 1944, 1-6; and Headquarters Eighth Air Force, INTOPS Summary No. 108, August 16, 1944, ibid., 93 Bomber Group, Box 254, Folder – 16 August 1944, Magdeburg, 1-9.

Mackey had almost downed a whole bottle, and to say he was a little high would be putting it mildly. We checked into the hotel, and Frank and I hoped that Mackey would lie down and go to sleep. Instead, he wanted to go to a shoe shop and get a pair of custom-made English shoes. Frank and I knew Mackey could not go alone, so we decided if we went with him and got him to walk enough he would sober up. We were walking in the elite shopping and banking district in the city. Mackey was stopping and looking in the windows, and Frank and I would wander along about a hundred feet in front of him. We were careful—we did not want the MPs to pick him up for being drunk.

All of the sudden Frank and I heard the sound of raised voices. We turned around and could not see Mackey. We rushed back down the street to see where he might have gone. It did not take long to find him. He was standing in front of an entrance to a bank. It was after closing time and a steel grill had been drawn across the front doors. I asked him what the problem was and he started laughing and said "Skip, I always wanted to pee on the Bank of England and now I am." He was urinating through the grill and the night watchman on the other side was hollering at him to stop. Frank and I both quickly turned and got to the end of the block. As we watched the event unfolding, Mackey finally walked away, still laughing and saying, "I always wanted to do that."

For the next hour or so Frank and I walked Mackey around and had him drinking tea and coffee when we could find it. Mackey eventually sobered up enough that we started trying to find a place to eat. We ran into a friend of mine, Jim Dyke, who I had not seen since we were in preflight in San Antonio some twenty months ago. He and a friend were looking for a place they had heard of where you could buy steaks. Frank and Mackey did not want steak so I decided to go with Dyke and his friend. We stopped at a street corner trying to decide where we might go to find out about this black market steak restaurant.[10] As we were waiting for the light to turn,

[10] Great Britain began food rationing in 1939 and maintained restrictions throughout the war. Meat was in very short supply.

three young ladies were also waiting and overheard our conversation. They thought they knew someone who could tell us where to go. They went down about three blocks and went in a pub. Five minutes later they came out with directions to a place they thought served steaks. They offered to take us to the address if we would buy their subway tickets. We rode the subway for what seemed like an hour or more.

We then walked for a while before we came to a set of stairs in an alley that looked like it was about to fall. We climbed three flights of stairs to a door. One of our escorts knocked on the door and got no response. After she knocked several times, someone finally opened it. Inside, the room looked like any other restaurant with tables, chairs, and even tablecloths. Army Air Forces personnel occupied most of the tables. The lights were dim, but it appeared they were eating steaks. We told the three young ladies we would buy them dinner if they would help us get back to downtown. The restaurant did not have a menu, so we had to eat whatever they brought us. It took forty-five minutes for them to bring our food. Sure enough, it was steak. We never knew what kind of steak though. It may have been horse meat or something worse but it did taste like beef. In fact, it was good. Any fresh meat would have tasted wonderful, because we had not had any for a long time. The next day we packed up and headed back to Halesworth and our base.

When we got back to the base, we found the group had not flown any missions while we were gone. The weather had been so bad that the entire Eighth Air Force had been grounded. The day after we returned I was asked to report to operations with my crew at noon. We were briefed that we would join two other planes on a mission to a target in western Germany. This would be a special mission and a new type of radar would be used to locate the target. I never did learn what or where the target was. The weather was dreadful over Europe and nothing more than a three-ship formation could be flown. The other two planes were from some other group that had been trained in this new type of radar. I would be the third ship and was going along to increase the bomb tonnage.

The Glenn Miller Band plays at Halesworth Field, August 1944. Glenn Miller disappeared on a flight later that year. (Courtesy of Jim Davis)

The weather was actually good, so to speak, over England, only scattered clouds. We were briefed that the two other planes would be over Halesworth at a certain time and I would join them and fly the right wing position. I had been around long enough to suspect that although this did not sound like a rough mission, it probably would be. The two planes arrived over our base on August 21 at the designated time, and I pulled in formation with them. We climbed out over the English Channel and soon reached 10,000 feet. I had the crew put on their oxygen masks and Mackey pulled the pins on the 250-pound bombs that we were carrying. Halfway across the Channel we encountered heavy clouds that were as dense as any I had ever been in. I had to fly really tight formation in order to see the other two planes. We continued to climb to 21,500 feet and changed course frequently. The only way you could tell we had changed course was by the centrifugal force that you could feel from time to time.

Had I had time to think about our situation, it would have been frightening. Here we were in dense clouds over western Germany and hardly able to see the ship on our wing. Because the visibility was bad and we were flying the right wing of the lead ship, it was impossible for Ed to fly from the copilot seat, and I had to do all the flying. We had flown for a long time when we started making some turns and doing a lot of maneuvering. It was during this maneuvering that we started getting antiaircraft fire, and we could feel the concussion and see the orange flash from the flak bursting around us. I thought we would never reach the target. Finally, the lead ship opened his bomb bay doors and we did the same. The bomb run was not very long—perhaps eight or ten minutes, but when you can see the orange glow of bursting flak in spite of the clouds, even one minute seems like an eternity. It was a relief to see the bombs drop from the lead ship as that was the signal to release ours.

Just as our bomb bay doors closed, the lead ship started a steep turn into me. I had to make a drastic turn to keep from colliding with him. My left wing was up so high that I lost sight of the lead plane. Afraid to straighten out, I continued a steep turn to my right and dropped down several hundred feet. I called my gunners and asked if they could see another plane, but they could not. I decided to level out. Here we were somewhere over western Germany, not knowing where. Flak was still bursting around us. In a situation like this, time seems to stand still. The only thing we could do was head west and hope we would hit England. If we missed England to the north, we would end up over the Atlantic—not a good prospect. England seemed very small and a long way off. Eventually, we started getting breaks in the clouds and saw water below us. It was not long before we could see land but we did not want to let down until we were sure the land was England. As we got close we recognized it as an area about two hundred miles north of our base. We got to the base, landed, and were thrilled to be back safe on the ground.[11]

[11] This is the only mission that Davis flew that cannot be independently verified.

It had been almost two weeks since the Eighth Air Force had been able to bomb Europe due to bad weather, so most crews and maintenance people were rested, and most of our planes were in good shape. On August 24 I was on an alert list, so it was another night of little sleep. When the curtain was pulled, it showed our route would be over the North Sea, across a peninsula just below Denmark, and down over the Baltic Sea to an aircraft assembly plant in Rostock, Germany. This would be a long mission, as Rostock was about one hundred miles west of the Polish border. We received some flak as we crossed the peninsula, and the flak in the target area was very intense. We did have some problems with another B-24 group. I do not know who was off course, but the groups had to do some maneuvering to avoid colliding. One plane was damaged so much that its crew decided it could not return to England and instead flew to Sweden, where they spent the rest of the war as internees.[12] The mission was over seven hours long.[13]

That evening when the alert list was posted, we were once again scheduled to fly. It was always hard to fly two missions back to back, but usually the second one does not get your attention as much as the first one. You are so tired after coming off of a long mission that to some degree you say "what the heck." At the briefing, the black line showing our course weaved into the heart of Germany to the I.G. Farben chemical plant in Ludwigshafen. It was the only target in the area, and the German high command defended it with everything they had. Because it was a very important facility to them and was somewhat by itself, they knew what you were after and were always ready.

---

[12] This happened occasionally. Crews would determine that their planes were too damaged to return to England and would instead fly to either Sweden or Switzerland. Because those two countries were neutral, the crews had to stay there for the duration of the war.

[13] Jim flew in a formation of 112 B-24s that attacked an aircraft production factory in Rostock. See Freudenthal, *A History of the 489th Bomb Group*, 147-50; Headquarters 2nd Bombardment Division, Tactical Mission Report, August 25, 1944, NA, RG 18, World War II Combat Operations Reports, 491st Bombardment Group, Box 2069, Folder – Mission Report 60, Schwerin/AF, 8/25/44, 1-6.

The fog was terrible that morning. It was so thick we could only see about two lights down the runway. There was virtually no wind, and we were very concerned about hitting the prop wash of the plane that had just taken off. For all practical purposes you would be taking off blind and the possibility of anything unusual happening was something you did not need to deal with. As the plane in front of us revved up its engines and released his brakes for takeoff, the vapor spirals that spun off the tips of his props made an odd picture. The plane would quickly disappear into the fog, leaving only the vapor circles hovering over the runway. The circles would linger for a short while and then disappear as you pulled out to make your own takeoff. Your concern now was to get this big, heavily loaded metal bird safely into the air. A blind takeoff like this was so demanding you would at least temporarily forget the hell you would experience over the target. For some reason I was more concerned about this mission than usual—maybe it was because of the intense pace, or perhaps it was because I knew it would be impossible to continue to beat the odds. Whatever the reason, I did not have complete confidence that everything would turn out all right.

We climbed through several layers of clouds and took our place in the group formation. Two groups were to bomb the chemical plant, and we were in the second one. We reached altitude just before crossing the enemy coast near Antwerp. We got our usual greetings of flak as we crossed the coast and started winding our way through Holland and Germany. From time to time we received barrages of light flak. The weather was reasonably good with some thin cirrus clouds that made visibility a little difficult. We knew the group in front of us was nearing the target because suddenly a heavy barrage of flak appeared over the target area. Then in the dark cloud of flak we would see a ball of red and orange. That was always a sickening sight, because you knew that you were witnessing an exploding B-24. I do not remember how many times we saw that sight, but at least five and maybe as many as seven. I think the antiaircraft fire on this mission was the most intense and accurate of any target I ever bombed. It was at this point that you had to draw deep on your courage. To watch the planes exploding and to know that with each one ten airmen had been lost was sobering. To realize that you also would have to go through the cloud of flak was frightening.

Just as we were entering the cloud of black smoke, our group's lead plane started making a turn to the left. We later learned that the group that had just gone through the target zone found it impossible to see it and radioed our group commander of the problem. Our commander led us to the secondary target, which was a railroad marshalling yard at Ehrang, Germany. We did not miss all the flak at Ludwigshafen, but we did miss some of it after we pulled out to go to the secondary target. We got enough flak at Ehrang, but it was nothing like the flak over the I.G. Farben Chemical plant. The flight back out of Germany was routine until we got to Holland. I do not know if the group had gotten a little off course or not, but for some reason we seemed to get pounded all across Holland. It was a relief to clear the coast in one piece. We had now completed nineteen missions and were becoming one of the older crews.[14]

The 489th Bomb Group was taken off combat operation from September 1 through September 8. After the allied armies broke out of Normandy and General Patton's Third Army swept across France, it often ran away from its supply lines, and in many cases the areas of France that were liberated would be without food. The need for immediate food and supplies made it necessary, at least temporarily, to build wooden racks in the B-24s to haul food as well as equipment to areas that needed help. On September 1, I flew to a field near Southampton and took aboard a load of bacon. It did not take long for them to load the plane and for us to take off for Orleans, France.

We flew low over the D-Day beaches with a skeleton crew made up of pilot, copilot, navigator, radio operator, and flight engineer. As

---

[14] Jim's bomb group attacked railroad marshalling yards near Ludwigshafen. See Freudenthal, *A History of the 489th Bomb Group*, 150; and Headquarters 2nd Bombardment Division, Tactical Mission Report, August 26, 1944, NA, RG 18, World War II Combat Operations Reports, 491st Bombardment Group, Box 2069, Folder – Mission Report 61, Ehrang, 8/26/44, 1-6.

we cleared the beach we turned to a 125-degree heading. It was not long before we cleared the Cherbourg Peninsula and entered more open and rolling country. From that point on it was unbelievable to see the destruction along the roads. Burned out vehicles of every kind, from horse-drawn carts to huge tanks, lay in waste. Some were still smoking. This destruction stretched for miles in what seemed like an endless string. The railroads that at times paralleled the roads were also littered with wreckage.

Flying at a thousand feet or less made navigation a real problem, because most landmarks had been destroyed a few days earlier, and as low as we were flying, we could not see a very large area. We were scheduled to land at Bricy Airport, which was just outside of Orleans. One thing we could not afford to do was overshoot the runway, because the battle line was no more than fifteen miles away. Bricy had a number of buildings, but most, if not all, lay in total destruction from the allies' recent bombing raids.[15] We were briefed that only one runway was available for landing, and even it had numerous bomb craters that we would have to maneuver around while landing and taking off. They were right. The plane had to be steered back and forth to miss the holes. We taxied up to a small building off the end of the runway where a fleet of army trucks was parked. I was one of the first planes in.

One thing I did not expect was the large crowd of French people who had gathered where we were to unload. I would guess fifteen hundred people were just outside the fenced off area. I was directed to a parking space and got the cut engines signal. After we got everything in order, we got out of the plane and could not believe all the French people who were cheering and motioning for us to come over to shake their hands. We did and were almost unable to break away. I had never been hugged and kissed so much in all my life. I guess for years they had heard or seen these big planes fly over

---

[15] One of the problems that the advancing allied forces faced was the destruction caused by early American and British bombing missions. When Davis flew his supply missions, Orleans had only been under allied control for a few weeks.

and had never been so close to one before. We were probably the first American airmen they had seen. With all of that and having just been liberated only a day or two ago, they could not have been happier or more gracious. They would also have something to eat, even though it was just bacon. They quickly unloaded us and it was time to leave. In a way I hated to go; we had been given such a great reception. It made us proud to have been a part of their liberation.

We had not been given any routes or courses to follow, so I decided on our return flight we would see as much new territory as we could. Our course took us across France, and I especially wanted to see the Mont-Saint-Michel. I remembered reading about it when I was in elementary school and was always fascinated about how it was built on this rock island. When the tide was out you could walk to it, but when the tide was in, it became an island in the bay. I also wanted to fly over the islands of Jersey and Guernsey. Although the clouds were a little higher than when we came over, we still had to fly low to stay under them. Everything went fine until coming upon a ridge that bordered Mont-Saint-Michel. Suddenly numerous bursts of flak appeared so close in front of us that as soon as they burst we flew through the smoke. I had been looking at the island and saw the flash from the guns. Without thinking I dropped the nose of the airplane and banked steeply to my right to seek protection from the ridge. I went straight to the deck and stayed there until we arrived at the coast. When we got back to the base we were told that the Germans still held the islands of Mont-Saint-Michel, as well as Jersey and Guernsey. I could not imagine how foolish I was nor can I believe how stupid the gunners on Mont-Saint-Michel were to have fired as early as they did. If they had waited just a minute or so I would have flown right over them, and they would have had a lot of time to really unload on me. I made myself a promise that I would never take a chance again. We were lucky to have survived my decision to fly over the area.[16]

Late in the afternoon of September 9, the alert list was posted for the mission the next day and my crew was on it. At the brief-

[16] Davis and his crew made three more supply trips to France.

ing the next morning, we found out the target was Ulm, Germany. This would be an unusual mission because it was a joint operation with the Fifteenth Air Force stationed in Italy. The Fifteenth Air Force was supposed to bomb their targets in the Ulm and Munich area. Then, the 1st and 3rd Divisions of the Eighth Air Force, composed mainly of B-17s, would make their bomb runs over the area. The 2nd Air Division, which contained the B-24 groups (including our 489th Bomb Group), was scheduled to reach the target last. This was the first time the Eighth and the Fifteenth had coordinated bombing targets in the same area. The weather officer briefed us that the weather would be good both going and coming back.

We took off and formed in the usual fog and layers of clouds. As we moved over the Channel to join the bomber line, we pulled the pins on the bombs, test fired our guns, and put on our oxygen masks. This would be a very long mission—perhaps over nine hours. While climbing up to take our place in the formation, something was not quite right about how the plane flew. The engines seemed to be performing well, but the flight attitude seemed to be unstable. No matter how we tried, we could not get the plane trimmed up and to the right attitude. As we flew over the Channel gaining altitude, it seemed to get worse the higher we got. We finally reached our mission altitude of 22,500 feet, and the plane flew like it wanted to set down. The enemy coast was fast coming up, so we had to decide if we were going to abort or not. It was now or never. I really believed we should return, but when everything is running well, it would be very difficult to explain why we did.

Halfway to the target area, I knew I had made a terrible decision not to abort and return to base while we were over the Channel. It was too late now, because we were well into Germany, and to abort and return alone was suicide. That was especially true today with good weather and no clouds in which to hide. We had to pull more power just to keep up with the group. It did not take a lot of calculations to tell us we were in serious trouble because of the excess fuel we had used. We did not feel we could go on, nor could we take the chance of returning home by ourselves.

I realized that we might have to try to reach Switzerland. If we were successful in crossing over the Swiss border and landing, the war would be over for us. Because Switzerland was a neutral country, we would be held as internees until the war was over. That was a real possibility, but it was a decision I would have to make after we cleared our target.

Other problems were developing with the mission that I was not aware of at that time. The Fifteenth was arriving to its targets late. Also, the weather was not cooperating—a dense formation of clouds now stretched from a low altitude to an altitude much higher than the B-24s or B-17s could fly. The 1st Division altered course to the right and the 3rd Division altered course to the left, each trying to find an opening in the clouds. In the meantime the 2nd Air Division, of which we were a part, had gained a little time on the 1st and 3rd Divisions because we were about ten miles an hour faster. The dense cloud formation was not very wide, so the lead plane commander decided that each group was to penetrate the clouds. It was almost like hitting a wall as we entered the cloud bank. The only thing you could see was the plane that you were flying right next to. We were in the clouds only a few minutes but it seemed like hours. Thinking about the number of planes that were in these clouds with you that you could not see was frightening. The only thing you could do was to hold a true course straight ahead until you cleared them.

After what seemed like an eternity, we broke out of the clouds as suddenly as we entered them. The group formation was scattered into small three ship elements. We did not know if we had lost any of our planes or not. After we got our bearings, the situation we found ourselves in was beyond description. In reality, it seemed that everyone got there at the same time—the Fifteenth and all of the Eighth. There were airplanes everywhere you looked—below us, above us, and coming at us from every direction. Add to that all the flak that was being fired and it was utter chaos. It became a game of each man for himself. I had to make a steep turn to the right to avoid three planes that appeared to be on a collision course with us. Then I had to turn to the left to avoid another group of three. The plane had no more than straightened out to a level position than bombs started falling just in front of the nose of our plane. I looked up and saw a group of five B-17s with their bomb bay doors open dropping bombs. They came frighteningly close to hitting us.

I finally decided to scuttle our bombs in order to lighten the ship and be able to maneuver better. An unexpected thing happened when we dropped our bombs. As they left the plane it suddenly started flying like it should have. The ground crew had loaded the plane incorrectly and gotten too much weight (or bombs) in the rear of the bomb bay, which made it fly tail heavy. After we dropped the bombs, the plane flew great.

During this ordeal, Van Hooten called me on the intercom and said "Skip, I don't know what it is, but it looks like there is a liquid of some kind coming out of the end of the right wing." I immediately knew what it was. Each wing had three gas tanks holding a total of 450 gallons. No doubt flak, which was intense, had knocked a hole in our right wing tip tank. I called Siegfried and told him to transfer all the gas out of the tip tank to the main tank in the fuselage as fast as he could. While Siegfried worked to get at least some of the gas out of the wings, we threaded our way in, through, and around the mass of planes until finally we got enough space to straighten out and take a reading of our situation.

I had asked Frank to determine exactly where we were because just in front and slightly to the left was Lake Constance in Switzerland. Siegfried had gotten all the gas he could out of the tanks but he did not know how much that was. I asked him to take a reading and let me know the best he could how much gas we had left. That was at best a glorified guess, because the gauges could not be counted on to be very accurate. When he returned I got with Frank and we estimated how long we could stay in the air with the fuel we had. No matter how we figured it, we could not get back to England. I got the crew on the intercom and explained that we did not think we had enough fuel to get back to England. We had one of two choices: either land and be interred in Switzerland, or head for home and fly until we ran out of gas and had to bail out. We had to decide quickly. I gave them a minute to think about it and then asked each one what they wanted to do. All of them voted to go to Switzerland. The more I thought about it the more I felt like we should head home and hope for a miracle. We now had twenty-four missions and hopefully we could finish our tour in a month. I called them and explained that for some reason I felt we could get back and that we should head for England. They each called me and said, "If you feel we should head back then we are all with you."[17]

We turned in the general direction of England until Frank could get a heading worked out. Shortly we saw a group of five B-24s going in the same direction we were, so we eased over and got into formation with them. I was very anxious as we pulled in close to them because it was a no-no for a strange plane out of the clear to come sliding into a group of planes in formation. The Germans had captured several B-24s and B-17s intact and had on occasion joined groups of planes and then would radio their ground stations the altitude, headings, and all kinds of information that would help the air defenses. The only reason I did this was because so many groups had been broken up and stragglers were forced to form groups to fly in formation, for protection against the Luftwaffe. At first I felt lucky to find some friends to fly back with, but it was not long before I decided we had to break formation because it was taking too much gas. We pulled out and cut our mixture and power as low as we could. We were now cruising at 140 mph rather than the 165 mph we usually flew, but we had to reduce speed to have any hope of getting back. I did not look forward to bailing out and would do everything I could to avoid it.

As we passed the coast of Belgium we pulled the power back and started a long power glide across the Channel, with our gas gauges indicating we were virtually out of fuel.[18] We began throw-

[17] Davis's navigator later claimed, "His was a gutsy call." See Morris, "Memoirs of the War," 38.

[18] A power glide means maintaining power to the engines while losing altitude. This procedure allows the plane to increase its speed a great deal and get to base quicker. Pilots commonly used it when they had injured on board or had mechanical problems.

ing everything we could overboard, such as our .50-cal. ammunition and almost anything else that was not tied down. Each of my
crew had his parachute on and was ready to jump if necessary. We
had our throttles as far back as they would go. We cleared the English coast, and I believed we might make it to the base. We called
the tower and told them we were out of fuel and were making a
straight-in landing. As we landed and taxied, the engines quit. The
thrill of being back home was beyond description.

This would be a day that I would never forget. Beyond a doubt
more airplanes flew in the small area over southern Germany than
ever before in the history of aviation. There were more than 1,100
B-24s and B-17s in the air. I believed I had to maneuver to avoid
a collision with each one. I am sure there will never again be that
many planes in such a limited area. The Germans contributed their
part by saturating the sky with flak. A strange thing about the flak
was that it was of secondary concern to avoiding a midair collision
with the other planes. That was the first and last time that something attracted my attention more than the flak, and I never thought
I would ever see that.[19]

On September 14 an alert list was posted for a briefing in the
afternoon. This was not normal and immediately we understood
we would be a part of an unusual mission. We were not disappointed. Some thirty-six crews reported for the briefing. The briefing
officer opened by saying we were a part of approximately 250 crews
that had "volunteered" for a special mission, one we would probably really enjoy. This mission would allow us the opportunity to do
something that we had always wanted to do but had been restricted
from doing. It would be a low level mission to drop supplies. This

---

[19] A total of 1,145 bombers, including 388 B-24s, flew missions that attacked
targets near Ulm, Germany. See Freudenthal, *A History of the 489th Bomb Group*,
162-3; Headquarters 2nd Bombardment Division, Tactical Mission Report, September 10, 1944, NA, RG 18, World War II Combat Operations Reports, 491st
Bombardment Group, Box 2070, Folder – Mission Report 67, Ulm, Ger., Sept.
10, 1944, 1-6; and Headquarters Eighth Air Force, INTOPS Summary No. 133,
September 10, 1944, ibid., 93rd Bomber Group, Box 253, Folder – 10 Sept. 1944,
Heilbronn, 1-9.

sounded too good to be true. We should have known at that time that there would be a price to pay, but the thought of buzzing legally was such a surprise we really did not worry much about the mission's details.

The allied army in Operation Market Garden had made plans to try to capture four bridges over three rivers before the German Army could destroy them. All of the bridges were in territory occupied by the German Army, and as a result, it would require a maximum airborne assault. Allied commanders were most anxious to capture these bridges and protect them from destruction so that they could use them when their ground forces arrived. It would be much easier to cross the river by bridge than by boat or on barges. The rivers were very wide and would not only present major difficulties to cross, but after crossing, they would have to depend on pontoon bridges to move the armor to the other side.[20] This was to be one of the largest airborne operations ever attempted. The plan involved the entire allied airborne army as well as many units of the Eighth Air Force, one of which was the 489th Bomb Group.[21]

The allied armies had captured most of Belgium and were moving north. The main road leading north from Antwerp crossed three large rivers—the Maas, Rhine, and Waal. At this point, the three rivers were only about ten miles apart. The U.S. 101st Airborne Division was assigned to capture the bridge at Grave, which crossed the River Maas. The 82nd U.S. Airborne Division was responsible for seizing the bridges over the Waal River at Nijmegen and the roads leading to it. The British First Airborne Division was to capture the bridge over the River Rhine at Arnhem. If successful, the allied armies would then have a much easier and faster route to the heart of Germany. For the next three days we practiced low level flying over the English countryside in three-ship elements and squad-

[20] Pontoon bridges are made from prefabricated bridge sections that army engineers can connect together to create a temporary river crossing.

[21] For overviews of Operation Market Garden, see Ambrose, *Citizen Soldiers*, 118-31; Murray and Millett, *A War to Be Won*, 438-43; Cornelius Ryan, *A Bridge Too Far: The Classic History of the Greatest Airborne Battle of World War II* (New York: Simon and Schuster, 1995); and Worthen and Berner, eds. *Monty's Folly*.

ron formation. It was natural that we considered this mission to be similar to the supply missions to Orleans, France. We would not receive mission credit for this operation, so we assumed we would not come into contact with the enemy. By this time we should have known better than to assume anything.

It was a treat flying without all the heavy clothes, electric suits, and oxygen masks. We would see Holland flying at a hundred feet or less—a thrilling ride. Our crew for the mission would be made up of the pilot, copilot, navigator, radio operator, a special supply drop person from the Services of Supply, and three of my gunners to help discharge the packages and parcels out the rear hatch. We would also carry bundles attached to the bomb shackles that would be released over the drop area. These parcels would be attached to parachutes hooked to the airplane via shroud lines, which would serve to open the chutes after they cleared the plane. One problem we would have to contend with after the drop would be the need for someone to go into the bomb bay and cut the shrouds loose, so we could close the bomb bay doors.

The mission on September 18 was much different than the usual combat mission. We had been briefed on the mission some four days in advance and had practiced low level flying for the last three days. Another difference was that we could sleep late because the briefing was not until 1:00 p.m. We ate breakfast about 10:00 a.m. I was in the chow line with Lt. Claude Lovelace, and we ate breakfast together. I had first met Lovelace in Ireland on our way to join the 489th Bomb Group. We had a close relationship because we were the only two crews left from the group of four that started our tour together. This was the eighteenth mission for Lovelace. We visited a long time and talked about the many close calls that we had, but that we did not expect any today. I guess we all were looking forward to this unusual mission.

At 1:00 p.m. we had our briefing and received all the details. We were not told about the possibility of enemy ground fire. I know that none of us expected any because we had been told this operation would not be credited as a combat mission.

We were going to fly at an altitude no higher than 2,000 feet, so we did not need any special clothes other than our life vests. Just in case, we wore our flak jackets. The briefing described what the landmarks would be so we could identify the correct area to make our drop. There were supposed to be ground markers as well as smoke flares to identify our particular drop zone. Because there would be many planes in the area, all at low altitude, it was most important for all planes to stay on course and drop in the correct zone. It was emphasized that the supplies we were carrying were critical for the paratroopers and glider forces to proceed and capture their specific areas. By no means were we to drop the cargo in areas that might be taken by the enemy.

Our bomb group would be leading the combat wing on this mission. I was anxious to see how the cargo was loaded because I was concerned that some of the bundles dropping from the bomb bay could get twisted or fail to detach from the shroud lines and become a flight hazard. We were scheduled to drop from two to four hundred feet and at a speed of less than 150 mph. That was fifteen miles an hour less than cruising speed, and with the bomb bay doors open, it was a speed that did not give you a lot of maneuverability. Each plane was assigned a sergeant who was trained in dropping supplies. I discussed what the potential problems might be, and we talked about what we might be able to do in case a problem developed. He was a nice young man; he assured me that he had checked everything and did not expect any problems.

Everything went well on takeoff and assembly. As we were crossing the Channel we overtook the final elements of C-47s pulling gliders loaded with airborne troops. Each C-47 was pulling two gliders and was flying at about 1,000 feet. They would be landing in the area where we were scheduled to make our drop, so we had to stay behind the gliders until they landed. The only thing we could do was to circle over the Channel to kill some time and allow them to get to the drop area and land. It was not a big deal to circle and use up some time, but the problem was that the groups following us would get involved and the whole schedule would be disrupted.

Unfortunately, we had no choice. After killing as much time as we thought necessary, we leveled out and headed for Holland.

As we approached the coast, what really caught my attention were the huge German coastal guns. I have no idea what size they were, but I had never seen gun barrels that large and long. It appeared that every one of them was pointed directly at us. I reasoned that they could not and would not fire at us because they would be too large and we were too close, but to look down the barrels was very scary. We were now flying in three-ship formations, and I was flying off the right wing of the lead ship. It seemed we just cleared the first dunes of sand by no more than fifty feet. At first the countryside looked like it must have been flooded. However, it was not long until we could see some houses and small villages. The first ones seemed to be evacuated, but soon we passed a small village that had people standing in the streets and on rooftops waving at us. We were so low we could see the expression on their faces. Many hazards appear when you are flying at fifty feet or less. High power lines were especially dangerous because you often would be on top of them before you could see them. Windmills and church steeples were also a problem.

It was at this time that I got a call from the waist gunner. "Skip, that haystack we just passed had some men that looked like soldiers and it appeared that they were firing a machine gun at us." Before I could digest that, I saw soldiers in the road we just passed with rifles pointed in our direction. Then I saw some vehicles and tanks with German markings on them. I suddenly realized we were over German territory and were catching a lot of rifle and small arms fire. We were low enough that I saw a soldier firing a pistol at us. I wished there was some way to get even lower or a lot higher. I do not know why we were not shot down. Our concern now was to get to the drop area, make our drop, and get out. Although my gunners were returning fire, it was almost impossible to see a target long enough to aim and fire before it disappeared. We could see ahead that the last of the gliders were releasing and heading toward the ground. The fields seemed covered with gliders, and as we approached, I wondered how they could find a place to land because of the large number of gliders scattered over the area as well as the fences and other obstacles on the ground. We passed over some gliders that were attempting to land without a clearing. I saw one in particular land on the ground only to collide with another glider, and I can still recall seeing bodies of soldiers as they were flung through the air. At that instant I was glad to be in a B-24 at fifty feet rather than in a glider.

We should have been at our drop area, but the key landmarks were missing. I could not find a radio beacon or smoke marker, and the railroad bridge that was supposed to be there was not. Everything indicated that we were in the drop area, except for the lack of landmarks and the markers. We decided to circle and hopefully find the markers and bridge that had to be there somewhere. As we circled we were exposed to continuous ground fire. Coming around the second time, we had to pull out of the area because another flight of B-24s was coming in. In order to avoid a collision with them we circled around again. I was going to drop my load on the next circuit—we could not continue with the ground fire we were receiving. We decided to drop into a mass of grounded gliders. As we came around the third time we climbed to 300 feet and opened our bomb bay doors, slowed down to 150 mph, and released the supply packages. The men in the rear were also throwing out the bundles in the back. I received a call that all the bundles had cleared the bomb bay and had released from the shroud lines. That was good news—I had worried about that from the time we took off. Now all we had to do was get our speed back up to 165 mph, cut our shroud lines, close our bomb bay doors, and move out of the area.

Before we could do any of that, the plane whose right wing I was flying off of made a sudden steep turn to the right, dropped its nose, and headed to the tree tops. I banked as steep as I could and dropped my nose, trying to avoid a collision. For an instant I thought we were going to collide. I had to pull so steeply to my right that I lost sight of him. We were only flying at 150 mph when we went into that steep turn, and the fact that the bomb bay doors were still open and the shroud lines were flopping in the air added a lot of drag. In fact, I had to turn so sharply that it almost threw the men in the rear out the windows. The airspeed was so low, the drag so great, and the turn so tight that the plane was shuddering and vibrating. We should have gone into a stall, but we did not. I realize that all of this happened in a very short time, but it seemed to go on forever. The men in the rear could not look out and tell me where the other plane was because they could not get off the floor. I decided we must be in the clear by now, so I slowly started lowering my left wing. As I leveled out, my airspeed built up. I looked around for the other planes but found none. I had no idea where they went, but all I wanted to do was get out of the area as fast as I could.

I told Frank that I was heading west and would try to avoid heavily populated areas because we were still getting ground fire. Soon the fire seemed to disappear, giving us a chance to get our wits together for the journey home. Somehow I felt safer close to the ground, so we came out of Holland at tree top level. About halfway across the Channel, I climbed up to a couple of thousand feet. Somehow the thrill of flying at tree top level had lost some of its allure.

We landed back at our base without any problems, taxied our plane to its stand, and cut our engines. The crew was anxious to go over the plane to see how much damage we had. They came to me with what appeared to be wooden bullets. At debriefing, it was confirmed that they were wooden bullets. The briefing officer said that the German ground troops often used wooden bullets for close fighting. The wooden bullet would splinter when making contact and would cause a much more serious wound than a solid one. They were only effective at very close range. Our first thought was that maybe they were short of material for rifle bullets, but the briefing officer assured us that was not the case. I wish many times that I had kept one. The wooden bullets were all found in the rear of the plane around the waist windows, which indicated they came into the plane through the openings there. We had a lot of holes in our plane from regular bullets, but not as many as I expected, considering the number that were fired at us.

Many things went wrong on that day that affected our drop. I understand the radio beacons were mistakenly sent to the wrong areas. Also, the railroad bridge that was a key landmark for locating our drop area had been destroyed. I never did find out what happened to the smoke marker. Regardless, we were told later that our drop was excellent and the ground troops were able to salvage eighty percent of the supplies.[22]

Later that afternoon, we learned that two of the 489th planes went down in the drop area. Lieutenant Lovelace's plane was hit by ground fire and crashed just short of a canal.[23] Capt. Robert White's plane was also hit by ground fire and apparently exploded before hitting the ground. The news really got my attention. That morning I had breakfast and a long visit with Lieutenant Lovelace. We had discussed the fact that his crew and mine were the only ones left of the four that arrived together. We both felt like our chances were good that we might finish a tour in September or early October. We even sat together at briefing just a few hours ago. I also found out that another good friend of mine, Lt. J. W. Berry, was critically wounded.

When we arrived for the briefing on September 22, we were told we had been scratched from the mission. The September 23 mission was also canceled because of weather problems. I had hoped that I could finish my tour in late September or early October, but at the rate we were flying it would take until November or December. I had reached a point that I was ready to fly as often as I could.

[22] Altogether 250 B-24s dropped supplies to the U.S. forces participating in Operation Market Garden. While Davis and his crew were able to deliver most of their supplies, Market Garden ultimately failed. Ground reinforcements were unable to reach British paratroopers—who had seized a bridge over the Rhine River at Arnhem—before they were overrun by German forces. See Freudenthal, *A History of the 489th Bomb Group*, 166-70; and Headquarters 2nd Bombardment Division, Tactical Mission Report, September 18, 1944, NA, RG 18, World War II Combat Operations Reports, 491st Bombardment Group, Box 2070, Folder – Mission Report 71, Ground Support, Holland, September 18, 1944, 1-4.

[23] While Lovelace and three others died, five members of the crew did survive and were captured. See Combat Questionnaire in Freudenthal, *A History of the 489th Bomb Group*, 169.

The next day my crew and I were given three-day passes. We decided that we would go back to London because we had been there enough that we were familiar with the city. We also knew that the heavy buzz bomb attacks had tapered off, because the allied ground forces occupied nearly all of the launch sites that the Germans used. We arrived in London and had no trouble finding hotel rooms. Virtually all the ground forces were on the continent, along with all the airborne troops. In addition, many fighter groups had moved to the continent. London seemed almost deserted of military personnel. About the only ones there now were Army Air Force crews like us. It was really nice because we could find good restaurants, catch cabs when we needed one, and go anywhere without a big hassle. It was very restful, and we hated to go back to our base.

B-24 crashing nose down during Operation Market Garden, September 1944 (courtesy of Jim Davis)

Flooding in Holland at the time of Operation Market Garden, September 1944 (courtesy of Jim Davis)

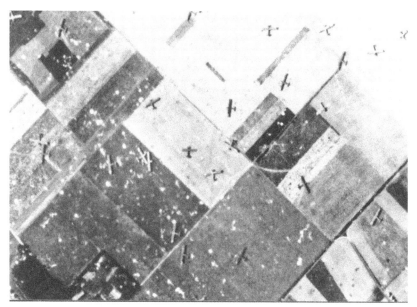

Gliders on the ground in Operation Market Garden, September 1944 (courtesy of Jim Davis)

Parachute drop during Operation Market Garden, September 1944 (courtesy of Jim Davis)

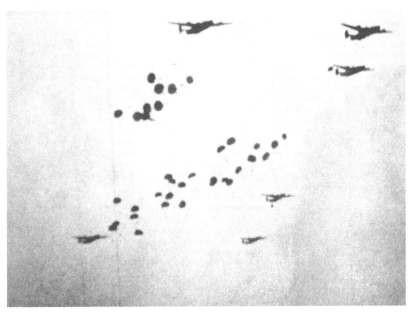

B-24 dropping parachutes during Operation Market Garden, September 1944 (courtesy of Jim Davis)

CHAPTER 8

Finishing Our Tour

WHEN WE RETURNED TO the base on September 29 we learned that our group had lost two planes a few days earlier when they had collided while returning from a mission. Lt. Frank Fulks was the pilot of one of the planes and a good friend of mine. We also learned that the 445th Bomb Group had suffered a disaster on the same mission. The 445th had proceeded down the bomber line as briefed. After they dropped their bombs on the target, they were supposed to have turned to the right to stay in the bomber line for maximum fighter protection. They made a mistake and turned left. The German Luftwaffe was always on alert for such a mistake, and this day they were in strength and position to concentrate a massive attack. In a period of five minutes they shot down twenty-five B-24s and damaged the rest of the planes in the group. Only three planes from the 445th group were able to make it back to their base.[1]

The first day back we found our name on the alert list. We had not flown a mission since the low altitude supply drops in Holland twelve days earlier. After breakfast it was back to the fog, rain, darkness, and long walk to the briefing room. Few people were talking. As the group commander and his aides entered the briefing room there was the usual "Attention," and everyone stood to attention.

---

[1] This mission had occurred on September 27, and the target was railroad works in Kassel. See Freudenthal, *A History of the 489th Bomb Group*, 178.

The briefing officer indicated our destination was the marshalling yard at Hamm, Germany.

We completed our preflight checks and had our crew inspection and meeting. The trip to Hamm was similar to most other missions. Clouds were a problem all day, but we were able to see the target and drop our bombs. We were greeted by light flak along the way and received moderate amounts over the target. The mission took five hours and fifty minutes. We were another mission closer to going home.[2]

We were alerted for a mission on October 2, but it was scrubbed. Later that day the alert list was posted, and our names were on it. The mission on October 3 was an airfield at Lachen-Speyerdorf, Germany. For the second mission in a row we did not have any serious problems, which was a record. It was a long mission, taking seven hours and twenty minutes.[3] It would be nine days before we flew another mission. We were on the alert list a couple of times but were scratched at briefing.

On October 11, we were on the alert list. Our target for the next day was Rheine, Germany, but because of bad weather we had to bomb the secondary target, which was Osnabruck. The Luftwaffe was up in force, but fortunately our fighter escorts picked them up before they could attack our formations. The most eventful thing that happened on this mission was that a young fighter pilot named Chuck Yeager made his first big step to fame by shooting down five German ME-109s, becoming an ace in one day. We could never express our appreciation enough for the job the fighter pilots did in keeping the Luftwaffe from reaching our bomber formations.[4]

[2] This was Jim's first mission back from leave and involved an attack on the railroad marshalling yards in Hamm, Germany. See Freudenthal, *A History of the 489th Bomb Group*, 180.

[3] On this mission, Jim's bomb group attacked an airfield at Lachen-Speyerdorf. Close to 300 B-24s participated in missions that day. See Freudenthal, *A History of the 489th Bomb Group*, 188-9; and Headquarters 2nd Bombardment Division APO 558, Tactical Mission Report, Field Order No. 1213, October 3, 1944, NA, RG 18, World War II Combat Operations Reports, 491st Bombardment Group, Box 2072, Folder – Mission Report 79, October 3, 1944, 1-4.

[4] The 489th Bomb Group attacked railroad marshalling yards in Osnabruck. See Freudenthal, *A History of the 489th Bomb Group*, 193-4; and Field Order No. 484, Bombing Analysis of 20th Wing Mission of October 12, 1944, NA, RG 18, 2nd

On the evening of October 13 our name was again on the alert list. The next morning, we found out our target was Cologne, Germany. There was a lot of noise from the crewmembers, because Cologne was considered to be the second most heavily defended city in Germany. Each one of us knew this would be no milk run. Briefing, preflight, startup, taxiing out, takeoff, and assembly went well, and soon we were on our way out over the Channel. We all were dreading this mission. Because of the heavy antiaircraft fire expected over the target, our commanders had decided to change up the group and squadron formations into smaller units of six planes. These would fly in different patterns in hopes of confusing the approximately three hundred heavy antiaircraft guns.

During a mission I usually would keep calling Frank, asking where we were and especially if we were close to the IP where our bomb run would start. I did not have to call Frank today to ask him how near we were to the target. A hundred miles out, you could see a huge black cloud developing over what you knew was Cologne. I had never seen such a heavy black cloud of smoke from exploding antiaircraft shells. To know we had to run that gauntlet of fire was chilling. However, it was a challenge. Whatever the price, no one would turn back because of the danger. The sky was so black you could not see through it. Inside the black cloud it was just as bad as it looked from the distance. Shells were bursting all around the plane. You could smell the foul odor, feel the concussion, and hear the fragments as they struck the plane. It seemed like an eternity before we finally broke out. We took inventory as quickly as we could. It seemed almost impossible, but no one was injured and we still had four engines running.

At this time we could relax some, although I was concerned that we might have damaged tires or broken hydraulic lines, which could mean difficulty in lowering the landing gear. We cleared the usual flak on Holland's coast, and as we started our descent about halfway across the English Channel, we felt such a relief. The ice

Air Division, Operations Report, Box 2727, Folder – 2nd Air Div. Operation Rpt. Osnabruck, October 12, 1944, 1.

buildup from condensation on the oxygen mask had been heavy that day, and as a result when we got back to the base area it began to melt, and my pants became wet. However, it did not matter because we were alive. We peeled out of formation and sweated out lowering the gear. It was great news when the waist gunners told me the landing gear was being lowered and appeared to be down and locked in place. This had not been a long mission, only six hours and fifteen minutes, but it had been a rough one, especially over the target. As I climbed out of the plane, I was hoping that we would not have to fly tomorrow.[5]

After we went through the debriefing process, we dressed and headed for the mess hall. After eating I headed back to the hut hoping to have some mail from home. No mail today, so I immediately fell asleep. A couple of hours later, I woke up and the first thing Mackey said was "Skip, we are on the alert list again." I hated to hear that. I was too tired to get too worked up about it though. After a lull in September it looked like we were back in the groove, and at this pace it would not be long until we could wind up our tour. As I lay there thinking about what tomorrow might bring I guess I concluded that most likely tomorrow's target would not be a rough one. I had to be a fool or an eternal optimist to dream such a dream. It was a long night of tossing and turning, followed by the usual wake-up, breakfast, and briefing. When the curtain was pulled back I nearly fell out of my chair. We were scheduled to go back to Cologne again. There were a lot of grunts and groans because a run to Cologne two days in a row was too much. But to Cologne we were going.

During our preflight check Dexter Bodin, my radio operator, told me, "Skip, you know when we started our tour I was concerned that we would never finish." He could not see how any one could survive the number of missions that were required. "Now," he said, "it looks

[5] A force of 250 B-24s participated in this attack on the railroad marshalling yards in Cologne. See Freudenthal, *A History of the 489th Bomb Group*, 193-4; and Headquarters 2nd Bombardment Division APO 558, Tactical Mission Report, Field Order No. 1239, October 14, 1944, NA, RG 18, World War II Combat Operations Reports, 491st Bombardment Group, Box 2073, Folder – Mission Report 85, Cologne, Germany, October 14, 1944, 1-4.

like our chances to finish a tour are pretty good." He explained that on all the missions we had flown, he was always on the flight deck at the radio operator's station. As a result, he had not seen any of the action going on outside. He had got to thinking that if we were to finish our tour and return home, he would hate to have someone ask him what it was like and to have to tell that person he never saw a thing because he was always back at the radio station. He finally asked, "Skip, would you mind if on our bomb run, I put on a portable oxygen tank and go to the hatch to the bomb bay and look out to see the bombs leave the plane, and maybe see some flak burst?" He also wanted to see the bombs hit the target, if possible. I told him it would be fine with me.

As we prepared to take off, the crew was somewhat quieter than usual because they all knew what we were going to have to do—run the black cloud gauntlet again. It was going well as we assembled and headed out over the Channel. After we had passed the coastline and flown for quite a while, I started looking for the black cloud that floated over Cologne yesterday. From my calculations we should have been within about fifty miles of Cologne, but I could not see any sign of flak. I called Frank and he assured me we were on course and about forty miles from the target. We reached the IP and started our bomb run—still no flak. I called Bodin and told him to get ready because it would not be long before we opened the bomb bay doors. He had gotten his oxygen tank, had raised the door to the bomb bay, and was lying on the flight deck looking down through the opening.

About two seconds before we released the bombs, all hell broke loose. Suddenly, bursting antiaircraft shells surrounded us. Just after our bombs left the plane we got a big burst right under us. The concussion of the blast made the ship lift upward. Apparently the blast had happened just in front of Bodin. No doubt all he saw was a huge explosion and nothing but fire. He jumped back up on the flight deck with such impact that I thought he might have been hit. I asked Siegfried to help Bodin because at that moment, seeing him and his reaction, I had no doubt he was injured. Siegfried got to him and got him back into the radio operator's chair. As it turned out he was not hurt, but he was shaken by the close call. Trego was giving me a picture of what was happening right behind us. Yesterday we had been further down the bomber line, and as a result we saw all the flak thrown up to the groups in front of us. On this mission, however, we were leading the groups. The Germans held their fire until we were over the target and then let it go. We got a lot of the initial antiaircraft fire, but the groups behind us really took a beating, just as we had yesterday.

The return flight was typical, with a few bursts of flak from time to time. We finally cleared the deadly coastal batteries and reached our base. After we filled out our reports, we gathered under the plane's wing to wait for a truck to take us to debriefing. While waiting, we had a lot of fun with Bodin. He was still a little pale and shaken from his first sight of bursting flak. He told me that he never would do that again.[6]

We had flown three missions in the last four days, and I was ready for a day off. It was good news when we heard that we would not fly the next day. All during September and October the weather had been very bad. We had taken off and landed in almost impossible flying conditions. During the last two missions, the weather had been terrible. The mission on October 14 involved approximately one hour of instrument time and on the mission yesterday, we had nearly two hours of instrument time. It is a difficult task to fly close formation in instrument weather. You are only able to see the planes nearest you, but at the same time you know that there are many other planes flying too close for comfort. One slight mistake or miscalculation by any plane could cause a chain reaction of mid-air crashes. Also, each mission's takeoff and landing was a challenge because of the rain and fog.

---

[6] Approximately 300 B-24s carried out attacks on the Cologne marshalling yards and other nearby targets. See Freudenthal, *A History of the 489th Bomb Group*, 196-7; and Headquarters 2nd Bombardment Division APO 558, Tactical Mission Report, Field Order No. 1240, October 15, 1944, NA, RG 18, 491st Bombardment Group, Box 2072, Folder – Mission Report 86, Cologne, Germany, October 15, 1944, 1-5.

We were on the alert list again on the 18th. After the usual routine we arrived at the briefing, and when they pulled back the curtain, we saw the black line zigzag to the railway marshalling yards at Mainz. As usual the weather was bad, and this was one of those days when the contrails were especially bad. We must have been traveling exactly the same course as the upper wind that day, because we were constantly battling the turbulence. The clouds reached up to 30,000 feet and made it necessary for the group to meander around them. About fifteen minutes before we reached the IP we encountered some heavy turbulence. A fully loaded B-24 flying at maximum altitude in close formation is living dangerously. Under those conditions when you suddenly strike prop wash, the plane reacts violently, and if you do not respond immediately you will find yourself in serious trouble. It creates a situation that could cause a mid-air collision.

Usually in that situation I would try to slide out immediately to the side as far as I could, to give me more room to wrestle the turbulence and avoid colliding with another ship, or to prevent another ship temporarily out of control from sliding into me. I had been able to slide a little to my right when I saw a ship just in front and above me suddenly rise up and slide to the left, all in the same motion. The plane's left wing lifted up, and in no time it was above the plane that it was flying next to. It seemed to hang there for some time, until it slowly settled down over the lower plane. The props on engines one and two actually sawed the other plane's fuselage in two about halfway between the tail and the rear edge of the wing. The impact broke the left wing off of the upper plane, and it dropped down. The props and some debris flew through the air, barely missing our plane. The most peculiar thing, which I cannot explain, was that the plane that was cut in two seemed to fly for some time with some space between the tail and the rest of the plane, until both sections finally dropped. The whole event seemed to unfold in slow motion. Bombers Moon and Pregnant Peggy, the two ships who collided, were gone just like that.

We made the bomb run in heavy flak, and many of our planes were severely damaged. We lost another plane on the way back from heavy flak damage over the target. We landed without any serious problems, and after we debriefed and ate, I was ready to lie down and rest for a spell. This was not a good day—we had lost ten percent of our group in the attack.[7]

I was sound asleep until Mackey and Frank came in and woke me up. They were really excited. They had been to the squadron office, where the clerk on duty said that he had just received orders for our crew to be put on temporary leave and assigned to a "flak house" for ten days.[8] I had not expected that, and immediately I asked Mackey if he had made a deal with Dr. Levine. He assured me that he had not. We were so close to the end of our tour that I was in a hurry to finish. Mackey and Frank were excited about going, while Ed did not really care. After thinking about it, I realized that just maybe ten days would not be so bad after all.

It was not long before we were to leave, so I got up and started putting some things together. At this point, ten days of rest and relaxing sounded super. It had been several days since I had gotten any mail, and I was really homesick. I could dream of all the good times Jean and I had experienced. Normally, I would not have slept much, but I was so tired that I had no problem this night.

It was late in the evening when we arrived at a country estate. We carried our bags in and were greeted by a nice lady. After reading our orders, she said that we were at the wrong place. The place where we were supposed to be was down near the coast in south England. This place was for fighter pilots who had finished their tour of duty and had volunteered for a second tour. They could come and stay at that facility for as long as ninety days before they

---

[7] Four crewmen, two from each of the planes that collided, survived. This mission to the railroad marshalling yards in Mainz involved more than 300 B-24s. See Freudenthal, *A History of the 489th Bomb Group*, 197-9 and 288-91; and Headquarters 2nd Bombardment Division APO 558, Tactical Mission Report, Field Order No. 1249, October 19, 1944, NA, RG 18, 491st Bombardment Group, Box 2073, Folder – Mission Report 88, Mainz, Germany, October 19, 1944, 1-4.

[8] A "flak house" was a location where an air crew could go for an extended leave.

would have to start their new tour. It was almost dark, so I asked her if perhaps we could stay overnight. She readily agreed. In fact, she said that if we wanted her to, she would make some telephone calls in the morning and get our orders changed so we could stay there the entire time. When she told us about the food and the fact that we could have anything we wanted, including going anywhere at any time, we were sold. She mentioned that they would serve fruit juice to us every morning in bed if we wished. I doubted that a better place existed, so we told her that we would like to stay. She bid us welcome and handled all the paperwork to get our orders changed.

This country estate was beyond description. Its name was Eynsham Hall, and it was several miles outside of Oxford. As far as I was concerned, it was a castle. The owner had leased it to the Red Cross while retaining the guesthouse for himself. Either his father or grandfather had become very wealthy through controlling almost all the copper that England used. Although the estate was not as well maintained during the war as I am sure it must have been before, it was still beautiful. The interior was built with the finest woods and cloth that existed. The walls were covered with silk, and the doors were a work of art. The bathrooms were the most outstanding of all. The most important thing was that there was plenty of hot water.

Ed and I shared a room. The next morning we went down to breakfast, and we had our first real eggs since we left the States. After our wonderful breakfast we walked around the grounds. We found tennis courts, a skeet range, and other recreation facilities, as well as a lake with very unfriendly swans that no doubt did not approve of our presence.

Each evening they showed a movie in one of the large parlors. It had been a long time since we had seen a movie, so it was really enjoyable. We decided to go horseback riding the next day. I was the only one who had ever ridden a horse more than once or twice. I was excited as it had been a long time since I had ridden. The next morning we boarded an army truck and rode six or seven miles to a farm. After getting the horses saddled, each of us picked the horse we wanted to ride. We mounted the horses, and this was a show in itself, as Ed, Frank and Mackey did not know what they were doing. We rode the horses out of the barnyard and down the road about a mile to a large field. By this point, we all felt like we were real horsemen. The farmer had a jumping facility and suggested that we might want to try jumping the horses over the hurdles. He placed the wood pole about two feet above the ground, and we all took turns jumping. It was not difficult to ride them over the low poles but after he raised them we all ended up around the horse's neck or flat on the ground. After that we rode the horses around the field and really enjoyed the day. On the way back to our hall that evening, someone suggested we go back tomorrow. Everyone agreed. The next morning when they got up, they were so sore that they wanted to back out, but I insisted we had already told the farmer we would be back and the best way to get over the soreness was to go riding again the next day. I was sore, but Frank, Ed, and Mackey could hardly walk.

On the way over to the farm we groaned every time the truck bounced. After much effort, we got mounted and headed to the field. It was a rather large field for England, about a quarter mile long and almost as wide. No one wanted to jump today; so, we decided we should race to the far end of the field. Ed was having some trouble with his saddle slipping, so I told Mackey and Frank to go ahead and race, and Ed and I would come as soon as I got the saddle fixed. The field was covered in weeds that were about two feet high and were so thick you could not see the ground. The horse I was riding was rather small, so Ed's horse, which was large, got out in front of me. We were both going full speed. We came to a small area that was almost void of the weeds, and in the center of the clearing was a board about eight feet long lying on the ground. When Ed's horse got to the clearing and saw the board, it suddenly dug all four feet into the ground and came to a sudden stop. Although the horse stopped, Ed kept going. He went sailing through the air like a bird. He pulled his knees up and did a complete flip. He hit the ground running and never did fall. This all happened not far from where Frank and Mackey were waiting. Mackey and Frank laughed so hard that they had to get off their horses. Ed was embarrassed, but we had a lot of fun kidding him.

We decided to race to the other end of the field, but once again I had to fix a saddle and was late getting started. Frank was riding a very large and fast horse. About halfway down the field was a telephone line connected to a couple of poles. The horses were all going full speed, and Frank was out front. As fate would have it, his horse headed straight for one of the telephone poles as if he did not see it. Frank felt like the horse surely would have enough sense not to run into the pole, but they were getting so close that Frank decided he should steer the horse away from a collision course with the pole. Just as Frank pulled the reins to the right, the horse decided he would go to the left. His abrupt change of course caused Frank to lose his balance, and he went sailing through the air. Unfortunately, he slammed into the pole in mid-air. It scared me to death, because I knew he had to be seriously hurt. He was lying motionless on the ground. After working with him for a few minutes, he finally got his wits together and as best as we could determine he did not have any broken bones—just a lot of aches, pains, and a few cuts and scratches. Ed and Mackey could not help but laugh—especially Ed, because Frank had had so much fun when Ed was thrown through the air.

When we arrived back at the estate, we did not see many of the fighter pilots who were staying at the hall. Several had gone to London and other places nearby. By the third day, many of them had returned. We were a novelty to them as much as they were to us. This was the first opportunity to visit with fighter pilots. They were a different breed than the bomber pilots and crews. Over the next few days I became close friends with several of them. They considered me to be a special person. Many times they expressed the opinion that they did not believe they could fly bombers and be so dependant on fighters to protect them. To the fighter pilots, the bombers seemed so helpless. They also could not understand how we could get enough courage to fly through the huge clouds of antiaircraft fire that was a part of every target.

One afternoon, five of them invited me to go up to their room to have a bull session and drink some champagne. The room was rather cool and the champagne was the best I had ever tasted. They each related different experiences that they had had during their tour of duty. Some were P-47 pilots who had spent most of their tour doing ground support missions. Others were primary escort pilots, flying cover for the bombers. Each one had had many exciting experiences, and most had been shot down or crash-landed. The stories they told that day could have been material for several very interesting books. They were all very brave and patriotic. However, I could not understand why they had chosen to fly another tour without returning home first.

During the bull session someone would take the bottle around and refill everyone's glass. I did not know how much I had drunk, and because the room was cold I never felt any effects of the champagne until I sat in front of the warm fireplace. Soon I was feeling somewhat lightheaded. Then, the fireplace started swaying and tilting. It did not take long for me to realize that I should go to my room and lie down. With great effort I was able to work my way up the first flight of stairs. My room was on the third floor and at that point I did not know if I could make it. I crawled up the last two flights of steps. I was glad that no one had seen me. When I finally reached my bed, I was elated. I knew everything that was going on, but I just could not do anything about it. I had difficulty lifting myself into bed. I was lying on my stomach and holding onto the bed. Even though I knew it was standing still, it seemed like it was rocking back and forth. That was the first and last time I ever got drunk. I found out the hard way that champagne could have a potent effect.

The days did go fast and soon we had to go back to the air war. On the Saturday night before we left, the Red Cross had a big party. They rolled back the rugs and a local musical group played for a dance. Bulletins were posted in the towns around the hall, and army trucks picked up any young ladies who wanted to attend. A lot more women ended up attending than there were men. We all ate, drank, and danced until two in the morning.

Finally, the day in late October that I dreaded came. It was time to pack up and head back to our base. The day that we left was the hardest that I ever lived. We had learned to relax and realize how wonderful life was. It is impossible to describe the feeling. I tried to reason with myself that we were almost through with our tour and would be going home, but then I would remember what it was like to go back to combat and all it took to safely complete a mission—so close but yet so far.

We did not have to start flying immediately, because our group was stood down from operations for three days to celebrate the completion of its 100th mission. The three-day group party was just that—an unending party. The officers who had the duty of sending trucks to the towns around the base to bring in women who wished to attend said it took twenty trucks to bring all the women in but only five to carry them home. The 100-mission party was anything you wanted it to be. We had lots of food, bands, stage shows, all day and night poker games, and what seemed like one big dance. I did not enjoy it as much as I should have because of just returning from our stay at the flak house. Mackey had a great time. I think he shot "craps" for two solid days and nights. He was winning, and on several occasions he gave me a handful of bills with instructions not to give him any of it back until the party was over. He must have won $2,000. Ed and I spent most of the spare time at the hut. I did catch up with the letter writing that I had neglected for some time.

On November 4 we were on the alert list for the next day. It was hard to get mentally prepared to fly combat again—it had been more than two weeks since we had flown our last mission. At the briefing the next morning we were told that we would be bombing some fortifications near Metz. When we got to the target area we found it to be too overcast to attack, so we bombed some marshalling yards as a secondary target. It was a long mission lasting just under seven hours. We encountered flak at several places along the way but did not have heavy flak over the target area. The weather had turned bad by the time we returned, with low clouds and heavy rain at times. With conditions like that you could not relax until you landed and got to the parking stand. I suspected that we would fly tomorrow if there were a mission. Sure enough, as soon as the alert list was posted, it was not long before word got out that we were on it. Because we were in the process of winding up our tour, I was not too sorry to be flying.[9]

At the next morning's briefing we were informed that we would be bombing a synthetic oil plant at Sterkrade. Once again the weather was terrible, but somehow all of the planes avoided collisions and eventually found their place in the formation. We encountered some flak on our way to the target and faced heavy and accurate flak in the target area. Germany tried to protect their fuel plants. The mission lasted five and a half hours. Once again we had terrible weather when we returned.[10]

Soon after we arrived back from this mission, we heard that the Air Force had issued orders for the 489th Bomb Group to be relieved of operational missions and returned to the United States within the next three weeks. All personnel would be restricted to the base. It caught everyone by surprise. It took a day or two to realize that it was real. By that time rumors spread about why. Some said we were going to be the first group transferred to the Pacific Theatre and the air war against Japan. One rumor was that we would be sent to the Pacific for submarine patrol. Another speculated that we would return to the United States, convert to B-29s, and then go to the Pacific. In one day's time you might hear a dozen rumors. Each one claimed to have direct information from the top of the command.

[9] Jim's bomb group attacked the Metz railroad marshalling yards. See Freudenthal, *A History of the 489th Bomb Group*, 211-2; and Field Order No. 510, Bombing Analysis of 20th "B" Wing – Mission of Nov. 5, 1944, NA, RG 18, 2nd Air Division, Operation Report, Box 2730, Folder – 2nd Air Div. Operation Rpt. Karlsruhe, November 5, 1944, 1.

[10] A total of 130 B-24s carried out the attack against a synthetic oil refinery in Sterkrade. See Freudenthal, *A History of the 489th Bomb Group*, 212; and Headquarters 2nd Bombardment Division APO 558, Tactical Mission Report, Field Order No. 1291, November 6, 1944, NA, RG 18, Eighth Air Force, Box 366, Folder – A-3 Mission Rpt. F.O. 1291, Germany, November 6, 1944, 1-4.

When we arrived as a replacement crew, the tour of duty was twenty-five missions before rotation back to the States. The Air Force was trying hard to build up the heavy bomber force of the Eighth Air Force to a level of 2,500 combat-ready B-24s and B-17s, and 5,000 combat-ready crews for maximum effort against German targets. During the spring, summer, and early fall of 1944, the Eighth Air Force was flying at maximum strength. The pressure on the crews and airplanes, as well as on all the ground forces who kept them flying, was at the very highest level. We flew in impossible weather at a pace that taxed one's physical and emotional strength. The missions were long—many as long as nine and a half hours. Although a steady flow of planes and crews were arriving daily, the losses were heavy. During the summer months, the Eighth Air Force lost approximately one thousand bombers.

The demand for men and machines was so great that the Air Force issued orders to increase the tour length. Finally, they said there would be no specified length of tour—crews would fly until they could not perform at a satisfactory level. The aircrews' morale was seriously affected. Most felt that it was a case of flying until you were shot down, killed, seriously injured, or captured. That does not make for a bright future. Those in Washington who issued the orders never were exposed to a similar situation. To counter the order, or at least to control the situation, the high command issued orders to all the groups that a crew would fly until they were considered too battle weary to continue. They also said that no crew would be expected to fly more than thirty-five missions except under certain conditions, which meant volunteering for a second tour. Only a few crews volunteered for another tour.

I could have left the group now because of the number of missions I had flown, but they asked me to stay. If I left the group, it would have taken six weeks, or maybe two months, before I could get home. The group was scheduled to leave within two or three weeks. Because I was in a hurry to get home I told them I would stay with the group, at least until we returned to the States. It is impossible to express the emotion you have when you realize that you are going home. It took days for it to really soak in, and to know it was not a dream. There were many times that I did not think that I would ever see Jean, all my loved ones, the good old U.S.A., and last but not least Texas.

One thing was for sure. The group did not want you to have much idle time during the last few weeks. I flew a training mission on November 9 with a new crew that had just arrived, even though the group was not flying any further combat missions. Even after we were told that we were going home, we still flew training missions. Some of the so-called training missions were flying some of our planes to other bases. One day I was asked to report to operations where I was told that I would fly a plane to a depot. When it turned out to be the plane that I had flown on my first mission, I contemplated declining the assignment. I never had refused to fly a plane, but the thought crossed my mind. I was afraid that fate would trick me and maybe on the trip to the plane's grave, it would take its last revenge and crash. Once again I had to revert to a frame of mind I had throughout my tour—I might be killed some day, but not today. So I went on and flew it without saying a thing. The grand old lady flew fine, and we had no problems.

The next two weeks were a busy time getting ready to go home and still flying training missions nearly every day. On November 29, we finally left by way of Bristol, England. The weather was horrible. The wind was blowing a gale, and as always it was raining. The sea was a monster. While we waited to board the ship, I visited with Dr. Levine. I told him that I was concerned that I might get sick because I had never been on a ship before. I asked him if there was something I could do or take to help if I did. He made me feel a little better when he told me that seasickness was all in your mind. He said that if you think you are going to get sick, you will. He further stated that he had crossed the Atlantic thirteen times and had never even felt queasy.

As we rounded the corner of the building and got a look at the ship, I immediately felt weak. It was not a big ship as I had hoped, and it was rising and sinking with the swells to the extent that the gangplank would drop out of place. The up and down motion of the ship was so drastic that it presented a problem getting aboard. The deck hands, in order to get us aboard, had us get to the edge of the dock, and when the ship started down, to jump as fast as we could so that we did not catch the upward thrust. Most of us hit the deck with such force that we fell. I kept telling myself I could endure anything because we were going home.

Once on board we were shown to our room. Lady luck had smiled on me. I shared a room in the center of the ship with seven other men. The ship was rocking and rolling so bad that it was impossible to stand up without holding on. The officer who occupied the bunk above me had already stowed his gear. He was so sick that he could not talk. He had already thrown up everything he could and now he had the dry heaves. He sounded like he was dying.

As soon as I got my belongings stowed, I decided to see where some of my friends were and ended up in a large room in the bow of the ship. It turned out this was no time to visit, because most of them were sick and just hoping to survive. I returned to my room and got into my bed. It was not long until the ship left. I was not anxious to go to the mess room that night. In fact I do not know if it was open or not. The ship pulled out into the harbor and dropped anchor. I went to sleep sometime during the night and slept well, because it was about seven when I woke up. All the others in the room were either asleep or felt so bad they had no desire to go with me to breakfast. I finally clawed my way to the dining room and the only other person sitting in the room was Dr. Levine. I got my breakfast and with much effort made my way over to him. I asked him if he felt sick, and he dropped his hands—his face was white. He immediately stood up and rushed to the door without saying a thing. I was hungry, so I sat all alone in the dining room holding on with one hand and eating with the other.

After we pulled out to sea to join the convoy, the sea became a little calmer, and we were able to spend time on deck. Living on a ship, you lose all sense of time. After the first few days, most everyone had gotten over being sick and started eating everything they could get their hands on. The cooks would bake white bread every day but would never have enough to satisfy everyone. We also could never get enough of their pies and cake. Some of the enlisted men who had kitchen duty found out that the ship's cooks would make four or five apple pies every night and put them in a secure area. The next morning when the cooks got up to fix breakfast, they would eat their apple pies. Some of the GIs found out about it and decided to relieve them of some pies. For two or three nights they found half of their pies gone the next morning. The cooks decided that they would put a stop to that by making some pies, putting soap in them, and deliberately putting them up front so that they would be the ones stolen. The next morning when the cooks went down to start breakfast, sure enough, the pies in front were missing. So they took the remaining pies and had their usual breakfast of pie and coffee. They did not realize that the GIs had found out about the pies with soap. When they got their pies that night they took the pies from the rear and pushed the pies with soap to the rear. The cooks ate the pies with soap in them and got sick. We did not have breakfast that morning.

It seemed like we had been on the ocean for a month, all the time rolling, rocking, and pitching. One morning after we had been on the ocean for over a week, I woke up and immediately sensed something strange. I could hear the steady groan of the engine and feel a slight vibration, but no motion. I could not imagine what had happened. I even thought that maybe we had been attacked by a U-boat, and I was dead and in heaven. Without taking time to dress, I rushed up the stairs that led to the deck and opened the door. The view was beautiful. The ocean was as flat and calm as a mirror. The only movement of the water was the wakes the ships were making. It was not long before everyone aboard ship was on the deck. Later that day I laid down to take a nap. I suddenly heard this loud noise and I immediately knew it was the ship's guns firing. I was sure that we must be under attack as I rushed up to the deck. I was relieved when they told me it was just practice.

We had now been on the ship for eleven or twelve days and began counting the days until we would be seeing the U.S.A. Finally, the day came. We were alerted that soon we would enter New York Harbor and sail by the Statue of Liberty. Everyone was on deck. It was hazy and cloudy that day, and we were close before it became visible. It was just as great seeing it as I had imagined—a sight and a day I will always remember.

After disembarking from the ship, we were carried to Bradley Field, Connecticut, where we were told that we would be given thirty days leave plus travel time. Because our return was so sudden and we were not allowed to tell anyone, our families and loved ones were surprised when we called. For two days I tried to call home. I was unaware that some mail sent to me in England had been returned advising my parents that I was "Missing in Action." As far as they knew I had been shot down and was probably dead. I never could get a call through, so I decided to send telegrams. I sent one to Jean, who was living with her mother in Tyler, Texas. Because my parents lived in a rural area, I sent their telegram to my brother. At first, I do not think they believed it. They thought someone was pulling a prank.

It took two days for us to be processed. I left on a troop train on December 22. We went through New York City, arriving just before 5:00 p.m.—what a show that was. It took five days to get to Texas. We traveled through Pennsylvania, Ohio, Indiana, Illinois, Missouri, and Arkansas. One afternoon as the train rolled across Indiana, I sat down by a sergeant and we got to visiting. We discovered that we had been stationed at several of the same bases, although not necessarily at the same time. We were discussing some of the unusual events that had happened while serving at those bases, and he mentioned an incident at Frederick Army Air Force Base in Oklahoma. He told me about a cadet who had flown to Snyder, Texas, and all the problems it caused because he did not know there was a Snyder, Oklahoma. He went into great detail about how the cadet had screwed up. I laughed but never did tell him that he was talking to that cadet.

We finally got to Texas, and I caught a bus to Tyler. Jean came down, and what a reunion that was. For many weeks and months I doubted that I would ever return. There is no way to describe the feeling of being home.

CHAPTER 9

Homecoming

THAT EVENING, JEAN'S MOTHER cooked fried chicken and made hot biscuits and gravy. She was a great cook, and because it had been a year since I had had a good home cooked meal, that made it that much better. We spent a few days in Tyler and then drove to Abilene to visit my family. It was a great homecoming. I was disappointed to learn that G. H. Blackburn, my closest friend growing up, had waited as long as he could to see me, but he had to leave before I could get home in order to go overseas as a P-51 fighter pilot. Unfortunately, he was shot down and killed six weeks later. It was strange to go back home and not see my hometown friends. All the young men were in service and scattered all over the world. A steady flow of people came by to see us. I was asked to speak at several meetings and even spoke to my church in lieu of the regular pastor's sermon.

My four weeks' leave went by quickly, and I had to report to Topeka Air Base. Jean and I left a couple of days early to find a room. We did not have many choices and finally rented a second-floor room. The room was not very large and the house must have been a hundred years old. We ran into Frank Morris at the base, and he introduced us to his new bride, Jerry. By the time he and Jerry arrived there were no rooms available in Topeka anywhere. Jean and I decided to invite them to stay with us until they could find something else. The two beds occupied almost every inch in the small bedroom. We put our bags under the beds and hung a bedspread on a wire stretched across the room between the two beds. That was togetherness, especially because Frank and Jerry had only been married a few days.

Rumors still floated around about where we were going and what we would be doing. The biggest rumor at Bradley was that we would be assigned new B-24s and would fly submarine patrol out of Hawaii. Because Hawaii was a place I wanted to see, that possibility sounded fine. The only thing I was not excited about was that we would be flying over water most of the time. Because I had flown the Atlantic and had so many problems and near disasters, I was not anxious to fly over the ocean, especially on a regular basis. After ten days we shipped out of Topeka on a troop train to Davis Mon-than Field at Tucson, Arizona. It was not certain but was generally accepted that we would pick up new B-24s and head for Hawaii.

Many of the officers had brought their wives with them when we reported to Topeka. We now had a problem because we were to go to Tucson on a troop train. This left the wives to get there the best way they could. One of my pilot friends had a car, so his wife asked Jean and two others to drive with her to Tucson. How they ever made it I will never know. The car was a big red Buick convertible with tires no thicker than paper. The best thing they had going for them was they were young and did not know better.

After we arrived in Tucson, Frank, Jerry, Jean, and I had to look for a place to stay. Once again we did not know how long we would have to be there but figured it would be no more than a month. We finally found a room at a motel that had two beds in it, so we rented it and once again we stretched a bedspread on the wire between the two beds. Although Jean and I had been married for a year and a half, we had spent very little time together, so I guess you could say we were still newlyweds. However, because Jean and I had been married longer than Frank and Jerry, we tried to go see a movie and not get in until midnight so they could have some time together.

It was now January 1945. It had been more than two months since we last flew after the long cruise home, the thirty day leave, and all the travel in between. We had to fly at least twelve hours every three months to draw flight pay, so it was necessary to get in some flying time. We were assigned an old B-24 whose best days were long gone. Because we had no training schedule, we got to fly anywhere we wanted to. My crew wanted to see the Grand Canyon, so we decided we would fly up to Flagstaff, then down the Grand Canyon and out over the western United States. During preflight, Van Hooten, one of my waist gunners, asked me if it might be possible for him to come up front during the flight to see what it was like to fly a B-24. I told him he could come up and even fly the plane. He was really excited about the thought of sitting in a pilot's seat.

We got the old girl into the air, and it seemed strange to be flying again. We flew up to northeastern Arizona and picked up the Colorado River. I called Van Hooten on the intercom and told him to come up. I had him put his feet on the pedals and hold onto the wheel. He then followed me through the turns and change of altitude. After fifteen minutes, I told him I was going to slowly let the controls go and let him fly. For some time I had to keep reminding him to keep the nose up and maintain the heading. He finally reached a point where he could, with a little help, hold the altitude and heading. After a few minutes, he was really getting excited about actually flying the plane. He had a smile a foot wide. He finally looked over to me and said "Skip, there is nothing to this flying. I thought it was hard." I told him "Just wait. It gets harder." At that point I started rolling some elevator trim in. As the nose would lower, I would caution him to get the nose up and he would apply a little more pressure on the wheel. It was not long until he was having difficulty pulling the wheel far enough back to maintain altitude. Before long the smile had left his face and he was beginning to sweat. He was unaware that an airplane had trim tabs and had no idea I had done anything to alter the flight characteristics of the airplane. Finally he said, "Skip, you better take over, because I am about to give out." I took the controls and rolled out the trim.

He stood behind the pilot's seats and finally said, "I don't know how you can fly these planes as long as you do. It certainly is harder than I thought it would be."

We were called to a meeting one morning where we were expecting to be told we would be sent to Hawaii for submarine patrol duty. Instead we were told we would be converted to a heavy bombardment group, which meant B-29s.[1] This changed everything. I was not sure I wanted to go to B-29s because that would probably mean the Pacific Theatre bombing Japan. The air war in Europe was winding down, and the big push to destroy Japan by bomber forces meant we would be right back in combat again. Our crews were split up and sent to various places to receive specialized training in B-29s. The pilots went to Maxwell Air Force Base in Montgomery, Alabama.

At first we thought we would go by train and take our wives with us, but because of the short time we had to get to Maxwell for the start of transition training, they decided to fly the pilots there. Jean and the other pilots' wives drove to Alabama in the same old car and with the same thin tires. We boarded the planes on February 8 for Maxwell and arrived early the next morning. The first thing after breakfast we went to headquarters and checked in. During the check-in process, I was interrupted by a captain. He said "Lieutenant, you know that we don't wear our leather jackets anywhere on this base except the flight line." I told him I did not know because we had just arrived that morning. He once again said, "You only wear them on the flight line." I thanked him and told him I would remember the rule. I went ahead with the process of checking in and about five minutes later he came rushing up to me and in front of all the staff at headquarters in a very loud voice said, "Lieutenant, I thought I told you that we don't wear our leather jackets anywhere except the flight line." I told him he did. He said, "Why do you still

---

[1] The B-29 "Superfortress" was built by Boeing and had a crew of eleven. It was the most advanced bomber of the war and was used in the Pacific Theatre. See United States Air Forces Museum, Boeing B-29 "Superfortress", http://www.wpafb.af.mil/museum/research/bombers/b3-30.htm, accessed on July 5, 2005.

have it on?" I tried to explain that I thought he meant for the next time but he would not let me finish. He yelled, "Get it off—now!" I embarrassingly slipped it off.

Two days later, we had eaten breakfast and were walking to the flight line. A lot of other pilots were on their way too, including several generals, colonels, lieutenant colonels, and majors. Two of us were walking along with our leather jackets under our arm because we did not want any problems. It was still early and the light of day was just breaking. Two officers walking about twenty feet in front of us had their leather flight jackets on because it was cool. A jeep came up the street behind us. As it passed the two officers in front of us, the jeep suddenly stopped and backed up. Out jumped the same captain who had gotten on me the first morning. He rushed up to the two officers, and they stopped. He told them the same thing that he told me, the leather jackets were to be worn only on the flight line and they were to get them off and to get them off now. Neither of them said anything, but they reached up, unzipped the jackets, and removed them. All this time the captain was watching them to make sure they got them off. When they removed their jackets, it quickly became apparent that one of them was a one star general and the other was wearing two stars. The captain jumped to attention and immediately saluted. They said "at ease" and continued toward the flight line. From that point forward, we did not have to worry about when we wore our flight jackets anymore.

On February 12, we really got a welcome. It was about 4:00 p.m. and several of us got together and decided to see what Montgomery looked like. It was a cloudy day and looked as if it was going to rain. Because we had to walk some distance to get to the cabstand, we waited until the rain passed. The weather was awful, with a lot of heavy thunder and lightning, and then the wind started blowing extremely hard. We were in a room at the end of the barracks that had windows on both sides and the end. Suddenly, we heard a terrific roar, and the trees just outside our room were almost lying flat. It soon passed and everything quieted down. We rushed down to the cabstand before the crowd got there. Broken tree limbs were lying in the street, but we never thought much about it. A cab came down the street, picked us up, and headed for downtown.

The further we went the more broken limbs and debris littered the streets. We got to the overpass over the railroad and found that some trees had fallen across the street blocking it. The driver knew a way around the overpass so he took off down a side street. We soon arrived at an area that had been completely destroyed. The houses and power lines were scattered everywhere. We stopped and did all we could to help the police, ambulances, fire trucks, and special crews clear the road and help the wounded. We got to town later that night, but the electricity was out and all the restaurants were closed. It was late before we were able to get back to the base. We had been on the outer edge of a vicious tornado that did a tremendous amount of damage in Montgomery. Twenty-six people were killed, and another 293 were injured.[2] I was glad we had decided to wait until the storm passed. If we had not, we would have been in the center of the storm instead of the edge.

Our wives arrived the next day after an uneventful trip. The first thing we needed to do was find a place to live. As usual, it was a difficult task to find a decent place to live. We were fortunate to find an upstairs bedroom in a beautiful old colonial home that included kitchen privileges. The stairs leading to our room were a work of art. We really enjoyed our stay there.

The day arrived for us to start our flying. I had never seen a B-29 except at a distance, but I knew it would be impressive. We met our instructor and he briefed us on what to expect in learning to fly the B-29. I never forgot the time in Fort Worth when our instructor took us out to the B-24. Then, I could not believe that a plane that large could fly. As we approached our first B-29, I felt the same way. It was much larger than the B-24. The instructor paused a moment and told me to look at the number on the tail of the plane. He pointed out that the number meant it was the thirteenth B-29 to roll off the assembly line. The closer we got to the

---

[2] The tornado registered as an F3. See the National Weather Service report at http://www.srh.noaa.gov/bmx/tornadoes/montgomery.htm, accessed on July 5, 2005.

plane the larger it got. It did not take long to realize the B-29 was in a class by itself.

To compare a B-24 to a B-29 would be like comparing a Model T to a Rolls Royce. The pilot's seat was roomy, and the controls were well placed. The B-29 was the first plane to have a pressure control system, meaning you could fly at any altitude without having to wear an oxygen mask and the temperature could also be controlled. It had sufficient room for crewmembers to move around without being cramped. There were also fold-down bunks that made long flights more comfortable, especially for the men in the rear section. All the gun turrets were remotely operated making them much safer to use. By being remotely operated, it was also safer. The turrets had dead spots that would stop the guns from firing at certain positions, preventing the gunners from accidentally shooting any part of the plane, such as the props, tail, and, wings. Before, a gunner in a B-24 would have to be cautious to not, in the heat of battle, follow an enemy plane so long that he would fire through the engines or wings of his own plane. In many cases that happened.

The first flight in a B-29 sold me on the plane. At Maxwell we put in a lot of long hours, made a lot of landings, and never had any serious problems. The time passed quickly, and soon our training at Maxwell Field was finished and it was time to return to Davis Monthan Field. In the middle of March we boarded a train that took us through Mobile and into New Orleans. We had to change trains at New Orleans. We spent a miserable night at the train station. The next day we finally got to Tyler. It was nice to spend a few days with Jean's mother and enjoy her great cooking. From there we went to Abilene to spend a few days with my parents.

It was again time for us to head to Tucson. We arrived at last, and as usual the first thing we did was look for a place to stay. As always it was a problem. After a difficult three days, Jean found a bedroom that also had kitchen privileges. We only stayed at that place about two weeks. The front yard had a fence around it, and the weeds had taken over. I know the landlady had at least sixty-five cats in, under, and around the house. The whole place smelled like a cat. The kitchen looked like a disaster. She never washed any of her plates or pans. Dirty dishes were everywhere. She had what she said was rabbit for every meal, and she would fry them. Even though she said they were rabbits, I suspected they might have been cats.

One day she and I were sitting on the porch, and she told me about a letter she had received from her son, who was in the Navy in San Diego. He had written her that he was in the hospital with a crushed hip and several broken bones. She wrote him back telling him not to pay any attention to the doctors, and when he was ready, he should just walk out of the hospital. She told me he could will himself well and walk out at any time. We decided it was best to look for another room. Luckily, we found one in a house about a block east of the University of Arizona.

When we arrived at Davis Monthan for our phase training, I was disappointed to learn that my crew would have several new members. Ed remained as my copilot. Technically, I was airplane commander, and Ed was listed as pilot. Frank Morris was relieved of flying duty because of his asthma. In his place I was assigned Lt. John Basch. I never knew why Ernest Mackey did not return to my crew. In his place I was assigned Lt. Joseph Girard. The B-29 also carried one more crewmember than the B-24, to act as the radar operator. Lt. Robert Gobrecht took this position. Dexter Bodin was still my radio operator. Technical Sgt. James Colley replaced Siegfried as my flight engineer. George Van Hooten and Robert Kluge both returned as gunners. My other gunners were Asahel Howard and Raymond Vandergrift. I was sorry to lose the crewmembers I had gone through so much with, but was fortunate to get an excellent group of replacements. Both of my crews were made up of outstanding young men and all were very capable.

That summer in Tucson was tough. The B-29 was a great airplane, except for the engines—they were the weakest part. Summers in Tucson were very hot and created problems with engine cooling. On some days the temperature reached 115 degrees. We would start our engines and taxi to the end of the runway in preparation for takeoff. As we revved up the engines, the temperature would climb through the red line into the danger area. We then had to sit until the temperature came down, sometimes as much as fifteen minutes. As soon as it was out of the red, we would pull on the runway and take off. The temperature would then quickly shoot back up to the red line. This stop and go activity hurt the engines' performance.

Takeoff procedure was changed in an effort to ease the abuse the high heat was causing. We were asked to get the plane in the air as quickly as possible, and once in the air to lower the nose and throttle back until the temperatures came down. This meant we could do some legal buzzing after takeoff. Some pilots would abuse this new procedure. A beautiful resort hotel was situated some distance from the end of the northwest runway. The hotel had a beautiful swimming pool and usually a lot of beautiful women were lying around it. Although the hotel was far enough away that the planes should have already reached climbing speed, for some reason many, or perhaps I should say all, would buzz right over the hotel. After the third day, the hotel was complaining about the planes being so low. Immediately we were told we could not use that particular runway except under certain conditions, and if we had to take off on that runway we were to climb quickly and stay well away from the hotel.

That summer took a toll on me. I had dropped to 128 pounds. On takeoff, when we had to sit and cool our engines down, it was hell. The B-29 had a glass nose, and with a temperature of 115 degrees beaming through it, the cockpit got incredibly hot. We sweated so much that our clothes were soaked by the time we took off. About halfway through phase training I developed a case of tonsillitis, and for two days I tried to stick it out but to no avail. One morning I woke up with a high fever. Jean called the hospital, and they sent an ambulance to pick me up. The doctors checked me, and late that afternoon a nurse came in and gave me a handful of pills. I counted twenty-six of all sizes, shapes, and colors. I asked her how often and which ones I was suppose to take. She said to take them all now. I went to sleep and did not wake up until about nine o'clock the next morning. I felt better but was so weak I could hardly walk. The nurses told me I had sweated so much they had to change my bedclothes and sheets three times during the night. I knew nothing about it. I was released in a few days but was grounded for ten days. Because I had fallen behind in our required missions, I had to do a lot of flying for the next month to catch up.

Because the bombing missions to Japan were approximately sixteen hours long, we flew a lot of long practice runs. A sixteen-hour mission actually means close to a twenty-four-hour event because it takes several hours to prepare. As the airplane commander I had to make myself familiar with every phase of the mission. I had to plan my own flight program to include navigational courses, time of various check points, loads and adjustments, alternate routes, emergency landing fields and their distance from our planned course, and a multitude of other information. Plans had to be made to cover any and all unexpected emergencies. A great deal of time was required before you ever thought about preflighting the airplane and starting the engines. After the flight was completed, you would then have fill out a number of reports and forms.

One day we took off for a cross-country flight from Tucson to Houston, up over Little Rock, over Kansas City, then down to Oklahoma City, and finally back to Tucson by way of Amarillo. There were three B-29s in this group. We were not far apart, but we never saw each other. On long missions like this, we carried prepared meals that could be heated on the plane. I always made it a point to never eat any prepared food during the time we were in the air, and I encouraged my crew not to either. I was always afraid of food poisoning. Instead, I would try and take some fruit, candy, nuts, crackers, or cookies. On this cross-country flight the weather had been good until we started encountering some cirrus clouds in western Oklahoma. Having grown up in this country and having taken basic and advanced training in central and western Oklahoma, I was aware that on hot summer days thunderstorms often developed, and the cirrus clouds would be caught in the westerly winds and carried east. I felt like the cirrus clouds we were encountering were the result of thunderstorms further to the west, so rather than maintain our altitude of 21,000 feet, I chose to drop down and stay under the clouds.

The clouds kept getting lower and lower. I received a call from Bob Gobrecht, my radar operator, that he found some bright echoes on his screen to the west and was not sure what they were. I concluded they were thunderstorms, and from all indications they were large and possibly severe. I had no desire to or intention of wrestling with a thunderstorm. We were now below 5,000 feet and just under the clouds. We had altered our course to the south near Lubbock. Our radar indicated the clouds were 50,000 feet high, too high for us to climb over the top. We either had to find a break in the clouds or go somewhere else to land. We saw an area where, although the storm was building, we could see some light. We were between Hobbs and Jal, New Mexico. Although the clouds were low and boiling, we decided to make a run for the lightest place and hope for the best. We were at about 2,000 feet and just under the clouds. We began to encounter terrific updrafts, and just as suddenly there would be severe downdrafts. After fighting the heavy turbulence, we finally broke through. What we did was probably a mistake, but we were tired and anxious to get back to Tucson. The next morning I found out the other two planes on the same cross-country flight with us had to make an emergency landing in Oklahoma City.

We learned that during the flight the crews in the other two planes heated and ate the prepared meals that the mess had fixed. The food was tainted and they all got sick. When they encountered the high cirrus clouds over western Oklahoma, they chose to fly through them rather than letting down below the clouds. They flew into a severe thunderstorm near Borger, Texas, flying at 25,000 feet going west. When the storm finally released them, they had lost 13,000 feet and were headed east. The storm had broken most of the glass in the planes, and the large hailstones had dented and vir-

B-29 on a training mission (courtesy of the Air Force Historical Research Agency, Maxwell Air Force Base, Montgomery, Alabama)

tually wrecked them. When I heard the problem they had, I paused and offered a prayer of thanks that we avoided the storm.

Two days later we were on a long night cross-country flight. We were flying at 23,000 feet and had the plane on autopilot. It was 2:00 a.m. and everyone was really tired and sleepy. It was a beautiful night, with few problems on the flight. We were flying over southwest Texas near the Big Bend country, and we could not see any ground lights. We had already been in the air twelve hours and had almost two more hours of flying before we got back to Tucson. Ed leaned over and asked if I minded if he took a nap. I told him to go ahead; I was wide awake. I never could sleep while flying no matter how tired I might be. I had never slept in a plane and was not sleepy at that time.

The engineer's compartment was located behind the copilot's seat in a B-29. The engineer was always busy checking his instruments and keeping logs on the flight. We had the curtains behind the pilot and copilot's seats closed so the light from the engineer's compartment would not reflect into the cockpit. Ed was sound asleep. It must have been twenty minutes later that we entered an area of turbulence caused by some mountains below. I must have been in a semi-sleep state and not fully aware of what was happening. The plane was bouncing around, and in so doing the curtains shielding the engineer's compartment began to flap. I was suddenly awakened with the plane bouncing and the light flashing off and on from the engineer's compartment. Well aware of what happened to the other plane two days ago, my first thought was that we were in a thunderstorm, so I immediately kicked the autopilot off. It must have been a minute or so before I figured out everything and realized that we were flying over a mountainous area and not in a storm, and the "lightning" was actually light reflecting from the engineer's compartment. The best I could tell, I had been asleep twenty minutes. None of the crew ever knew that I had fallen asleep.

One night in early May we were on a cross-country route and were returning to Tucson. Again we were over West Texas. It was about 2:00 a.m. and we were in contact with the aircraft controllers in El Paso. They wanted us to keep them informed exactly where we were every ten minutes. We had never had to do this before. As it turned out, we were in almost constant contact with them. They were telling us exactly where to fly and when to alter course. They continued to monitor our course and location until we were almost to Tucson. It was strange, and I suspected there was a good reason for the close monitoring of our position. We later learned that the United States tested parts of the atomic bomb that day, just a hundred miles northeast of El Paso and a few hours after we had flown by.

On another practice mission, we left on a cross-country flight one Sunday to Mobile, Alabama, and back over San Antonio. The weather was beautiful and clear. The B-29 we were in only had twelve hours of flying time, so we were cautious and paid close attention to the engines. About 150 miles northwest of San Antonio, the oil pressure started to drop on one engine. Soon it had dropped enough that we decided we could not afford to take a chance, so we feathered the prop. We had to land at the nearest base that could take a B-29. The closest and most logical base was Pyote Army Air Force Base, which was located about two hundred miles east of El Paso. The crew asked if maybe we should just stay over until tomorrow, because it had been a long day and it was now about 4:00 p.m. I told them it would be fine with me.

We got close enough to call the tower for landing instructions. They alerted the other planes around the field and instructed us to come in and land on the northwest runway without flying the traffic pattern. As we got to the lower altitudes the air became very bumpy. I saw the usual fire trucks, ambulances, and other cars with flashing lights that await anyone making an emergency landing. Because of the hot air I came in a little faster and with more power than usual. I felt the plane settling in, but for some reason it seemed to level out and became stable and steady. I thought we were floating just above the runway. I became concerned about the airspeed because I could tell we should be on the ground, but I never felt when we touched the runway. I then realized we were on the runway. It was the only perfect landing I ever made—not a bump or squeal of tires or any noise or motion indicating we had touched the ground. It was an eerie feeling but one that I was most proud of—a perfect landing with an engine out on a hot bumpy day.

All of my crew was from the east, midwest or west coast. The country around Pyote is flat with nothing but bushes. My crew looked around and said "My gosh, where are we? This looks like a desert." They asked me how close the nearest town was and I told them Pecos was to the west about thirty miles. They asked how many people were there, and I told them maybe two thousand. They asked if any other towns were around and I told them that Monahans was about thirty miles east, and they wanted to know how big it was. I told them it was about two thousand people. They said, "We can't stay here tonight, there's no place to go and nothing to do. This is the worst landing place we've ever seen." A jeep came to the plane and the captain wanted to know what our problem was. He said that it would be tomorrow before they could get to it. The crew said "You mean that we are going to have to spend the night in this dump?" I told them they would and that they would probably like it.

While we were waiting for transportation, they started talking and said, "Because you think it's an instrument problem rather than something wrong with the engine, maybe they could check the oil pressure gauge and see if it was faulty. Then we could change it and be on our way." So that is what they did. It was dark when we prepared to start our engines and head back to Tucson. During our flight preparation we were pulling the props through to be sure there were no locked cylinders. As fate would have it, the number two engine had a lock and we could not pull the prop through. Once again we had to decide if we would stay or find which cylinder was locked and fix it. The crew decided to do it themselves. We had to take the cowling off the engine and remove the plugs from each cylinder until we found the one that was locked. As it seemed to always happen, we checked sixteen cylinders before we found the one that was locked. It was past midnight by the time we got that fixed. Once again we got ready for takeoff. The engines were running and we were taxiing to the end of the runway when I got a call from one of my waist men. He had checked the wheels with his flashlight and could see some liquid squirting out from the right gear. That could mean only one thing—a ruptured hydraulic line. I turned the plane around and went back to the flight line, parked, and cut the engines. Now we had to decide whether we would make the repair ourselves or spend the night in Pyote. The crew decided they wanted to fix the hydraulic line. It took a while but we replaced the line again, started our engines, and taxied out to the runway. I really expected something else to happen, but we finally got clearance for takeoff. It was after 4:00 a.m. when we left the ground. We worked part of an afternoon and nearly all night repairing our plane just so we would not have to spend the night in Pyote!

We were being pushed through phase training so we could go to the Pacific for the accelerated air war against Japan. We were given our orders in the middle of June and told that we would report to Fairmont, Nebraska, to pick up our new B-29s. Once there, we would check out the new ships and complete any training requirements that we had failed to do in Tucson. The flight crews packed their footlockers and sent them to Seattle, to be shipped with the ground crews and the other units of ground personnel.

Jean and I took a train to Abilene and spent a few days with my parents. We had a great time, but soon we had to pack and get ready to leave. We went to Fairmont to pick up my new B-29. It took a long time to get to Fairmont, as we had to change buses often. The only available place to stay was a small two-story hotel. Our room was on the second floor with only one bathroom for the entire floor. Each morning someone from each room would stand by the door and as soon as the person who was using the bathroom would open the door and exit, we would all rush to the bathroom. The first one there was the winner and the losers would have to wait until that person left. After a few days of this, we were able to find a room in a residence.

The next few days were similar to what we had gone through about fifteen months earlier at Topeka. The processing and flying was very demanding and passed much too quickly. We were told that we would be leaving at the end of July. Jean and I decided that she would leave the night before I was to leave. Our time at the bus station was sad. The bus came, and we said our goodbyes. I went back to the barracks and got everything ready for departure the next morning. I did not sleep a wink that night.

Early the next morning we went to breakfast and to the flight line for our briefing. We were told the first leg of our trip would take us to Travis Army Air Force Base just north of San Francisco; from there we would fly to Hickam Field in Hawaii; from there to Guam; and finally to Okinawa, where the Corp of Engineers was just finishing the air base from which we would fly our missions to Japan. The trip sounded like fun, and I really looked forward to it, but I was not at all anxious to enter combat again. We gathered up our gear and were carried out to our plane. After completing our inspection, we boarded the plane and started our engines. We got taxi instructions and taxied out to the runway. It was strange that the tower was not clearing any of the planes to take off. Three planes waited in front of me to take off and several more were behind me. We sat there for some time before the tower told us to return to the flight line, park our planes, and return to the briefing room. None of us could imagine what was going on. When all the crews had returned to the briefing room, we found out that a typhoon had struck Okinawa, seriously damaging the air base that we were to occupy. They could not say how long it would take to repair the base—at least a week to perhaps a month.

The first thing I thought about was how I might get in touch with Jean and tell her to return to Fairmont, but I had no way to contact her until she got home. We were both sorry that she had left the night before, but we also decided it was best for her to stay where she was because it was possible we would be leaving again in a few days.

Days passed, and still no word about when we might leave. On the weekends we would usually go to Lincoln or Omaha, both of which had some good hotels and restaurants. During the week we were still going through training, but the uncertainty about leaving was getting hard to take. Then the news broke that an atomic bomb had been dropped on Hiroshima, Japan, on August 6, 1945. At first I did not know what an atomic bomb was, but from the news of the destruction it caused I knew it was powerful. We all hoped that the bomb would cause Japan to surrender, and we might not have to go to Okinawa. Then, on August 9 the United States dropped another atomic bomb on Nagasaki with similar destructive results. This gave us more encouragement that the war was almost over. The whole world was now waiting to hear from Japan. Finally, Japan announced on August 15 it would surrender. I was tower officer that day. When the announcement came over the radio we all felt like jumping out of the control tower. At last the war was over, and it would not be long before I would be back in civilian life. For the next several weeks we heard all kinds of rumors as to what would happen to us. It was not long before we were told we would not be going overseas.

We were given forms to fill out to indicate whether or not we wanted to be discharged or to continue in military service. I had decided long ago that I did not want to make the military a career. It was not long before I received orders to ferry a B-29 from Fairmont Air Base to Tinker Air Base in Oklahoma City. From there I proceeded to Camp Chaffey at Fort Smith, Arkansas, where I was discharged from active military service, although I was required to continue in the Air Force Reserve. I continued in the reserve until 1961. I had nineteen years of active duty and reserve time when I was finally discharged.

Epilogue
by David L. Snead

Jim Davis likes to claim he is just an ordinary man. He grew up near Abilene, Texas, on a small ranch and endured the trying days of the Great Depression. He helped his family scrape by in the 1930s and was able to graduate from Abilene High School in 1940. After the war, the Air Force required him to stay in the reserves until 1962 because of his qualifications as a B-29 commander, but beyond his limited annual training commitment, he was able to return to civilian life. He tried his hand at farming and ranching for a few years before beginning work at Central Texas Iron Works, a steel fabricator, in Abilene in 1948. The company produced frame work for buildings, built street sweepers, and constructed athletic stadiums. In 1958 the company decided to build a plant in Midland, Texas, and asked Jim if he would manage it. After careful thought, Jim and Jean made the difficult decision to leave Jim's hometown and accept the position. He managed the plant in Midland until he retired in 1984. Jean worked part time for a local businessman and rancher until she retired in 2001.

Jim and Jean have lived a very active life, first in Abilene and then in Midland. They had one daughter while in Abilene and now have two grandchildren. Jim remains very active in the Second Air Division Association and with the Commemorative Air Force.[1] Jim

[1] The Commemorative Air Force is a wonderful organization in Midland, Texas, that exists to preserve aircraft from World War II. In addition, it maintains

and Jean have also traveled extensively in their retirement. They have visited Japan, China, Australia, New Zealand, Tahiti, all the Baltic countries, and Russia. They have also traveled to Alaska, Canada, Europe, and Mexico. However, their favorite destination remains Hawaii.

As often as Jim likes to say how ordinary he is, I reflect on his experiences in World War II and realize just the opposite. Jim, along with all of those men and women who served in the trying times of World War II, represents something special. While he was and remains small in stature, he has lived a full life. To this day, he does not completely understand why he survived the war and many others did not—a common question for most veterans. However, it is clear that his determination, skill, and bravery had a lot to do with it. Jim persevered through extensive training that forced some very qualified men to fall to the wayside. He willingly flew into clouds of flak on numerous occasions to complete his missions knowing that being shot down, captured, injured, or killed were distinct possibilities. Although maybe not unique among World War II veterans, Jim still deserves his country's full admiration.[2]

While determination, bravery, and skill without question helped Jim survive, he will be the first to tell you that many good men sharing similar traits did not survive. This is the mystery of war—why do some men live and some die? Jim has told me frequently that luck and from his perspective, divine intervention, must be considered. Several times shrapnel came within inches of killing him, yet he survived virtually unharmed. On the other hand, Paul Redden, a gunner on the plane flying next to Jim on his first mission, died in a most horrific fashion. Unfortunately, this riddle has no definite answer. However, Jim believes, at least in his case, there may have been a reason.

---

an excellent museum, the American Airpower Heritage Museum. Its website is http://www.commemorativeairforce.org/index.shtml, accessed on July 5, 2005.

[2] For an excellent tribute to the World War II generation, see Tom Brokaw, *The Greatest Generation* (New York: Random House, 1998).

Jim once told me a story about how he had almost died while a child. For weeks he suffered from a high fever, and his family's doctor told his parents that he probably would not live for more than a few days. In the depths of despair as neighbors came to comfort his family, his mother left for about twenty minutes. After she returned, the family asked her where she had been, and with a smile on her face, she said she had been out behind the hen house on her knees praying to God to save her precious son's life. She said God promised her Jim would survive. Later that night his fever began to drop, and he began a slow recovery. Jim later explained to me that during World War II there were multiple times when only miracles could have saved him from sudden death, and on each of those occasions, he could not help but remember that night and think that his mother must have been out behind the hen house again.

Jim is only one man among many who participated in what Supreme Allied Commander General Dwight Eisenhower called the "Crusade in Europe," yet his story reveals the importance of all the participants.[3] He served his country with determination, commitment, and courage, and provides a reminder of just how difficult war really is. For his service, and that of all others like him, we should remain forever thankful.

[3] Dwight David Eisenhower, *Crusade in Europe*, reprint edition (Baltimore, MD: Johns Hopkins University Press, 1997).

Appendix
Jim Davis's Combat Missions

Date (1944)	Location (all locations in Germany unless indicated otherwise)	Target(s)
July 7	Aschersleben	Factories, Oil Plant
July 8	near Paris, France	Railroad Facilities
July 11	Munich	Transportation and Industrial Facilities
July 12	Munich	Transportation Facilities
July 20	Erfurt	Aircraft Production Factories
July 21	Kempten	Aircraft Production Factories
July 24-25	near Normandy, France	Ground Support for Operation Cobra
August 4	Wismar	Aircraft Factory
August 5	Brunswick	Tank and Aircraft Production Facilities
August 6	Hamburg	Oil Refinery and Fuel Storage Area
August 11	Saarbrucken	Railroad Marshalling Yards

August 12	Laon, France	Airfields
August 15	Wittmundhafen	Airfield
August 16	Magdeburg	Oil Refinery
August 21	Western Germany	Unknown
August 25	Rostock	Aircraft Production Facilities
August 26	Ludwigshafen	Railroad Marshalling Yards
September 10	Ulm	Ordnance Factories
September 18	Nijmegen, Netherlands	Supply Drop
September 30	Hamm	Railroad Marshalling Yards
October 3	Lachen-Speyerdorf	Airfield
October 12	Osnabruck	Railroad Marshalling Yards
October 14	Cologne	Railroad Marshalling Yards
October 15	Cologne	Railroad Marshalling Yards
October 19	Mainz	Railroad Marshalling Yards
November 5	Metz	Railroad Marshalling Yards
November 6	Sterkrade	Oil Refinery

Glossary

Abort. When a plane could not complete a mission and had to return to base, it was aborting the mission.

Aerobatics. Performing a variety of turns and rolls in an airplane.

Advanced Training. The third phase of training for Army Air Forces pilots. It generally lasted nine weeks and was where cadets began to train for the type of aircraft—bomber or fighter—they would fly in combat.

Air Speed. The speed of the aircraft in relation to the speed of air. This speed was often different from the speed of a plane on the ground because wind speed could either increase or decrease the airplane's air speed.

Aileron. Moveable flaps on an airplane's wing that control rolling and banking movements.

Army Air Forces. During World War II, the American strategic bombing command was part of the Army Air Forces. General Henry "Hap" Arnold commanded the Army Air Forces. It consisted of the Eighth and Fifteenth Air Forces in the European theatre.

AT-17. The AT-17 "Bobcat" was a two-engine trainer and light transport that was built by Cessna.

Attitude. The plane's attitude refers to its axis relative to a fixed point, like the horizon.

B-17. The B-17 "Flying Fortress" was a four-engine bomber built by Boeing to hold a crew of ten. Along with the B-24, it was the primary American bomber in the European Theatre.

B-24. The B-24 "Liberator" was a four-engine bomber built by Consolidated to hold a crew of ten. It had a maximum speed of around 300 mph, a cruising speed of 175 mph, and a range of more than 2,000 miles when fully loaded with munitions. Along with the B-17, it was the primary bomber used by the Army Air Forces in the European Theatre.

B-29. The B-29 "Superfortress" was built by Boeing and had a crew of eleven. It was the most advanced bomber of the war and was used in the Pacific Theatre.

Basic Training. The second phase of training for Army Air Forces pilots. It typically lasted nine weeks.

Biscuit. A hard pillow about thirty inches by thirty inches. A person placing three of them together could use them as a mattress.

Bladder. A hollow rubber device on a wing that could be inflated to break off accumulating ice.

Bomb Group. The 1st, 2nd, and 3rd Air Divisions were broken into bomber and fighter groups. Jim's division, the Second, consisted of fourteen bomb and five fighter groups. Each bomb group had up to 72 planes and each fighter group had between 111 and 126 planes.

Bomb Squadron. The smallest unit within a bomb group. Each bomb squadron had up to 18 planes.

Bombardier. The bombardier was the crewmember who controlled the targeting of a bomber's payload.

BT-13. The BT-13 "Valiant" was a single-engine trainer built by Vultee, with two seats—one for instructor and one for the cadet.

Buzzing. Buzzing was when a pilot flew his airplane at a very low altitude, generally to get attention.

C-47. The C-47, built by Douglas, was the military version of the DC-3 commercial airliner that transported troops and cargo, pulled gliders, and dropped paratroopers.

Carpet Bombing. A bombing mission where a large number of planes drop their bombs on a very small area, in order to clear a path for advancing ground units.

Celestial navigation. Taking measurements, derived from using a sextant to study the stars, moon, and/or planets, to determine a plane's course.

Check List. The formal directions for preparing a plane for take-off.

Check Pilot. A test pilot assigned to evaluate whether a cadet was meeting the training qualifications.

Crew Chief. The crew chief and his men were in charge of the maintenance of a plane on the ground.

Crosswind. A wind that is blowing at right angles to the direction of the airplane.

Davis Wing. A specially designed wing by David R. Davis for the B-24. It provided little drag and extra lift.

Eighth Air Force. One of two air forces that were part of the Army Air Forces in Europe. It was based in England.

Elevator. Part of the tail wing that helps control the direction of the airplane.

Feathering. Turning an engine off and changing the blade angle of the propeller in flight because of mechanical problems or battle damage. It was done to prevent the propeller on a disabled engine from turning, and in the process, causing an extreme vibration.

Fifteenth Air Force. One of two air forces that were part of the Army Air Forces in Europe. It was based in Italy.

1st Air Division. The Eighth Air Force was composed of three divisions of bombers and their support units. B-17s flew in the 1st Air Division.

Flak. German antiaircraft fire.

Flaps. Part of an aircraft's wing that controls the amount of lift or drag on an airplane.

Flight controller. Someone directing the takeoff and landing of aircraft from the ground.

Flight Engineer. The crewmember who was responsible for the mechanical operation of the plane while it was in the air.

Formation Flying. The organization of bombers in the air as they flew on a mission.

FW-190. The Focke-Wulf FW-190 was a single-engine German fighter plane.

Gunner. The gunners manned the antiaircraft machine guns on a bomber. There were four gunners on a B-24.

Headwind. A headwind is a wind blowing in the opposite direction of the direction of an airplane. It will slow the plane and increase fuel consumption.

Icing. When ice builds up on an airplane's wings while in flight. Icing adds extra drag on a plane and will reduce fuel consumption.

Initial Point (IP). The initial point marked the start of the bombing run when the bombardier guided the plane to the target.

Instrument Flying. In conditions of low visibility, pilots would have to rely on the plane's instruments to fly the plane.

JU-88. The Junkers JU-88 was a twin-engine German fighter-bomber.

Kick the Rudder. Hitting the rudder hard to quickly adjust the nose of the airplane.

Lead Crew. The bomber crew that controlled the flight pattern of the bombers flying in formation.

Luftwaffe. The German Air Force.

ME-109. The Messerschmitt ME-109 was a single-engine German fighter plane.

ME-262. The Messerschmitt ME-262 was a single-engine German jet fighter. It was the first operational jet fighter.

Morse Code. A basic signal code consisting of dots and dashes that can be used in audible or visual signals.

Navigator. The navigator provided the pilot with the proper directions to and from a target.

P-38. The P-38 "Lightning," built by Lockheed, was a twin-engine fighter with external fuel tanks. It provided a valuable escort for bombers.

P-47. The P-47 "Thunderbolt," built by Republic, was a single-engine fighter that also served as a ground support aircraft.

P-51. The P-51 "Mustang," built by North American, was a single-engine fighter generally considered one of the best fighters in the war.

Phase Training. The final period of training for Army Air Forces pilots. It generally lasted about two months.

Power Glide. Maintaining power to the engines while losing altitude. This procedure allows the plane to increase its speed a great deal and get to base quicker.

Preflight Check. The process of checking the airplane and making sure everything was in order before starting a mission.

Preflight Training. The initial training that a cadet would receive once in the Army Air Forces. Assuming he passed the training, a cadet would then begin the process of becoming a pilot. If not, cadets would be assigned to other areas of training, such as a navigator or bombardier.

Primary/Secondary Target. Every bombing mission had a primary target, but because the bombers could not always reach it or see it due to bad weather, other secondary targets were also available.

Primary Training. The initial phase of training for Army Air Forces pilots. It generally lasted nine weeks.

PT-19. The PT-19 "Cornell," built by Fairchild, was a single-engine trainer with an open cockpit and seats for an instructor and a cadet.

Radio Operator. The radio operator controlled communication on the bomber.

Replacement Crew. Crews used to replace those crews lost in combat or being rotated to other assignments.

Sand bagging. When you were assigned as a copilot with a crew that was not your own.

2nd Air Division. The Eighth Air Force was composed of three divisions of bombers and their support units. B-24s flew in the 2nd Division.

Shoot a Landing. During training, cadets often would practice the approaches to landing but would not actually land on the runway.

Stacked Up. When planes were delayed from landing because of bad weather or for other reasons, and had to circle an airport at different altitudes.

Tail End Charlie. Also called Coffin Corner Slot, this was the worst position in a flying formation: the last aircraft in a bombing formation. In this position, the pilot had to react to the movements of all of the planes in front of him and was in the most vulnerable spot if attacked by enemy aircraft.

3rd Air Division. The Eighth Air Force was composed of three divisions of bombers and their support units. B-17s flew in the 3rd Division.

Torching. Occurs when a plane emits smoke, sparks, and occasionally fire from the exhaust.

Turret. Where the airplane gunners manned their machine guns.

UC-78. The UC-78 "Bamboo Bomber," built by Cessna, was a two-engine training and light transport plane.

V-1 Bomb. The V-1 Buzz Bomb was a surface-to-surface missile or flying bomb used by Germany against Great Britain.

V-2 Missile. The V-2 was the first ballistic missile used by Germany against Great Britain.

Vertigo. Occurs when a pilot loses his equilibrium and is unable to determine whether he is flying up or down or left or right.

Wind shear. A rapid change in wind direction or velocity, particularly dangerous during takeoff and landing because the pilot has little room to maneuver.

Bibliography

Primary Sources

Ardery, Philip. *Bomber Pilot: A Memoir of World War II*. Lexington: University Press of Kentucky, 1978.

Army Air Forces Statistical Digest: World War II. Office of Statistical Control, 1945.

Astaire, Fred. *Steps in Time*. New York: Harper & Brothers, 1959.

The B-29: Airplane Commander Training Manual for the Superfortress. Headquarters, Army Air Forces, 1945.

Carigan, William. *Ad Lib: Flying the B-24 Liberator in World War II*. Manhattan, KS: Sunflower University Press, 1988.

Eisenhower, Dwight David. *Crusade in Europe*, reprint edition. Baltimore, MD: Johns Hopkins University Press, 1997.

Frederick 43-K Army Air Field. 1943.

Freudenthal, Charles H. *A History of the 489th Bomber Group*. Private publisher, 1989.

Gremlins: Hicks Field, Ft. Worth, TX. 1943.

Harwell, Ursel P. *Jaws over Europe: B-24 Bombers in World War II*: Private Publisher, no date.

High Pitch: 43-K, Enid Army Air Field. 1943.

Kray, William. *Bluie West One, Secret Mission to Greenland, July 1941*:

The Building of an American Air Force Base. Bennington, VT: Merriam Press, no date.

Morris, Frank E. "Memoirs of the War." In author's possession.

Myers, Jack R. *Shot at and Missed: Reflections of a World War II Bombardier*. Norman: University of Oklahoma Press, 2004.

Record Group 18 – Records of the Army Air Forces. National Archives of the United States, College Park, Maryland.

Stewart, John L. *The Forbidden Diary: A B-24 Navigator Remembers*. New York: McGraw Hill, 1998.

Stiles, Bert. *Serenade to the Big Bird*. 1947. Reprint Carthage, TX: Howland Associates, 1974.

The Strategic Air War against Germany, 1939-1945: Report of the British Bombing Survey Unit. London: Frank Cass Publishers, 1998.

Worthen, Frederick D. and Carroll A. Berner, eds. *Monty's Folly: Operation Market Garden.* Carlsbad, CA: California Aerospace Press, 1999.

Secondary Sources

Ambrose, Stephen E. *The Wild Blue: The Men and Boys Who Flew the B-24s over Germany*. New York: Simon and Schuster, 2001.

_____. *Citizen Soldiers: The U.S. Army from the Normandy Beaches to the Bulge to the Surrender of Germany, June 7, 1944-May 7, 1945.* New York: Simon and Schuster, 1997.

Astor, Gerald. *The Mighty Eighth: The Air War in Europe as Told by the Men Who Fought It.* New York: Dell, 1997.

Birdsall, Steve. *Log of the Liberators: An Illustrated History of the B-24.* Garden City, NY: Doubleday, 1973.

Brokaw, Tom. *The Greatest Generation*. New York: Random House, 1998.

Calder, Angus. *The People's War: Britain 1939-1945*. New York: Pantheon Books, 1969.

Carigan, William. "The B-24 Liberator—A Man's Airplane." *Aerospace Historian* Spring (March 1988): 11-24.

Childers, Thomas. *The Wings of Morning: The Story of the Last American Bomber Shot Down over Germany in World War II*. New York: Addison-Wesley, 1995.

Clifford, J. Garry, and Samuel R. Spencer, Jr. *The First Peacetime Draft*. Lawrence: University Press of Kansas, 1986.

Crane, Conrad C. *Bombs, Cities, Civilians: American Airpower Strategy in World War II*. Lawrence: University Press of Kansas, 1993.

Craven, Wesley Frank, and James Lea Cate, eds. *The Army Air Forces in World War II, Volume 1 – Plans and Early Operations, January 1939 to August 1942*. University of Chicago Press, 1948.

_____. *The Army Air Forces in World War II, Volume 3 – Europe, Argument to V-E Day, January 1944 to May 1945*. University of Chicago Press, 1951.

_____. *The Army Air Forces in World War II, Volume 6 – Men and Planes*. University of Chicago Press, 1955.

Daso, Dik Alan. *Hap Arnold and the Evolution of American Airpower*. Washington, D.C.: Smithsonian Institution Press, 2000.

Davis, Larry. *B-24 Liberator in Action*. Carrollton, TX: Squadron/ Signal Publications, 1987.

Eighth Air Force Historical Society. http://www.8thafhs.org/index. htm.

Freeman, Roger A. *B-24 Liberator at War*. London: Ian Allan, 1983.

_____. *The Mighty Eighth: Units, Men and Machines (A History of the US Eighth Army Air Force)*. Garden City, NY: Doubleday, 1970.

_____. *Mighty Eighth War Diary*. London: Jane's Publishing, 1981.

_____. *Mighty Eighth War Manual*. London: Jane's Publishing, 1984.

Glenn Miller Birthplace Society. http://www.glennmiller.org/ history.htm.

Hatcher, John J. "Camp Barkeley: Abilene, Texas," *Texas Military History* 3 (Winter 1963).

Hess, William N. *Hell in the Heavens: Ill-Fated Eighth Air Force Bomb Group Missions*. North Branch, MN: Specialty Press Publishers and Wholesalers, 2000.

Hoseason, James. *The 1,000 Day Battle*. Suffolk, Great Britain: Gillingham Publications, 1979.

Johnsen, Frederick A. *B-24 Liberator: Rugged but Right.* New York: McGraw Hill, 1999.

Levine, Alan J. *The Strategic Bombing of Germany, 1940-1945.* New York: Praeger, 1992.

McManus, John C. *Deadly Sky: The American Combat Airman in World War II.* Novato, CA: Presidio Press, 2000.

Mighty Eighth Air Force Museum. http://www.mightyeighth.org/.

Murray, Williamson, and Allan R. Millett. *A War to Be Won: Fighting the Second World War.* Cambridge, MA: Belknap Press of Harvard University Press, 2000.

Narsarsuaq Airport. http://iserit.greennet.gl/bgbw/contact.html.

Neillands, Robin. *The Bomber War: The Allied Air Offensive against Nazi Germany.* New York: Overlook Press, 2000.

O'Leary, Michael. *Consolidated B-24 Liberator.* Oxford, Great Britain: Osprey Press, 2002.

O'Neill, William L. *A Democracy at War: America's Fight at Home and Abroad in World War II.* Cambridge, MA: Harvard University Press, 1993.

Overy, Richard J. *The Air War, 1939-1945.* New York: Stein and Day, 1980.

Ryan, Cornelius. *A Bridge Too Far: The Classic History of the Greatest Airborne Battle of World War II.* New York: Simon and Schuster, 1995.

Schaffer, Ronald. *Wings of Judgment: American Bombing in World War II.* New York: Oxford University Press, 1985.

2nd Air Division, Eighth Air Force, USAAF. Second edition. Paducah, KY: Turner Publishing, 1998.

Sherry, Michael S. *The Rise of American Air Power: The Creation of Armageddon.* New Haven, CT: Yale University Press, 1987.

United States Air Force Museum. http://www.wpafb.af.mil/museum/index.htm.

United States Strategic Bombing Survey. *The Effects of Strategic Bombing on the German War Economy.* Washington, D.C.: Government Printing Office, 1945.

_____. *Over-all Report (European War)*. Washington, D.C.: Government Printing Office, 1945.

Wright, Stuart J. *An Emotional Gauntlet: Life in Peacetime America to the War in European Skies*. Madison: University of Wisconsin Press, 2004.

Index

Abilene, Texas, 204
Abilene High School, 207
aborting a mission, 129-31
Adkins, E.C., 2
Antilley, Leonard, 4
Army Air Forces, 3-6, 21, 133
Aschersleben, Germany, 95, 210
Astaire, Fred, 132-33
AT-17, 36-38, 43, 48
atomic bombing of Hiroshima and Nagasaki, 205

B-17, 71, 86, 154-56, 158, 183
B-24, 47-58, 60-61, 76, 78-79, 86, 101, 112, 115, 127, 138, 140, 151, 158, 166, 168, 175, 183, 191-92, 194
B-29, 182, 192, 194-98, 200-202, 207
Basch, John, 196
Bauer, H.M., 2

Belfast, Ireland, 82
Benson, Thornton, 58, 69
Berry, J.W., 165
Biggs Field, 59, 62
Blackburn, G.H., 189
Bluie West One, 71
Bodin, Dexter, 58, 69, 172-74, 196
Bradley Field, 187
Bristol, England, 184
Brunswick, Germany, 135, 210
BT-13, 30-32, 34, 41

C-47, 161
Camp Barkeley, 2-3
Camp Chaffey, 206
Caple, Frank D., 21
carpet bombing, 126-27
Central Texas Iron Works, 207
Colley, James, 196
Cologne, Germany, 171-74, 211
Commemorative Air Force, 207

223

Creighton, Francis L., 21

Daugherty, Louis H., 21, 49-50
Davis, Ernie, 15
Davis, James "Jim": after
    the war, 207-209; classes
    in training, 13, 18, 23;
    discharge from military
    service, 206; enlistment, 3-
    6; injured, 127-28, 141-42;
    Jean and, 5-8, 16-17, 21-22;
    return from tour of duty,
    184-88; wartime marriage,
    32-34, 37, 40, 57, 64, 66-
    67, 87-88, 107, 176, 188-
    90, 194-97, 204; wedding
    day, 26-29; work at Camp
    Barkeley, 2-3
Davis, Jean, 5-8, 21-22, 26-29,
    34, 40, 56, 67, 188-90, 207-
    209
Davis, Richard, 8
Davis Monthan Field, 190, 196
draft (Selective Service), 1, 3-6
Donahue, Fred, 29
Dyer, W.L., 49-50
Dyke, Jim, 145-46

Eanes, E.C., 49-51
Edom, Texas, 7
Ehrang, Germany, 151
Eighth Air Force, 67, 86, 96,
    103, 114, 126, 146, 149, 154,
    183
844th Bomb Group, 86
82nd Airborne (U.S.), 159

Eisenhower, Dwight, 209
Enid (Vance) Army Air Force
    Base, 30-31
Erfurt, Germany, 124, 210
Eynsham Hall, 177-81

Fairmont, Nebraska, 204-205
Fifteenth Air Force, 67, 154-55
1st Air Division, 86, 154-55
First Airborne Division
    (British), 159
Florcyk, Edwin, 126-27
formation flying, 111-12
445th Bomb Group, 169
489th Bomb Group, 83-84, 86,
    151, 154, 159, 165, 182
Frederick Air Force Base, 36,
    44, 187
Fulks, Frank, 169
FW-190, 102

Genre, William, 31
Girard, Joseph, 196
Glenn Miller Band, 139-40, 147
Gobrecht, Robert, 196
Goose Bay, Labrador, 71-72
Grenier Field, 68, 71

Halesworth, England, 82, 85,
    124
Hamburg, Germany, 138-39,
    211
Hamm, Germany, 170, 211
Harville, Floyd, 108
Hester, Margaret, 5

Hicks Field, 20, 31
Howard, Asahel, 196

JU-88, 95

Kemptan, Germany, 125, 210
Kluge, Robert, 58, 196

Lachen-Speyerdorf, Germany,
    170, 211
Laon, France, 142, 211
Levine, Leo, 128-29, 140, 142,
    176, 184-85
Liverpool, England, 82
Loadholtes, Joe, 120
London, 118-24, 131-33, 144-
    46
Lovelace, Claude, 84, 160, 165
Lubeck, Germany, 134
Ludwigshafen, Germany, 149-
    51, 211
Luftwaffe, 102-103, 124, 136,
    139, 142-43, 157, 169-70

Mackey, Ernest, 58, 69, 89-90,
    107-108, 115, 118-20, 131-
    32, 145, 176, 178-79, 196
Magdeburg, Germany, 143-44,
    211
Mainz, Germany, 175-76, 211
Maxwell Air Force Base, 192,
    195
McDonnel, Donald A., 21, 24-
    26

ME-109, 124, 170
ME-262, 125
Metz, Germany, 181, 211
Midland, Texas, 207
Mont-Saint-Michel, 153
Montgomery, Alabama, 193-94
Morris, Frank, 58, 62, 69, 77,
    89-90, 107-108, 118-20, 131-
    32, 136, 156-57, 164, 170,
    176, 178-79, 189-90, 196
Morris, Jerry, 189-90
Munich, 115-17, 210

Napier, Ezekial, 112, 129-30
New York City, 187
Nijmegen, Netherlands, 159,
    211
Normandy, France, 126-29, 210
Nowaski, John, 58-59, 64

101st Airborne (U.S.), 159
Operation Cobra, 126-29
Operation Market Garden, 159-
    68
Orleans, France, 152
Osnabruck, Germany, 170, 211
Oxford, England, 177

P-38, 103, 109
P-47, 103, 109, 180
P-51, 103, 110, 189
Paris, 110, 113, 210
passes (leave), 118-20, 131-33,
    144-46, 166, 176-81
Patton, George S., 151

Pearl Harbor, 1
Prestwick, Scotland, 81
Prichard, C.L., 1
PT-19, 21, 30, 32
Pyote Air Force base, 202-3

rationing, 7, 45
Red Cross, 113, 116, 177, 180
Redden, Paul, 103, 209
Rostock, Germany, 134, 149,
    211
Royal Air Force, 144

Saarbruecken, Germany, 140-
    41, 210
Salt Lake City, 59
San Antonio Aviation Cadet
    Classification Center, 8
2nd Air Division, 86, 154-55
Second (2nd) Air Division
    Association, 207
Siegfried, Arthur, 58, 62, 69, 93,
    111, 136, 156, 173, 196
Steeve, Edward, 64, 66, 69-70,
    108, 111, 118-20, 124, 132,
    140, 143, 145, 148, 177-79,
    181, 196
Sterkrade, Germany, 182, 211
Sweden, 149
Switzerland, 155-57

Tanner, Lewis, 91
Tarrant Field, 45, 47
3rd Air Division, 86, 154-55
Tinker Air Force Base, 206
Topeka, 189-90
training: advanced, 36-56;
    basic, 30-36; B-24 phase
    training, 59-66; B-29 phase
    training, 196-204; preflight,
    9-18; primary, 19-30
Trego, Herman, 58, 69, 93
Tucson, Arizona, 190-91, 195-96

UC-78, 37
Ulm, Germany, 154, 211

V-1 Bomb Attacks, 120-24, 133
Van Hooten, George, 58, 69,
    141, 156, 191-92, 196
Vance, Leon, 31
Vandergrift, Raymond, 196

Webb, Byron, 96
White, Robert, 165
Wismar, Germany, 134-35, 210
Wittmundhafen, Germany, 142,
    211

Yeager, Chuck, 170

CPSIA information can be obtained
at www.ICGtesting.com
Printed in the USA
JSHW080038130423
40260JS00002B/12